Praise for

A Cure for Gravity

Straightforward, self-effacing, and wonderfully detailed. . . . Jackson is as adept on the page as he is between the grooves.

T. C. Boyle, author of *The Road to Wellville*

A Cure for Gravity is, to pick up on one of the title's implications, an antidote to the chest-puffing fantasy of many rock memoirs.

Paul Sexton, *Billboard*

Full of humorous tales of his early, raucous days as a working musician.

Boston Herald

Clear, precise, and often witty . . . Jackson certainly has the talent to be a literary star.

Jack Lechner, *San Francisco Chronicle*

The young musician will find *A Cure For Gravity* insightful, a witty compendium of to-dos and to-avoids; the veteran will find the book reassuring.

Dallas Observer

Witty, sharp, and crisply written. . . . The book is sprinkled with engaging and self-effacing stories.

Adam Langer, *Book*

Wise, funny, and honest . . . [*A Cure for Gravity* is] hugely informative on music and the ways of working with it, as well as how to stay true to your beliefs.

Glyn Brown, *Sunday Telegraph* (London)

An engaging, unfailingly honest book.

Tony Clayton-Lea, *Irish Times*

A deeply personal account of Jackson's inner life as a child and teen. . . . He writes better than most people who consider themselves full-time authors.

Madison

A Cure for Gravity should be required reading for anyone who's ever attempted to start a band, either for fun or to make it as a professional musician. And even those who've only thought about it as a passing fancy will find much delight in this touching musical journey.

Kirkus Reviews

An honest, gritty look inside the music business and the mind of a musician.

Library Journal

The real surprise here lies in the disarmingly frank and often beautifully observed personal details.

***Eye* (Toronto)**

A Cure for Gravity

A Cure for Gravity

Joe Jackson

ACKNOWLEDGMENTS

Most of the people mentioned in this book were extremely helpful in filling in the gaps in my memory. I'd like to thank them all for their generosity, though special thanks are due to Mark Andrews and David Cairns, and to Kim Hilton for her detective work.

Many thanks also to Amy Scheibe and Ferdia MacAnna for helping me to knock the book into shape, Kris Dahl and Zoe Waldie for selling it, and John Saddler and Lisa Kaufman for publishing it.

J. J.

Printed in the United States of America.

Book design by Mark McGarry
Set in Monotype Dante & Gill Sans

Cataloging in Publication data is available from the Library of Congress.

ISBN 0-306-81001-8

First Da Capo Press Edition 2000

Published by Da Capo Press
A Member of the Perseus Books Group
http://www.dacapopress.com

1 2 3 4 5 6 7 8 9 10—04 03 02 01 00

Contents

Prologue: The Piss and Punchup Club

I'M SITTING in a Transit van in Basingstoke, a battered once-blue Transit van full of drums and amplifiers, in a dirty white concrete car park under a dirty white sky, and I'm thinking: What am I doing here?

The rest of the band has gone for a walk, in search of civilization, and I'm keeping an eye on things. Pretty soon I'm dozing, though it's too cold to sleep. It's the sort of useless gray Saturday when everyone should just stay in bed with a good book. A blank on the calendar. Christmas and New Year are gone, and 1975 is having trouble getting started.

I'm having some trouble getting started myself. Last night's gig was a late one and I have a lingering hangover. Not a pounding-head, churning-guts kind of hangover, but the kind where you feel sort of OK as long as you do everything *slowly.* I'm not sure I feel like doing a gig tonight. But if we must, I wish we could get on with it. This happens all the time: We're told to show up for a gig at, say, five o'clock, but the place is locked, silent, deserted. Eventually, around six or seven, a minion will appear, rattling a bunch of keys like some ghoulish jailer. He will eye us suspiciously. He'll ask if we're the band, and one of us will say, No! We're just four long-haired youths who like to hang around in empty car parks for hours on end in a van full of drums and amps and guitar cases. Or something to that effect. Grudgingly, the minion will open up and we'll get to work.

In the meantime, I'm dozing and thinking. Of *course* I can't sleep. I was blessed and cursed with a hyperactive brain. I ask myself age-old and portentous questions: If a tree falls in the forest and no one is around, does it make a sound? Or: Does music even exist, if no one's listening? I reckon it does. We don't have to actually be listening to know that masterpieces of music are always there. It's like they're just sleeping, between the pages of a score, or in those black vinyl grooves; Sleeping Beauties waiting for the kiss of our attention.

I admit it: I have a philosophical bent. I wonder not only why I'm doing this, but why anyone has ever done it, and *how*. How did Beethoven manage to write that incredible Violin Concerto? I'm listening to more Bowie than Beethoven these days, but I'm thinking of taking up the violin again. It was my first instrument. If I can figure out a way to amplify it, I can use it in the band. There's a little pickup I've seen people use on acoustic guitars; it would go on the bridge of the violin . . .

I'm thinking I should listen to that concerto again, and then a big chunk of it comes flooding into my mind. It's *in* there! Like a record or a tape, it's actually imprinted on my brain. I can *hear* the part where the lyrical second theme of the first movement soars up an octave, gathering perfect little embellishments around it. Every time I hear that part, I feel tears pricking my eyelids. There's no other way the music could possibly go at that point, not one note you could add or subtract or change; and I start to wonder whether the composer really wrote it at all, or read it in the mind of God.

And here I am worrying about a gig in Basingstoke at something called the Pen and Parchment Club. How it got a name like that I can't imagine. But, who knows, it could be the best gig we've ever done. There's a musical equivalent of the hair of the dog. You can be less than excited about performing—dreading it, even—but once you get up there, with real live people in front of you, something happens. Suddenly it's for real, you have to *deliver,* and all your senses are sharpened. And sometimes the worst places can turn out to be the most fun, if you can get the audience on your side.

Someone is tapping on the van window. I sit up with a start. A face with bushy black eyebrows is peering in.

"You the band?" asks the face.

"Are you the minion?"

"Wot?"

"Yeah, we're the band, of course we're the band, open up, will you?"

Keys rattle, and the rest of the band is sauntering across the car park.

Once inside, the Pen and Parchment Club looks like a pretty typical "social club," a place where, for an annual membership fee, working men and their wives or girlfriends can go and drink cheaper than they could in a pub. And, on certain nights, be entertained by a raffle, or a comedian, or a struggling pop group. In this case, a struggling pop group on the way to becoming a struggling rock band.

Either way, tonight we're going to have to struggle without the aid of a stage. What passes for a stage at the Pen and Parchment is a nine-inch-high platform about five feet square.

We never know what we're going to find when we walk into a gig. The stage might consist of six rickety tables held together with electrical tape, or there might be no stage at all. So we have some staging of our own in the van: a pile of wooden boards with slots in them, which fit together ingeniously to form either one large or two smaller platforms. We stole them piece by piece from the drama department of Fareham Technical College, where Dave, our drummer, works as a "groundsman"—in other words, as gardener and general dogsbody. At first, we took just enough to make a drum riser. But the slotted-wooden-board habit got into our blood. We had to have more! Now we can make small stages bigger. Provided, that is, that the height differential between "our" stage and "theirs" isn't too great: On some nights people trip up in the middle of guitar solos and go crashing into my keyboards or knocking over cymbal stands. Where the platforms really pay off, though, is on those rare occasions when we get a big stage, a real, honest-to-God theater stage, and we can create two tiers: the drums and keyboards towering over the front line. Like a real concert!

Tonight we can't come up with a configuration that works. So the drums will go on the existing "stage," and I'm going to have to set up my keyboards on the floor, which I hate. I've done floor gigs before. Usually, to add insult to injury, the band has to play in front of a huge stage that has already been commandeered by a power-crazed DJ. People stand behind me while I'm playing and make sneering comments and breathe down my neck and flick fag-ends onto the keyboards. But the Pen and Parchment isn't a dance club, and most of the floor space tonight is taken up by Formica-topped tables and chairs. With a bit of luck the punters will keep a more or less respectful distance.

I set up my keyboards: two electric pianos. The better of the two is a recently acquired Fender Rhodes, although it has a gammy leg and tilts at a slight angle. First I have to look inside it and check the tines—the metal bars that are struck by little hammers, like in a real piano, to produce the sound. These tines are temperamental. If they're not properly aligned, the hammer doesn't strike squarely, and instead of a pure tone you get a sound like a teaspoon on a milk bottle. Tines also break a lot, and then you get no sound at all. I seem to spend hours like a mechanic with the lid off the bloody thing, cursing and kicking one of its good legs.

The Rhodes is behaving itself today, so on top of it goes a neatly folded, slightly rancid leopardskin blanket, and on top of that, an old, legless, Hohner Pianet. The Pianet has its own problems: several notes buzz and distort, but that's OK. I actually like the buzzes, and I've decided to let the instrument sink into a natural state of decrepitude.

Next we need beer crates. Mark, the guitarist, and I both have speaker cabinets that we can hear better when they're raised slightly off the ground. And we're in luck, because the bar, which runs along one whole side of the club, is opening up. I go over to ask for a couple of empty beer crates, and get the fright of my life. First, two colossal Alsatians jump up on the bar, barking and snarling. Then the barman turns around. Not only is he a tattooed monster straight out of Hell's Angels central casting, but he has no hands—just two shiny steel hooks.

And no, there are no empty beer crates.

So we finish setting up, and then we ask the man from the committee (these places always have a committee) where our dressing room is. This is said as a joke, really, and taken as one, too. The closest thing to a dressing room (says the man, who's a nice enough bloke) is behind that door out there in the lobby, the one marked Gents. But if we like we can take a slight short cut to the "stage" through the bar, under the hatch at the end. We thank the man from the committee for his help. We're a gigging band, we're professionals. We'll change in the van.

Now we have an hour or two to kill, so what do we do? We go to the pub. What else? Sometimes we buy a bag of chips, or some egg fried rice from a Chinese takeaway. Usually we nurse a couple of pints and some crisps for as long as we can. We don't like to drink too much before a show. It might make us sloppy, and cause lapses in the professionalism we're working so hard to cultivate these days. Besides, we can't afford it.

An hour later we're in the van, all trying to change at the same time, and I get fed up with being elbowed in the face. I decide to change in the club toilet after all, which is a bad move, since there's about three inches of water on the floor. I lock myself in a cubicle and somehow improvise a technique of changing while alternately balancing on one foot, cursing, and propping myself against the toilet seat. Finally, I emerge resplendent in a pair of burgundy flares, dark red platform shoes, a cheap off-white nylon shirt, and a gold Lurex waistcoat with black starburst motifs.

Meanwhile, back in the van, Graham, the bassist, is getting into his lemon-yellow crimplene suit. Crimplene, it turns out, was not the ideal material for that friend of his mother's to make the suit from, since it's starting to stretch and lose its shape here and there. But it doesn't look too bad yet, especially when worn with a black shirt, red tie, and aviator shades. Graham, dark-haired and currently bearded, looks like a particularly effeminate Mafia hit man.

Dave, the drummer, is putting on his favorite black-and-white striped satin shirt and baggy pants cut off just below the knee, which he wears over black tights, with hi-top basketball boots.

Mark's outfits are always the most flamboyant. After all, he's the front man. Tonight he's wearing gold lamé hipster flares, a floral-print blouse, and a black chiffon scarf. Graham's sister isn't here tonight, but Mark's doing his own makeup now, just like she taught him: mascara, eyeliner, a little bit of rouge. Mark likes the whistles he gets when we walk on stage. You have to get a reaction, he says. Every night I cross my fingers and hope it's the right kind.

We're taking a bit of a chance with our clothes, but we got fed up with the band uniform we started off with: matching black-and-silver patterned sweaters and black flares. Hideous, but we had to make an effort. As we're constantly reminded by the small-time agents and club owners who book us, a gigging band has to be *smart*, in places like these! You can't just wear any scruffy old tat, like the bands in those big-time London rock clubs! So smart is what we've tried to be. More recently, though, we've come under the heady influence of glam rock. Now the bookers can't quite decide whether we're smart or not. So far, we seem to be getting away with it.

And finally . . . Showtime!

Time, once again, to disarm and charm that great beast called The Audience. Time to focus all our energy into making a connection, into making something *happen*. We can feel it, when we're winning them over, and it feels good. Everyone, band and audience, merging into one entity. And on a really good night—and this rarely happens, but we get glimpses of it—we're flying. It's as though music has the power to neutralize the force of gravity. We're like those lunatics you see on TV who jump out of planes and link arms in free fall. They never look as though they're actually falling, but floating, as though time is standing still. And maybe those glimpses are what keep us going, like a drug fix taking us out of the clatter and grind of normal life.

The first of our three forty-five-minute sets is uneventful, but this is normal. People are still trickling in. Most of them seem to be middle-aged bruisers with long sideburns who won't leave until they've had at least eight pints. Their pudding-fed wives are dressed, if not to kill, then at least to inflict grievous bodily harm, in shiny metallic stuff and earrings like Christmas-tree ornaments. Then there are old folks who drink bottles of stout and stare at us blankly through thick spectacles. God only knows what they're thinking. And at the other end of the scale, sullen greasy-haired youths, a year or two underage, who'll be either our biggest fans or our worst tormentors.

Most nights, early on, we're ignored, which is good. A *bad* gig is where they unplug your amps in the middle of a song and throw them out into the car park, and you can forget about getting paid. Hopefully, as the evening rolls on, we'll get scattered applause, a few shouts of "bollocks" and "get off," some drunk howling like a wolf at the back, and a few people dancing. And that'll be a good gig.

But tonight the drinking seems more reckless than usual, and the drunks are not happy drunks. They're oi-what-are-you-lookin'-at drunks, shut-up-when-you're-talkin'-to-me drunks, drunks in imminent danger of getting Out of Order. Even the laughter has an aggressive edge. The barman with the hooks has taken on a sweaty, psychotic look, and the Alsatians are barking. By the time we're halfway through our second set, we're getting nervous. There's something in the air here that we've come across before. We can almost smell it. It's hard to define, exactly, but it sure isn't peace and love.

Right in front of me a quartet of rough girls is getting seriously plastered on vodka and lime and vodka and blackcurrant and vodka and vodka. And one of them thinks it's very funny to come over now and again, make faces at me, and bang on one of my keyboards, to sowlike squeals of delight from her pals. By the third set, the ladies have been joined by a couple of guys who've drunk enough to make the ladies look good, and something's got to give. The point of no return comes when we hit the Scottish medley.

And what is the Scottish medley? Our third set is meant to be rabble-rousing good fun, and on a good night it is. It includes songs by Elvis and the Beatles that everyone knows, a '50s rock 'n' roll medley, and a lot of jokey, clowning stuff, including me slipping behind a curtain and reemerging (to wild applause and hoots of laughter) as Angus McSporran, wearing a long false ginger beard and a kilt (actually a tartan skirt that used to belong to my mother). We start with "Donald, Where's Yer Troosers?" I play a couple of jigs on an accordion, and we end with a rousing chorus of "Auld Lang Syne."

This is too much for the Vodka Girls. They have to know what's under the kilt. The one who's been banging my keyboards all night bounces up and starts tugging at it, revealing the rolled-up burgundy flares underneath, and I've had enough. I shove her away; she throws a vodka and orange over me; I throw a pint of bitter over her; and *whooosh!* the Pen and Parchment Club erupts. A bruiser who wants to defend the honor of the ladies starts a fight with a guy who says they're just a bunch of slags and they were asking for it. Another guy wants to fight *him,* and another tears off his shirt, revealing rippling muscles, just wanting to fight *anyone*. Chairs start flying and we escape under the bar hatch and out to the car park just as the dogs are set loose.

We lock ourselves in the van. We could be here for some time. At some point we'll have to go back in, pack up our equipment—or what's left of it—and try to get some money out of these bastards. Meanwhile, we watch the carnage. We hear glass shattering and women shrieking, and then sirens as three police cars arrive. A couple of bruised and bleeding drunks stagger outside. One has had the collar torn from his shirt. The other props himself against the wall and throws up—almost, but not quite, missing his shoes.

"You started this!" says Graham.

"Me?!" I say, incredulous. I didn't start anything! Suddenly I feel like throwing up, too. All I ever wanted to do was to play the piano. All I ever wanted was to make beautiful music, like Beethoven, like Charlie

Parker, like the Beatles, performer and audience merging into one entity . . .

"Another gig bites the dust," says Mark, and we all groan. That's what our previous drummer Steve Hollins, the one we sacked, used to say after every bloody show.

"The Pen and Parchment Club," says Dave. "What sort of stupid fucking name is that for a club, anyway?"

"Piss and Punchup Club, more like," says Mark.

Then we just sit in silence. I close my eyes and take a deep breath. Who *did* start this, anyway?

Here goes the hyperactive brain again. Who started *music*? Surely it was always there. In the Beginning was the Note. A deep, deep note it must have been, at least six octaves below middle C. Higher harmonics slowly came into being, until a vast chord of stars and planets hummed throughout the universe. Primitive creatures crawled out of swamps to listen, and pretty soon (we're talking in Cosmic Time here) they were walking on two legs and howling Cro-Magnon arias at the moon. And over that ever-present Note, a Greek plucked the strings of a lyre, a Chinaman bashed a cymbal, and so it goes across the ages, as musical empires rise and fall: Byzantium, Vienna, New Orleans . . . Basingstoke.

I open my eyes. I'm sitting in a Transit van in Basingstoke and I'm thinking: How the hell did I get mixed up in all this?

Sailors and Seagulls

I WAS BORN in August 1954 in Burton-on-Trent and spent the first year of my life nearby in a place called Swadlincote, on the border of Staffordshire and Derbyshire. "Swad," as everyone called it, was a gloomy place of soot-blackened brick and slag-heaps. My mother cried every day. She missed Portsmouth, where I'd been conceived, where there were friends and family and the air was fresh and salty. She'd met my dad there, in a dance-hall, when he was in the navy. Later, when they had a family, my dad was the head of it. But my mum won the biggest battles early on. She didn't want to be a navy wife, and she wouldn't live in "Swad," not for all the tea in China. So Dad became a plasterer, and we settled not in his hometown, but hers.

Everything about Portsmouth—"Pompey," as it's been called for centuries—seemed right and logical. In the middle of the south coast. Big, with close to 200,000 people, but not too big. Bounded on three sides by water, and to the north by the long chalk ridge of Portsdown Hill, a sort of afterthought to the South Downs. Sailors in the streets and seagulls in the sky. The smell of seaweed down by the harbor, and the vinegary tang of fish and chips. Lots of pubs. My mother had grown up in a pub, scrubbing floors and emptying spittoons. Her mother (who died before I was born) ran the place, and her father (whom I remember vaguely as an old bald geezer) drank in it, which I suppose made them quite compatible, in a way.

We lived in a cramped council flat in Paulsgrove, near Portsdown Hill, not far from the Chalkpit, where great grotesque machines dug chalk out of the hillside by the ton. My brother Chris was born in Pompey a few months after I arrived there. We shared a bed. My brother Pete was born six years later and slept in the same room in his pram.

I remember the flat in shades of gray. In the earliest photo I have, I'm eating a boiled egg, aged six or so, with quietly hideous gray '50s wallpaper in the background. The design, I suppose, is Floral, although no flowers like these were ever found in nature. Above my head is the one piece of decorative art we possessed: a plastic fishbowl, like a globe sliced in half and bolted to the wall, with a plastic arch across its top, a channel through which the pathetic little goldfish could swim, around in circles—what a treat! Sometimes he'd swim too fast, miss the channel, fly out of the bowl, and lie wriggling on the floor.

Now, I can appreciate the fishbowl as kitsch. Then, it was just plain weird.

Portsmouth was better than Swad, but hardly idyllic. We lived in what was probably the roughest part of town, and we had no money. Sailors and seagulls; there *is* a romantic side to the place, if you use a bit of imagination, but I don't think we saw it then. In Pompey sailors were "skates," and the women who came down from London by the coachload when there were a few ships in were called "skate-bait." As for the seagulls, we called them "shitehawks." In other words, we didn't exactly sit around composing odes to their grace in flight. Their most significant feature was that they might, or might not, shit on your head.

I once met a man who lived for a year in the arctic north of Sweden. It was dark for eight months, then sunny for just a few weeks, when huge mosquitoes would come out of hiding and eat you alive. But the most amazing thing about the place was that people had a real affection for it. They moved away, and worked or studied in London or Toronto or Berlin, but they went back. For them it was the center of the world. People are strange, but predictable! Portsmouth still seems the center of the world to me, even now. In my youth there were times when I detested the place, but part of me has always loved it, too, for no particular reason—or none that I can explain.

Pompey was home, but, throughout my childhood, we made regular trips to Swadlincote to visit my paternal grandparents. They lived in a strange, ramshackle, Addams Family type of house. The oven was built into the fireplace, and my grandmother, a short plump white-haired woman who never said much except "All right, me dook?" would plunge her chubby arms through fire and boiling fat, impervious to pain, to serve us dinner. My grandfather was tall and bald and didn't say much either. No one in my family ever said much. Grandad was in the ninety-fifth, and last, year of his life before he told me that my great-great-grandfather's name had been Joe Jackson, and that he ran a greengrocers' shop in Burton.

This is as much as I know about my ancestors. My mother's side of the family tree is even more mysterious. In the absence of any sense of family history, I can only imagine an unbroken line, stretching back into the Dark Ages, of faceless peasants. Where did the music come from? I have no idea.

Grandad Jackson, who'd been in the army, related to my dad and my three uncles not so much as father to sons, but as sergeant major to privates. His sternness was legendary, although I can see now that he had a sense of humor, too, a gloomy northern sense of humor. My brother Chris remembers him answering a knock at the door one day in the middle of a torrential rainstorm. A drenched postman stood there, and made a feeble and redundant observation about the weather. Grandad's reply was, "Ah well, there's no one out as matters."

My grandparents' house seemed to have been cleverly designed to be as inhospitable as possible to human beings. Not only did Grandma have to stick her hands in the fire every day, but Chris and I had to sleep in a bedroom that could only be reached through the bathroom. Occasionally we'd be trapped in there for all eternity while someone took a bath. The toilet, though, was at the bottom of the garden. It had a rough wooden seat and I lived in dread of having to find my way through the whole dark house, including the unseen horrors of the coal cellar, to use it in the middle of the night. There was a chamber pot under the bed, but somehow that seemed even worse.

The house perched on a slope overlooking a graveyard on one side, a slag-heap on another, and a disused pipe factory on a third. My grandfather and great-grandfather had both worked for the pipeworks, mostly underground. In Portsmouth they dug for chalk; up here they dug for clay. In its heyday, the pipeworks had turned out everything from clay pipes for tobacco to giant water and sewage pipes through which a grown man could walk upright. Now pieces of pipe of all shapes and sizes lay scattered around an overgrown field for kids to play on. This unearthly landscape still haunts me. Every time I see a science-fiction film that takes place in the aftermath of a nuclear apocalypse, I think of Swadlincote.

After a week or so of climbing up and down slag-heaps in the rain, it was always a relief to start the long journey home. Looking at the map now, it seems a minuscule distance, but at the time, Staffordshire was the far north to us. The journey seemed to take forever, by coach, changing at Cheltenham. Even later, when my dad got a car, it was still a day-long epic of packed lunches and thermos flasks, frequent stops, and plastic bags to throw up in. My dad had been to the Mediterranean and the Caribbean with the navy, but the distance to somewhere in the "real" north of England—say, Newcastle—seemed as unimaginable to my parents as it was to me. London, only seventy miles away, might as well have been another planet.

Mum and Dad were cautious people. They named me David Ian (Joe came later, as a nickname, and finally as my real name). My brothers were Christopher Paul and Peter Ronald, Ron being my dad's name. The names were carefully chosen: They were all "normal"; none of them could be made fun of by the other kids; and they could all be inoffensively shortened, to Dave, Chris, and Pete. They'd thought of everything. The middle names were "normal" too. You couldn't even make anything rude out of the initials.

My parents mostly obeyed the first rule of English working-class life: Never appear to be odd, eccentric, artsy, stuck-up, or in any way different from everybody else. Their greatest hope for me and my brothers seemed to be that we'd manage to get through life without being noticed too much. But for better or worse, I felt different.

I don't claim to have been "special" in some magical, precious way, a child genius dropped from the sky by all-seeing angels. But I did feel, as a child, that I'd somehow gotten stuck in the wrong place with the wrong parents. My real parents, surely, were explorers or actors or circus performers, who would some day come back and take me away. I was imaginative, curious about the outside world, and extremely sensitive. None of these traits were exactly encouraged in Paulsgrove. Maybe that was why I couldn't breathe.

My earliest memory is of being convinced, at the age of three, that I was going to die. So you could say I've been ahead of the game ever since. We were driving, as a treat, in my Uncle Sid's car on a summer afternoon, and suddenly I couldn't breathe. My mother opened all the windows, but it didn't help. In a panic we drove to the doctor. The doctor explained to my mum and dad that their son was, and most likely always would be, an asthmatic.

My parents were horrified. This would keep me off the football field and set me apart from the other kids. It wasn't much fun for me, either. From the age of three until my early twenties, I suffered from crippling attacks that lasted for weeks at a time. During them, I could hardly move —later, when we moved from the flat to a house, my father had to carry me up and down the stairs to go to the toilet. I was off school for weeks, drinking Lucozade until my teeth turned orange, suffering the embarrassment of classmates being delegated to pick up and deliver my homework. I became a guinea pig for every injection and inhaler, every indigestible pill and vile-tasting medicine known to medical science.

I was hospitalized twice, and put in an oxygen tent, which terrified me. My mother untucked a corner of the tent from under the mattress and slipped her hand over mine. At least she could indulge in the dream of her own childhood: She'd wanted to be a nurse. Still, I must have worn her out. When I wasn't having asthma attacks, I had hay fever, bronchitis, and pleurisy, which was accompanied by a fever so intense that I hallucinated. Sinister globular things popped out of the ceiling and grew and grew and tried to crush me. And the asthma attacks kept coming, and I did physical therapy, which just made me wheeze more, and took medications that I was allergic to, which made me wheeze even more and made my face turn purple and swell up like a balloon.

In other words, I was a sick kid.

I tried to deal with it the way I saw my father deal with things: stoically. All right, I'd tell myself: I was spending most of my life in my bedroom, which was cold (only the living room was heated, by a coal fire) and dark (it faced north to Portsdown Hill and got no sun). My bedside cabinet (an apple box covered in the same sickly wallpaper as the living room) was piled high with medicines. *But it could be worse.* I wasn't blind, deaf, or dumb. I had two arms and two legs. Stiff upper lip! The second rule of English working-class life: Suffer stoically. What kind of state did you have to be in before you could be allowed—or allow yourself—a little bit of sympathy?

Inevitably, I became a bit of a loner, a bit of a misfit. I didn't want to be that way. It just seemed to happen.

I loved books and still do. Near our council flat there was a little branch library in a black-creosoted wooden hut. I used to sit on the floor for hours, leafing through books. The floor was dark red linoleum. That little library was my favorite place in the world; if I close my eyes and try hard enough, I can still smell it. My favorite books were about astronomy and space exploration, and my hero was Dan Dare, Pilot of the Future, in the *Eagle* weekly. I was quite convinced that by the time I grew up, England would have a space fleet. I'm still disappointed it hasn't happened.

Back on Earth, the local bullies were picking up where the asthma left off. I was punched, tripped, and taunted in the playground. My head was pushed down toilets. I was kicked in the eye and got a huge sty which leaked pus for weeks. I was strangled with my school scarf and passed out, once again convinced I was going to die. I was surrounded one evening after school by a circle of older kids on bikes. Every time I tried to escape, my legs were battered by their wheels, and they wouldn't let me go until I finally broke down and cried.

I rarely told anyone about the bullying. When I did—say, when my dad demanded long and hard enough why I was looking so bloody miserable—he'd just tell me to fight back. "Stand up for yourself! Hit 'em back!" he'd say, and he would make me furious. It was obvious to everyone but him that I couldn't beat up a geriatric hamster. Hit 'em back? Sure, give them a good laugh before they kill me. Why were parents so incredibly, embarrassingly stupid?

I don't know what I would have done without Dan Dare. He was one thing to look forward to each week. Without that, my stoicism might have given out. I might have been forced to admit that I was, in fact, having a pretty miserable childhood.

White Trash

I'M SITTING at the counter in my favorite New York diner, tucking into eggs over easy with hash browns—very English, the breakfast fry-up, but very American, too. I'm washing it down with cranberry juice—caffeine is probably the only vice I don't have—and someone turns on the radio.

Most of the time, I don't *hear* music. My brain just tunes it out. We're all bombarded with some sort of music on a daily basis—in shops, TV commercials, restaurants, lifts—most of it simply noise pollution, deadening us to the real joy of music. So I only listen when I really want to. But the Puerto Rican waitress has turned on a Spanish channel, and a seductive salsa rhythm seeps into the room. It's a *charanga* band—a traditional group that uses flute and violin over the standard latin rhythm section of congas, bongos, and timbales—and now I'm half-listening. Then the violinist takes a solo, and I'm hooked. He's a great, inspired player. The band is playing a simple three-chord vamp, and he follows the chords closely, and yet still manages to come up with witty, ingenious, melodic twists. And the way he plays with the time! Dragging a phrase, and then ending it right on the beat. Setting up syncopations—accents that go against the beat—and then turning them around, playing them backwards. Then he hits an unexpected high note, and it's like a shaft of light going right through my body, filling me with warmth. Without even thinking, I cry out—"Yeah!" or "All right!" or something—and I marvel at the way that music, after all these years, can still surprise me.

The guy next to me just goes on munching his cheeseburger. But something special has happened, even if I'm the only one who knows it. The band on the radio are most likely second- or third-generation Puerto Ricans who were raised uptown, *way* uptown—in the Bronx—in a different world from me. But through the music, they've connected with an Englishman way downtown, in a way that would otherwise never happen.

"You've lost yer roots, mate." I remember a local yob saying that to me one night in a Portsmouth pub. He said it with a sneer, to emphasize his personal distaste at the fact that I'd been living in New York City, on and off, for years. I was hurt, until I thought about it later and realized: He doesn't know me, doesn't even know that I recently bought a place in my hometown, and he's talking out of his arse, because you *never* lose your roots. It's just that you have *branches,* too. I have a lot of branches in New York, but my roots will always be in Paulsgrove.

When I was six or seven, and brother Pete was getting too big for a pram, we moved from our council flat to a semidetached council house just up the road. I was shattered—I'd tentatively befriended a kid who lived close to the flats, and I thought I'd never see him again. How small the world of our childhood is! But the new house seemed spacious and friendly enough. Chris and I graduated to bunk beds—no more cover-pulling and shin-kicking during the night. The house even had a small back garden, luxury after the patch of damp concrete we'd shared with the other tenants of the flats.

For a while, my mother's father moved in with us. He was on his last legs, and having some difficulty coming to terms with the twentieth century. I'll never forget my brother's panic-stricken voice coming from inside the house, as my mother and I stood in the garden: "MUM! GRANDAD'S BOILING HIS SOCKS ON THE GAS IN A PLASTIC BOWL!"

Like my Grandad, Portsmouth, I've always thought, has character rather than charm. Unlike Brighton or Bournemouth, which were built for seaside fun, it's always been a working port, with a funfair and pier added as afterthoughts. Old photographs show it as a prettier place, but World War II put an end to that. Naval ports were prime targets, and my mother cowered in an air-raid shelter behind her mother's pub, the Binsteed Arms, as twenty-five thousand incendiary bombs rained down on the city. Even now, she's frightened by thunder and lightning as a result.

As for poor old Pompey, the architects and town planners of the '50s and '60s did their best to finish off the job that Hitler started. Our neighborhood was ugly even by those standards. Paulsgrove consisted of council flats and semidetached council houses, like ours, the top halves of which were covered with corrugated iron, which was in turn covered with peeling paint and dents made by bottles, stones, and cricket balls. Some of our neighbors were kindly, but many of them were sinister, subhuman creatures. Their houses had broken windows, permanently patched with bits of wood, and kids sprawled outside them in a miasma of dirt and rubbish, dismembering toy soldiers or rusty tricycles. Mothers screamed at them through clouds of fag-smoke. Fathers were at work or in the pub. Some of the kids were truly wretched, snotty-nosed guttersnipes right out of *Oliver Twist*. Once, on my way home from school, I passed a house where a young boy was calmly taking a shit on the front step. He returned my look of astonishment with a rude gesture.

What was the music of Paulsgrove? I can hardly remember any. Those Puerto Rican kids in the Bronx grew up beating out salsa rhythms on boxes and tin cans. Their music was part of their identity, and I envy them. I don't remember feeling anything like a sense of identity.

Many years later, I went back to Paulsgrove and found it much the same but smartened up a bit. Thanks to Maggie Thatcher, people were starting to buy their own council houses, and quite a few had celebrated by building tiny extensions out from their front doors, too small to serve any practical purpose, but richly symbolic. A boy of about twelve asked me if I had a cigarette for him, and when I said No, he informed me that in that case I could Fuck Off.

Later still, I returned with my American girlfriend, who was curious to see where I'd grown up. By now Paulsgrove was cleaner and greener still, but enough of the old neighborhood remained for her to tell me there was a name for this kind of place, and this kind of people. The name was "white trash."

I couldn't argue. Still, since white trash was all we were and all we knew, we were at least free of racial or class conflict. School was all boy, all white, all working class. As a student, I quickly set a pattern that never changed. I was exceptionally good at English, and attracted in a vague way to the arts—vague, in the sense that I didn't really know what was out there, and I wasn't being given too many clues. I was utterly hopeless at maths and sciences, and sports didn't even enter the picture. I tried to play football precisely once. My asthma was dormant at the time, but after five minutes the ball hit me right in the face. I was led off the pitch in a daze, blood gushing from my nose. After that, I was further humiliated by being forced to compete in the long jump, on the pretext that I was "tall." I *was* tall, but I was also weak, skinny, awkward, and a nervous wreck. I ran up to the line where I was supposed to jump, and then froze on the spot. Boys jeered and teachers groaned with frustration.

The teachers, taking a very general, godlike overview of my progress, considered me a slightly below average student. Their prescription to bring me up to par was to ignore my strengths and force me into daily confrontation with my weaknesses. For the rest of my schooldays, physics and geometry and algebra were stuffed down my throat until I wanted to puke. I never improved but just got more and more resentful.

In my spare time, almost as a kind of revenge, I started writing stories and illustrating them. I seemed to have a talent for drawing. Pretty soon I'd created my own space hero, Xavier Megan (I picked the names from a "Name Your Baby" book of my mother's). It was a shameless rip-off of Dan Dare. One day I told my father about my creation. He glared at me through narrowed eyes and said, deliberately, "You stupid child."

I wasn't quite sure why, but I was devastated. He might as well have amputated my right arm with a chain saw. Whether this was the start of my resentment of my father or just a step along the way, I don't remember. But I know that once I'd pulled myself together, I was more determined than ever to do something creative, however stupid and childish it might have been.

My dad could not have been accused of creativity, although he was what was commonly referred to as "handy." As well as plastering, he could lay a few bricks, make things out of scraps of wood, and so on. He wasn't a bad guy, but we never really understood each other. I think now that he had a sensitive side, which had been almost beaten out of him by his own father, and which he was ashamed of. So when he looked at me and saw a sensitive misfit in the making, he tried to beat it out of me, too. Not that he was cruel. It was for my own good! But it didn't work, any more than forced mathematics. One night, after smacking me around a bit, he sat down on the edge of my bed and tried to explain that it didn't mean he didn't still love me. I couldn't have been more than six or seven, but I remember thinking: I'm not buying this.

Thus, I came to fear my father without really respecting him. Still, he could be kind and generous. I remember him buying me hot salted peanuts from Woolworth's, and taking me to W. H. Smith's to look at the books—not to buy any, you didn't buy books when there was a library down the road. He took me to my first movie, *Ben-Hur*, which thrilled and terrified me, and later to my first concert. Just when I would start to hate him, he would do exactly the right thing. For as long as I can remember, he puzzled me.

My mother, on the other hand, was like a fixed planet to orbit around. She was a housewife and mother, and seemed not only content with her lot but positively delighted about it. She was Florence Nightingale, she lived to take care of us, and she seemed not to have the foggiest idea of what she herself might think or feel or want as an individual person. She was self-effacing to a degree that would later drive me mad with frustration. But through all the gray years before music came along, I have to say that it was my mother who kept me going. I felt, on a basic level, cared for. My problems would have more to do with not feeling understood.

I was soon working in earnest on my homemade comic books. I got another boy at school to help out, drawing or coloring panels here and there. His name was Gary, he was slightly more popular than me—which wasn't saying much—and he had an impressive way of drawing explosions, with bits of metal framework flying everywhere.

The tough kids sneered, but the others liked what we'd done, and somehow our efforts managed to circulate around the classroom intact. We started a weekly serial. We were actually having fun, until one day, an announcement in the classroom: The headmaster wanted to see us in his study.

We were terrified. It had to be about our comic: It was the only thing the two of us had in common. In the headmaster's study, we squirmed in our seats as the headmaster sat reading it in front of us for what seemed like hours. We were absolutely convinced we were about to be caned. Finally he spoke.

"Are you boys responsible for this?"

"Yes sir," we mumbled in unison, staring at our shoes.

"It's jolly good," said the headmaster. "Very exciting story. Are you going to do some more?"

I was too stunned to speak. Gary stammered "Y-Yes, sir."

"Jolly good!" said the headmaster. "Keep it up. Well, run along."

Once the shock wore off, and I realized there wasn't a catch, I was walking on air. This was the first time in my life that I had my own creative efforts recognized, approved of, even encouraged. It was like a shot of pure oxygen, like being able to breathe again after an asthma attack.

I suppose the incident sticks in my mind because it shows how rare this kind of encouragement was in the homes, schools, and streets of Paulsgrove. Imagine, two kids expecting to be caned for making a comic book! What must it be like to be a child prodigy like the young Orson Welles, who was constantly told by everyone around him that he was a genius? You'd probably develop a monstrous ego. But then again, half the battle of creating a *Citizen Kane* is simply believing you can do it.

Pretty soon I became known as "the kid who wrote stories." This made me nervous at first, until I realized that it wasn't getting me beaten up any more than before. There was even a certain grudging respect from some quarters. By the time I was ten, I was starting to see a way forward, a road I could take through life. It was pretty vague, but it had something to do with being a fascinating eccentric and writing stories. I was going to be a writer when I grew up. It wouldn't occur to me for another couple of years that a writer could use anything other than words.

Kryptonite

AT LEAST THREE different people I can think of have been quoted as saying that writing about music is like dancing about architecture. In other words: Music takes us to places that words cannot, and maybe that's the whole point.

But it's surely not *impossible* to write about music. Quite a few writers (Proust, Shaw, Joyce, Thomas Mann, Milan Kundera) have done it very well, as have certain articulate musicians (Berlioz, Bernstein, Copland). The problem is that it's a threefold challenge. First, you have to really understand the music. Second, you have to translate into a different language: the language of words. And third, you have to use the words to produce a good piece of writing. And even if you can manage all that, you may have written *about* music, but you still won't necessarily have *explained* it.

So, if it's so tough, why do we all keep writing, and talking, about music? Nonwriters and nonmusicians, too, talking about it at endless length, in reams and reams of newsprint, at parties, in fanzines, on the Internet?

For myself, I *have* to write about music. My thoughts about music and my experiences as a musician are inseparable from any kind of memoir I might attempt. If, on the other hand, I tried to write a book purely about music, it would be full of stories from my own life. So it seems I have no choice but to do both. And as I approach the task, I don't feel like I'm dancing about architecture. I feel more like a lemming rushing towards the edge of a cliff. My only excuse is that, like millions of lemmings before me, I just can't help myself.

What's the first music I remember? Maybe that's as good a place as any to start. My early environment, musically speaking, was quite barren. But I do remember certain songs.

The first was called "The Runaway Train." I must have been five or six, and my parents had just bought a radio. It was a Saturday morning—late morning—and I was luxuriating in bed. I never, even as a kid, liked to get up early. Besides, I shared a bed with my brother, and when he got up I liked to sprawl and roll around. And from the next room came a tune with a very American, more-or-less country sound, and a rolling, rumbling beat, like a train steaming across the prairie. The melody was almost a direct steal from the Civil War anthem "When Johnny Comes Marching Home." It's a catchy tune, I think now as I sit at the piano and pick out the notes. But as I fill out the melody with the chords that I remember, I realize it has one odd little twist. The first two lines are in a major key. Then, on the third line, it switches quite unexpectedly to the minor, with a descending line that ends up once again in the major. So this simple ditty takes on a note of seriousness halfway through, a question mark, a moment of tension, which is then released. Maybe this was what set it apart from other simple ditties I must have heard.

Scholars with bigger brains than mine have debated for centuries the question of why major keys sound "happy" and minor keys "sad." Of course, there are instances of minor-key tunes that are lively or jaunty or at any rate not exactly tragic. But that minor third, just the lowering of the third note of the scale by a semitone, imposes at least a certain gravity. If, as an experiment, you alter that one note and transpose a minor-key tune into the major, there's a lifting of shadows, a lightness, which might not be what you want. It might be like too much sugar in your coffee. But something definitely happens, and it's as undeniable as purple turning to light blue.

The next Saturday morning, I begged my parents to turn on the radio. I thought that if you turned on, same time, same channel, every week, you always heard "The Runaway Train"! I was crushed to find out that this wasn't the case. Never mind, said my dad, they'll play it again soon. Which, after a few weeks, they did, and I bounced up and down on my bed for joy.

Another tune sticks in my mind. Several years later—I must have been nine or ten—my family went to the Navy Days gala down by the harbor. Navy Days was by far the most colorful thing that happened in Portsmouth. Once a year, the navy would celebrate its preeminence in the town, fly flags from every mast and turret, and invite the public to clamber all over its ships. It was a hot summer day, the ice-cream vans were doing record business, and the whole town, the whole world, was happy. I was thrilled to descend into the bowels of a battleship. I laughed at the mudlarks, urchin kids who used to roll around in the harbor mud at low tide and dive for pennies we threw from the pier. And somewhere amongst all this festivity, I passed by a parked car, its windows open, just as its radio played the theme music from the movie *Exodus*.

I was transfixed by this music. It was sad, but strong; noble, but with a yearning quality that brought tears to my eyes. Everyone else was partying, but I felt as though I'd discovered a secret truth: that beneath it all was sadness. Not that the happiness and the pomp and circumstance were false, but that the sadness was always there, in a delicate balance with it. It suddenly seemed to me unbearably poignant. And I knew that no one else would understand.

And no one could, or ever will. When music hits you like this, it cuts through logic and soars like a pole-vaulter over the walls of your rational mind. It reaches you in a visceral way that is unique to your own experience. No two people hear the same music.

Now that I'm older, and hardened, and a clever bastard, I still find *Exodus* a good tune, if a bit sentimental. I have to remind myself that there are worse things than sentimentality. The Russians, for instance, revel in it—they believe it's at least halfway to real emotion, and therefore better than nothing.

Experience also tells me that part of this tune's poignancy comes, like "The Runaway Train," but more so, from an artful juxtaposition of major and minor. In this case, a tune in a minor key is repeatedly harmonized with major chords, at points where the ear seems to expect a minor chord, so that we always feel the clouds are just about to lift—but they never quite do. This is where the yearning quality comes from.

Does it matter? Should I, at this point, apologize to all lovers of the *Exodus* theme? Have I spoiled it for you?

More than one person over the years has suggested to me that to study music in depth, to pull it apart and analyze it, must be to strip away its magic. I'm happy to report that this has never, ever, happened. I know, for instance, what major and minor chords are, how to play them on a keyboard, and how to write them on paper, but I still don't know how or why they produce their *effect*. Studying the scores of great symphonies has only increased my respect for them. And although I've learned to manipulate the materials of music, I still feel that I'm working with something intangible. It's as though I've learned, like a carpenter, how to measure and cut and mold and join. But whereas a carpenter knows that wood comes from trees, my material is like some sort of Kryptonite from another planet. It's not quite solid, or liquid, or vaporous. When all's said and done, I really don't know *what* it is, or how it got here. And the more I think about it, the more ephemeral it seems, as though it were something I'd dreamed.

So it's not so much that the power of music can't be explained. You *can* explain it, break it all down to its atoms and molecules, show how it works, cut it open and reveal its beating heart, measure it and classify it and talk about it till hell freezes over, and it's *still* a mystery. And in many cultures, that which is beyond words and beyond rational explanation is a definition of God.

Uncomfortable with mystery, we try to explain the power of music by the memories, smells, associations it evokes. Sometimes this works. But *Exodus* is associated in my mind with Portsmouth and Her Majesty's Navy, and that doesn't explain anything.

The next big musical impression in my life came from my other hometown, Burton, and that doesn't explain much either. Rather than one specific song, it's a sound: the sound of mid-'60s British pop.

My father had one brother a couple of years older than him (gloomy, cadaverous Uncle Jack, who rarely said anything beyond "Ey oop") and two much younger brothers. They were almost two generations within the same family. And my younger uncles, Ken and Terry, were in what was called at the time a beat group. They were called the Diamonds, and I have a photo of them: Burns guitars, shiny suits, and Brylcreemed hair, facing the world in their one publicity photo with shy half-smiles. They were quite popular for a while in local clubs and dance-halls. The highlight of their career was opening a show for P. J. Proby, a bona fide pop star, albeit one who was more famous for splitting his trousers on stage than for his music. My uncles then gave it up and "settled down." I'd been too young to see them play, but the kind of music they were playing was all around me, once I started to notice it. There were the Beatles, of course, but at the time I made no particular distinction between them and the Merseybeats, or the Swinging Blue Jeans, or Billy J. Kramer and the Dakotas. It was all clanging guitars, sizzling cymbals, and raw voices.

I sat on the floor in my grandparents' house. The floor sloped alarmingly, so much so that the rugs would crumple and have to be straightened out at the end of each day. The house was starting to collapse. Outside it rained as usual, but I would be immersed in a pile of pop fan magazines belonging to one of my young aunts. The idea of being in a group was intriguing. It would be like your own little club, a secret society. I even entered a "Win an Electric Guitar" contest and drew pictures of the band I would form when I won. I was quite convinced I'd win, and my group would be called the Meteors. Much more recently, a band has actually recorded with that name, but spelled correctly. If my band had used the design I drew for the front of the bass drum, we would have been called the Metoers.

My spelling was usually better than that—after all, I'd made up my mind to be a writer. But now I was thinking about a second option. Being in a pop group might be more fun. Strangely enough, though, I didn't particularly relate it to *music*. It didn't seem to have anything to do with the revelation I'd experienced on hearing *Exodus*. It was as though you could either try to penetrate the mysteries of musical art, or you could be in a pop group.

What if you wanted to do both?

Eleven-Plus

In 1965, the *annus mirabilis* of rock 'n' roll, I was ten years old. Not living in the big city, not having a hip older sibling, what I knew of pop culture was only the tip of the iceberg. My parents had acquired a primitive record-player, but they never bought many records. They liked music, but I don't think they really knew what to buy. I remember Frank Ifield singing "She Taught Me to Yodel," and a Lonnie Donegan 78, which I accidentally trod on and smashed.

Still, I managed to become a pop fan of sorts. My favorite group was the Searchers. I liked their chiming twelve-string guitar sound, and there was a plaintive quality about their songs. Already, I seemed to have a taste for music with a melancholy flavor. It's a taste not everyone understands. People equate melancholy with misery and depression, but it's something different, and it can be deeply pleasurable.

I started to pick up secondhand singles from junk shops and jumble sales. The first one I bought was "Telstar" by the Tornadoes. I loved the cheesy organ sound—I had no idea what kind of instrument was playing—and the "modern," sci-fi image it conjured up. Mostly though, I found recent singles by British beat groups: "Juliet" by the Four Pennies, "The Game of Love" by Wayne Fontana and the Mindbenders, "Glad All Over" by the Dave Clark Five. I bought neon-pink bubble gum, which I hated, but which came with picture cards of pop groups.

I looked in vain for a secondhand copy of the Kinks' "You Really Got

Me," which I'd heard coming from a radio one sunny day on the stony beach at Southsea, the seaside-resort area of Portsmouth. I was thrilled by the fuzz guitar sound, which Dave Davies apparently got by sticking knitting needles through his speakers—a technique pioneered back in the late '50s by Johnny Burnette and the Rock 'n' Roll Trio.

I heard that fuzz-tone again when the Rolling Stones played "Satisfaction" on *Top of the Pops.* All the other groups suddenly seemed insipid. There was an air of menace about the Stones. They were less like a secret society than a gang. I felt a surge of pubescent adrenaline—which is powerful stuff—and said out loud, to no one in particular, "When I'm older, I'm going to have a group just like that."

My mother, knitting, utterly unmoved by the Stones, said "That's nice, dear," or something to that effect. As though I'd said that when I grew up I was going to have the world's biggest stamp collection.

It was time to take the Eleven-plus exam. A pass would send me, probably, to Portsmouth Grammar School, which is where someone with my sensitivity and artistic bent probably should have been, but an equally likely fail would send me to a no-hope comprehensive. I just scraped through, and I was sent to the Portsmouth Technical High School, the only school in town that was somewhere in between.

The Tec, as everyone called it, was big and harsh and it scared the hell out of me. My hopelessness at maths and sports was soon an object of ridicule, while my advanced reading age and interest in books and drawing were sullenly resented. As soon as I arrived, having barely opened my mouth or even looked at anyone, I was labeled a "weirdo." People just knew.

They seemed to know everything. Who the tough kids were (they were called 'ard-nuts or 'oolies—short for hooligans). Which teachers were "queer," and which ones would beat the living crap out of you just for tying your shoelaces wrong. They knew all kinds of local folk wisdom: for instance, that the nearby Isle of Wight was more correctly called "The Pile of Shite" and that all its inhabitants were inbred. In a local joke, an Island boy gets married, but after a week it's all over, and he's back with his parents. "What happened?" asks his dad. "Oi found out she was a virgin," says the son. "Ah," says the old man, "you done the roight thing. If she ain't good enough for her own koind, she ain't good enough fer you."

I laughed at this, but I didn't understand it. Nor did I understand the constant references to what happened on Portsdown Hill—"going up the 'ill" was a nudging, winking euphemism for illicit sexual activity. I'd always thought of the Hill as a place where bored youths hung around waiting to beat you up. Sex was apparently connected in some way with violence and lawlessness. I felt a kind of nausea as new feelings stirred inside me, like a boat losing its direction on a sea that was much, much bigger than I'd imagined. Soon I'd be a teenager, good God, childhood had been bad enough, what now?

I gradually figured *some* things out. Like where to get that fabulous occasional treat, a bag of chips after school—Greasy Ada's, where one kid once found a fag-end in his.

I found out which shops would sell you a packet of ten cigarettes and which prefects would turn a blind eye if you smoked them on the bus. I became obsessed with the fear that I'd be called on to smoke a fag in public and wouldn't know what to do. I got a packet of ten Players No. 10s from a machine round the back of the Guildhall and practiced when no one was looking. I held match after match to cigarette after cigarette and got nothing but an unpleasant singeing smell. Finally I gave up. I didn't know you were supposed to inhale to light them. I didn't know anything! I stewed and squirmed in shameful ignorance. How was I to know that most of the other boys probably felt the same?

The teachers at my new school were no less frightening than the hard-nut kids. One maths teacher, a huge red-faced man, would pick boys up by the hair and throw them bodily across the room. And there was a physics teacher with the luridly piratical name of Bill "One-Lung" Blood, who stood at the back in school assemblies, scowling, rattling coins in his pocket, and coughing horrible gurgling coughs, a result of having (so they said) only one lung.

Just a few weeks into my first year at the Tec, another maths teacher, firing questions at boys randomly, spotted me as a mathematical dunce.

"Don't you know your eight times table, Jackson?" he demanded.

"Yes sir! I mean ... well, I'm not sure, sir."

The maths teacher dragged me out to stand in front of the class.

"This boy will now recite the eight times table," he announced.

I felt faint. I got as far as four eights being thirty-two until my mind went blank.

"What's the matter, Jackson?" asked the maths teacher.

"I'm just thinking, sir," I said, but I could have thought until Christmas, it wouldn't have helped. Eventually, I took a couple of wild guesses until I got five eights.

"Go on, Jackson," said the teacher.

He wasn't going to let me go. My mind went blank again.

"I can't do it, sir," I pleaded.

"Of course you can, Jackson. You can't possibly have reached the age of eleven without knowing your eight times table. Go on."

You bastard, I thought, you sadistic bastard, you're going to make me stand here until I struggle all the way through to twelve eights. I'll be here all day. I stood for several minutes in defiant silence. Then, suddenly, tears rolled down my cheeks.

The teacher sighed and told me to sit down. Every face in the class turned towards me with an expression of sheer loathing. They didn't really care that I was a mathematical idiot. But crying, that was another thing. I'd gone from being a weirdo to an outcast, an untouchable.

Getting out of bed in the morning got harder and harder. I put my alarm clock in a saucepan on the other side of the room. It would rattle and clang like all the torments of hell and I'd be forced to get out of bed to silence it. I was just going to have to cope with the Tec. I took comfort from small things, like the fact that there was one—exactly one—other boy in the school who was taller, skinnier, and more ghostly pale than me. He looked like a skeleton animated by voodoo. And if I was a weirdo, at least I wasn't manifestly insane, like the kid who tried to hang himself in the toilet with his school tie. Or paranoid delusional, like the kid with enormous, thick lips who constantly followed me around the place telling me that *I* had big lips.

After a while I graduated from Dan Dare to Marvel comics—Spiderman and the Fantastic Four. Trading comics with other kids got me accepted up to a point. But if I ever stood a chance of becoming one of the gang, I soon blew it in a big way.

I enrolled in a violin class. Despite its "technical" manifesto, the Tec apparently had some musical possibilities. The best thing about the violin class, though, and my main motivation, was that it took place during the sports period, which I was desperate to escape.

It's hard to imagine anything on earth more excruciating than the sound of a snot-nosed rabble of eleven-year-old boys attempting to play the violin. Just thinking about it makes me want to take several aspirins and go to bed with a hot water bottle. Still, one good thing about the early stages of learning an instrument is that progress is reasonably quick, and follows a pretty continuous upward curve. It's only later that the curve flattens out, and the real work begins.

I made good progress on my cheap fiddle. I liked the instrument, the feel of the wood, the way it smelled, the feel of the rosin on the bow. The Strings are hard to play, but they're the most "organic" instruments, satisfying in a way that no synthesizer can ever be. A violin is nothing, after all, but wood and varnish, with catgut and steel for strings. Even an instrument as simple as a trumpet or clarinet seems like a drunken riot of plumbing by comparison.

Nevertheless I soon realized that it wasn't so much the instrument itself that intrigued me as the opportunity to learn more about music. Learning to read music was fun. Notation was pleasingly logical, and should be to anyone who has some sense of rhythm and isn't irredeemably tone-deaf.

Around the same time, some of my peers must have been making their first assaults on guitars, and most of them *still* don't read music. They use all kinds of strategies to avoid it, and only make things more difficult for themselves in the process. Some of them have confessed to me a fear that reading "the dots" would take away their "feel" or their "soul." Where do people get these ideas? You might as well say that learning the alphabet will hamper your ability to write poetry. Musical notation certainly made a hell of a lot more sense to me, at eleven or twelve, than physics.

In fact, as I learned notation and the fundamentals of music theory, a whole new world started to open up, a sort of parallel universe in which everything made sense. I was no prodigy, but I was told I had a good ear. I also had an urge (although, typically, I sensed it wasn't allowed) to wander away from my scales and exercises, and try to make up my own tunes. I wasn't scared of the parallel universe. I wanted to get in there and explore.

The "real world" was more problematic. Apart from the expected, by now stoically endured beatings and asthma attacks, I was soon floundering in the early terrors of adolescence. I had strong sexual feelings about both girls and boys, and not a clue what it all meant. My parents, and everyone else's as far as I could tell, denied the very existence of sex. So, like generations of British schoolboys before us, we had to pick up clues from each other. How (can anyone tell me, please) were we supposed to do this? All the while pretending to each other, of course, that we had it all figured out?

One day, on a rare occasion when I hadn't been able to escape from sports, a kid was tossing off in full view in the middle of the locker room.

"You dirty sod!" said one boy.

"Piss off!" said the masturbator.

"That's what you have to do to have a baby," said another boy.

"No it's not!" said another.

"Hobson can make smoke come out of his," said a third.

"You mean spunk!"

"No, smoke, I saw it."

"What's spunk?"

And so on and on, the blind leading the blind, and always in awe of the slightly older kids who boasted (at fourteen and fifteen!) that they knew what it was all about. Stained sheets, shame, and confusion. And we weren't even Catholics. Why any adult thinks—and they still do—that they're doing children a favor by "protecting" them from sex is utterly beyond me.

Guilt, shame, and a terrible yearning. Like the tension of major and minor. Like the melody that always seemed to lie just out of reach of my groping fingers.

Crumbs

Nothing much changed in the next couple of years. My brother Chris joined me at the Tec, but he was two years below me, a big barrier at that age. We sometimes took the bus together, but, following family tradition, we never talked much. We got on well enough, but we'd never quite figured out how much we had in common. And while I was shy, Chris was an obvious introvert, less awkward than me and with a sweeter disposition, but largely silent, and as stoical as my father. I didn't even know that he, too, was becoming very interested in music.

We both tried to look out for Pete. We thought he was cute. He was both the baby and the extrovert of the family. He climbed trees, fell out of windows, and buzzed about, as my mother said, like a blue-arsed fly. He talked too fast, cracked jokes, and got words wrong: He called the Isle of Wight hovercraft "the horrorcraft," which still makes me smile now, as I imagine a boat full of skeletons and dagger-wielding hands coming out of every corner.

I kept working at the violin and the theory. By the time I was fourteen, I was starting to think of myself as a musician. Things were looking up. I didn't know it, but I was lucky, too: I was starting out in music by getting some solid technical ground under my feet, before I knew that—this being the '60s—discipline had become a dirty word. The older truth, that discipline is actually the road to true freedom, would be out of fashion for quite a while.

I was encouraged by the school music teacher, Reggie Wassell. Reggie was a distinguished-looking man with longish slicked-back silver hair, who wore a bow tie and trousers so high-waisted that the braces that held them up seemed no more than a few inches long. He looked, now I come to think of it, exactly how a music teacher should have looked.

Reggie towered saintlike above the rogues' gallery that was the Tec's teaching staff. He'd done a remarkable job of creating a musical oasis. Like any good concentration camp, the Tec had an orchestra, which was an unwieldy assortment of whatever instruments were currently being taught in the neighborhood. There might be only one viola but five clarinets, for instance. Reggie's sister came in to play the cello. We called her Bunhead, because of the lacquered hair-sculpture that perched on top of her head and shook backwards and forwards in time with her vibrato.

The school orchestra played Handel's *Water Music*, over and over again, for years. I played second violin, sometimes from the music, sometimes, with varying degrees of success, by ear. This once got me a kick in the shin from the older kid next to me when the line I was busking turned out to be the first violin part.

Then, at one rehearsal, fate and Reggie Wassell conspired to give me the job of playing the timpani—without a timpani part. The music had gone missing, and Reggie, in an extraordinary display of trust and generosity, told me to just listen to the rest of the orchestra and make up my own part.

Reggie must have seen me fooling around on the battered old kettledrums during breaks. But I don't know how he'd guessed that I also had the kind of ear that could tell me, for instance, what kind of things to play on them in a given piece. I didn't even know that myself. But I knew that the timpani, alone in the drum kingdom, could be tuned to specific notes, and since this piece was in D, I tuned them to the most useful ones: D and A. And as the orchestra played, I listened for the right timpani moments, which I instinctively felt should be few, but dramatic. I bashed out the obvious loud cadences, lay in wait in the quiet passages, attempted a crescendo roll, and ended with a flourish. Reggie was delighted, and he used my performance to illustrate a first lesson in Orchestration.

"You see," he beamed, "he didn't just bang the drums any-old-where. He waited for the right moment and didn't play too much. He played a small part, but you *heard* it! That's the secret. If you just keep bashing away nonstop, on any instrument, you don't *hear* it any more!"

Apart from being a great ego boost, this was one of the best music lessons I've ever had. Orchestration, or in jazz and pop parlance, arranging, is the art (to put it crudely) of deciding who in a group of musicians plays which part, and when, and how. And it started for me with an old but indestructible principle: Less is more. It might seem obvious, but I still hear demo tapes by bands in which everyone plays flat out all the time. They can't work out why it sounds monotonous, and they're searching for the right thing to *add*.

Just as a painter starts from a blank canvas, a musician should start from silence; and one of our most essential skills is the ability to simply shut up and listen.

The other thing I learned from my first timpani performance was that I could trust my musical instincts. I was getting excited by the idea that maybe, just possibly, I'd found something I could be really good at.

I threw myself into music, passionately, voraciously. I read every book I could find in the library about composers and music history. An oboe and bassoon teacher arrived at the Tec one term and I took oboe lessons, while Chris surprised me by taking a short-lived crack at the bassoon. He had to stop because of the braces on his teeth, which made it impossible to play for more than fifteen minutes at a time without agonizing pain.

I didn't want to be an oboist, really. I just wanted to have as many opportunities as possible to get involved in music-making. I got a timpani book and practiced my rolls, and learned how to tune the drums during a performance by putting my ear to the drumhead and flicking the surface with a fingertip. I sneaked into the assembly hall during breaks and noodled on the piano.

I even started going to the big Central Library, behind the Guildhall, after school, to borrow orchestral scores. One of them, Beethoven's Ninth, I thought I'd lost, but the next day Reggie Wassell played the "Ode to Joy" theme on the piano and asked if it meant anything to anyone. I shot my hand up—thank God the score had been found! But there weren't too many kids taking Beethoven scores out of the library, and once again, Reggie was delighted. My classmates weren't so sure, but among the blank stares and sneers, I thought I detected a hint, here and there, of a different attitude. It wasn't respect, not quite; an instinctive deference, perhaps, that at least some kids felt toward someone who seemed to be gifted at something they could barely understand.

One Saturday, I was walking down Lake Road, which at that time was lined with junk shops, and I spotted a pile of records. They were Beethoven symphonies, and they were cheap. I couldn't believe my luck. I bought three and rushed home to play them. They sounded weird, booming and groaning like they were coming from the bottom of the harbor. Then I tried them on 45 rpm, and finally on 78. That was more like it! Too bad there were only two minutes of a symphony on each side.

How could anyone, even a provincial kid in the late '60s, have been so ignorant? I lived, as eighteenth-century missionaries said about the American Indians, "in outer darkness." Both my parents had left school at fourteen: my mum to help her mother in the pub, my dad to go "down the pit." They both came from large, poor families in which no one ever asked anyone anything or told anyone anything. At seventeen my father had quit digging clay and joined the navy, but his experiences of the world were never discussed. Whatever they were, they seemed to have been pushed to the back of his mind, lest they disturb the tranquillity of an existence where it was apparently enough that you had food on the table and weren't being bombed by the Nazis. What more did you want?!

We really were ignorant. We called the Elite Fish and Chip Shop down the road "The Ee-Light." My dad brought home yogurt one day as a special treat, and none of us could understand why it tasted sour. "I know," said my mum, "you're supposed to put sugar in it!" So we did.

I went back to Lake Road and managed to get complete sets of the Second and Seventh Symphonies. Beethoven was becoming my hero. He was an ugly bastard and a misfit and no one understood him, and I could relate to that. But he was also a genius and sooner or later everyone had to admit it. He was tragic, too, going deaf in the prime of his life. He had a beautiful soul but he was tough and determined and he died in a thunderstorm shaking his fist at the sky.

Changing the discs every two minutes wasn't the best way to get acquainted with the works of the master, but LPs were out of my reach. Anyway, there was something I liked about collecting sets of things. I was still collecting comics, too, rummaging around in every back-street junk shop I could find.

One day I stumbled across a dingy sweet-shop in Southsea where there were three or four piles of secondhand comics in a corner, going for a couple of pennies each. As I looked through them my heart raced. They were priceless back issues of Marvel comics, in perfect condition, dozens and dozens of them. Someone's collection had come down from the attic, and they hadn't a clue what treasures they were throwing away. I bought as many as I could afford and came back over the next three days with as much money as I could scrape together. I built the backbone of a collection, which I still have and which is now worth thousands of pounds. I bought double copies, and valuable issues of titles I didn't collect, to use in trades. The other collectors at school were awestruck. I had a secret connection. Why me? It was as though, once in a while, a crumb fell from God's table. I was the insect who found the crumb, and it kept me going for weeks.

I made a couple of friends, too. One was a dedicated cellist, whose other great love was sports. Music classes being at the same time as sports was a big problem for him.

This made no sense to me, although it's clear enough now. Athletes and musicians actually have a lot in common. From a coldly rational point of view, what we do is useless, unnecessary. Yet we pour years of dedication into it, training our bodies and minds, striving to transcend human limitations. We work in teams, we take solos, we go on tour. We're heroes and role models, and then again—as someone is always on hand to point out—we're just entertainers, and we should all be bloody well grateful if we can make a living doing something we like.

My cellist friend was seriously torn between the two, and I was aghast. Nowadays I'm a baseball fan, but sports, at that time, were something for me to define myself *against*.

Tom, another boy I hung around with, had another talent beyond my comprehension. He knew how to pick up girls. He was handsome and confident, and gorgeous nymphets flocked to him. Whether he really got beyond clumsy groping with any of them, I'll never know, but I envied him with a burning fury. Why did he hang around with me? I think he saw me as a charming eccentric. Or perhaps, like Sherlock Holmes or Batman, he needed a sidekick to reflect his glory. I bumped into Tom, more than twenty years later, in a Southsea pub. I barely recognized him; his face was scarred by adult acne. He'd become a male nurse, and he'd been faithfully married for many years to a rather plain local girl.

"You know, it's funny," I said, laughing nervously at the absurdity of it all, "but I always remember you as this good-looking charmer who got all the girls. I'm sure it wasn't really like that."

"Yes it was," he said.

At fourteen, I wasn't charming anyone, but my musical horizons were expanding rapidly. My dad took me to my first concert: the Hallé Orchestra, at the Guildhall, playing Beethoven's Seventh. I was overwhelmed. Like a headbanger at a heavy metal gig, I shook my head and pounded my feet to the symphony's stomping folk-dance rhythms—at least, until I was glared at and loudly tutted by a group of old matrons behind me.

"For God's sake keep still!" my dad hissed into my ear.

Why? How could anyone be so indifferent to this glorious, life-affirming music? Why weren't there more kids there? Why weren't people dancing in the aisles?

The pop music I'd enjoyed just a few years earlier seemed childish to me now. The Beatles, I thought, were just four clowns shaking their heads and howling "Yeah Yeah Yeah." I wasn't paying attention to how pop was changing and growing. But I heard Stravinsky's *Rite of Spring* on Radio Three, and I was astonished. It was weird, and I could barely figure out what was going on, but it packed more of a punch than a hundred Merseybeat groups. I didn't yet have the know-how to delve more deeply into twentieth-century music, but Stravinsky's visionary score, which still, ninety years on, has the power to stun an audience, got under my skin. I sat with my violin on my lap, plucking jagged approximations of what I'd heard.

"What's that racket?" asked my dad.

"It's ... er, Abstract Music," I said. It was the only term I could come up with for music that was "modern" and didn't seem to obey any of the laws of harmony or tonality.

To be fair, I have to say that my father was quite supportive of my early musical efforts. He'd repaired the broken case that came with my violin, and seemed to approve of my having a relatively harmless pastime. At the same time, both my parents were rather bemused by it.

One day I sat in the living room listening to Beethoven and following the orchestral score.

"Are you following that music in that book?" asked my mother.

I said that I was.

"What, reading it at the same time?" asked my dad.

"Yes!" I said, mildly annoyed. What did they think, that I was pretending? But they weren't so much suspicious as amazed. I used to feel like I was in the wrong family, and wonder how these two people had managed to produce someone like me. Now it struck me that they were probably wondering the same thing.

A musical score, to my dad, might as well have been something that had dropped out of a UFO. A brick, now, that was something he could understand. He soon came through for me again, though, in a big way. I'd been making noises for some time about wanting a piano. I was at an awkward, struggling phase with the violin, but I'd fooled around on the school piano enough to know that the keyboard was the gateway to the musical knowledge I wanted. There, literally in black and white, was the whole musical universe, eight octaves of it, every sharp and flat, every chord and scale, laid out in a logical diagram. I had to have a piano. My parents were skeptical—surely we couldn't afford a piano, and what if I lost interest after a few months? But they asked around a bit, and eventually one of my aunts found one. An elderly couple was getting rid of a pretty decent upright, and wanted no money for it, as long as it was "going to a good home."

My dad, along with a workmate called Bill and a friend whom I knew as Uncle George, hauled the piano up a couple of scaffold boards over the front step and into the hallway, where it stayed. My mum gave its ex-owners a basket of fruit, and I set about teaching myself to play.

The main reason I wanted the piano, though, was that I'd decided what I wanted to be when I grew up: not a writer, but a composer.

Hardnuts

I'M LISTENING to Beethoven's *Eroica* Symphony—the first LP I ever bought, aged fourteen—and as the finale starts, with its crazy cartoon fanfare, all blaring trumpets and manically scurrying strings, I wonder what the audience at its first performance must have thought. This was, after all, by far the longest symphony ever written up to that time—truly "heroic" in scope—and by the time this rude fanfare arrives, half the audience had probably either dozed off or walked out in disgust.

As the fanfare comes to a halt, there's a pregnant pause: What's this lunatic going to do now? And what we get is a silly little tune, a nursery tune, plunked out by pizzicato strings. It's repeated, with woodwinds echoing each note a beat later. And every now and again the trumpets interrupt with more little fanfares. Sheer nonsense.

Then Beethoven starts to weave other contrapuntal lines around the tune. Is he serious? Is he really going to try to build a whole movement on this? But then the music swells, as though the wind has caught its sails, as first the woodwinds and then the violins play a lovely melody. Now we realize that Beethoven has played a trick on us. That idiotic little tune he started with was actually the *bass line* of this, the real tune. At this crucial moment in his magnum opus, Beethoven has made a joke. He then goes on to transform his real theme into a magnificent set of variations.

What does it mean? Some commentators think that Beethoven is showing off. Look what I can do, he's saying, with trivial material.

Personally, I think Beethoven is reminding us that silliness is as much a part of life as heroic struggle, and telling us that, like us, he sometimes finds life absurd. He's also showing us that great and beautiful things can grow out of the seemingly insignificant.

Did I understand all this at fourteen? I believe I did. I may not have been able to express it so well, but I "got it," all right. I treasured my one LP. It was secondhand, scratched, in a battered cover with no inner sleeve. But finally I could listen to that whole last movement, without interruption, and it was like a journey from the earth to the stars.

I saw music then as white magic. Pure energy, pure emotion, pure spirit. I thought that musicians, regardless of what kind of music they played, were beyond reproach, like firefighters or nuns. Other people had other ideas. Carrying a violin case around at school or on the bus, I was a moving target. Practicing the piano in the school assembly hall, I was an outcast. I thought there had been looks, here and there, of grudging respect. Well, maybe I'd imagined it. Mostly there was sneering, jeering, and the occasional blow.

Sometimes I think things haven't changed much. I still have more or less the same feeling about music, and the sneerers and jeerers are still around. I don't take it so personally any more, but it still amazes me how much scorn some people can muster for musicians—or the wrong kind of musicians. The biggest fights are not necessarily between, say, jazzers and folkies, or rockers and baroquers. The greater the distance between two genres or subcultures, the more likely they are to be irrelevant, even invisible, to each other. It's ironic, but this is the way that grudges and rivalries seem to work. Poor people don't envy the rich nearly as much as they envy the poor person who gets a break. People in Portsmouth reserve their bitterest hatred for the city of Southampton, a similar port town of about the same size, in the same county, less than twenty miles along the coast. No one seems to have a problem with Edinburgh or Leeds.

The history of rock 'n' roll teems with such wars of attrition. At fourteen, I saw the '60s—that magical decade—give way to the '70s, a decade we're still not quite sure what to make of. Already, there were performers who dressed as scruffy as possible, and played the People's music for the People, and wanted to be indistinguishable from the People. You can trust us, they seemed to be saying; we buy our clothes from the same thrift shops as you; we're just like you. And for them, that was the whole point.

But pretty soon a new tribe would arise, strutting across the stage like peacocks, romantic figures, larger than life. They would dye their hair green, perform wearing nothing but the underwear of the opposite sex, bite the heads off of live bats—anything, as long as it was an alternative to humdrum, jeans-and-T-shirt reality.

Camp followers on each side of the divide, of course, heartily detested each other. But if, in a blindfold test, you were to just compare the *music,* you might have found it hard to tell the difference.

Of course music per se is not always the issue, and it's impossible to completely separate any kind of art—or any kind of product—from the preoccupations of its time. I like to say that I have no agenda. I say it because I don't run with any particular gang, and because agendas are often no more than defensive postures we take up against other people's agendas. But I do have an agenda of sorts, or a guiding conviction, and I may as well be honest about it. Music is either an art form or it isn't, and I say that it is: the greatest of the arts, and one of the closest approaches we mortals have to the divine. And try as I might, I can't seem to reduce it to the level of the matching handbag that goes with this year's jacket. Nor can I inflate it to the level of tribal warfare.

So, presumptuous though I may be, I try to speak on behalf of the goddess, or the muse, of music itself. The best music is universal and transcends fashion. Not in some high-flown intellectual way, but in a way that's humble and honest and real. There's no one right path for everyone, and I don't think myself any better than those who are on the front lines of the style wars. I may even be among their fans. It's just that, to be true to myself, I have to be a conscientious objector.

Most of us, as we pass out of the rock 'n' roll century, are becoming more and more open, more likely to sample all kinds of music, and less defensive about our tastes. But skirmishes still erupt, and they can be as nasty as they ever were.

Mods versus rockers. Punks versus skins. Guitars versus synthesizers. Techno versus trance. Not just polite differences of opinion, but real Cosa Nostra vendettas, with critics and fans alike heaping onto "enemy" musicians the kind of vitriol which, it seems to me, ought to be reserved for people like Charles Manson or Pol Pot.

By the time I was fifteen, the rock 'n' roll revolution, post-Altamont, had moved into phase two, but I wasn't listening. I was the closest I'd ever get to defining myself as a "classical" musician. A stupid label, "classical," covering hundreds of years, everything from Gregorian chants to Strauss waltzes to avant-garde expressionism. It's a label I can't bring myself to use without quotation marks. But it will have to do. I was a "classical" musician. It was as though I didn't know there was a war on.

Phase two, in any revolution, is the point at which the revolutionaries lose sight of the Glorious Cause—hedonistic youth versus the Establishment, in this case—and start quarreling amongst themselves. By 1970, the quarrels were simmering nicely. In another six or seven years, they would explode.

In the meantime, I was an anomaly. Which side was I on? I was profoundly uncool. But in my own way, I was rebelling, too. I wouldn't have been able to explain it at the time, but my way of rebelling was to pursue what I loved, and what made me feel alive, in the face of gray conformity. I rebelled by pursuing excellence in a world that didn't seem to expect much.

In that world, a "classical" musician was either irrelevant or uniquely unpopular—hated in his very own special way.

One day, on my way home from school on the bus, the armed forces of conformity converged on me in the form of four or five older kids: "hardnuts." I was going home late, after practicing on the school piano, and the upper deck was empty except for me and them. They spotted my violin case and moved in like hungry sharks. First they taunted and jeered.

"Ooh, look, it's Little Lord Fauntleroy!"

"Where's Mummy then? Does she let you go on the bus all by yerself?"

"Are you a poofter mate? Do you fancy me?"

They pooled their collective knowledge of classical music and came up with a couple of old jokes about Tchaikovsky's nuts being cracked and Beethoven's last movement lying steaming on the piano stool. One of them tried to sing "Come Into the Garden, Maude," which wasn't exactly classical but was at least "posh." Then they all chimed in with variations on the theme.

"For fucksake get in 'ere to the fuckin' garden, Maude!"

"Maudie, get in here and give us a wank!"

"Maude, stop scratching yer bum and come into the fuckin' garden!"

"Oi Maude, come into the garden and stop picking the scabs off yer arse!"

This was the funniest thing they'd ever heard in their lives. They all fell about with laughter. Then one of them snatched my school scarf and started to set fire to one end with his cigarette. Another wrestled my violin case from me, took out the violin, and messed about with it. Surrounded, there was nothing I could do except sit there, terrified. The posh kid's violin was no Stradivarius, but it had cost all of three pounds and wasn't likely to be replaced.

After what seemed like hours, but was probably not much more than ten minutes, the hardnuts lost interest and got off the bus. My scarf was ruined, but the violin escaped with just a couple of scratches.

I never saw the hardnuts again. For all I know, they may have grown up to be model citizens. But sometimes I think I see them, and hear their braying voices, on TV, in the newspaper, in the local bar. They're the politicians who rail against government support for the arts. They're the businessmen who think that only money can measure the worth of things. They're the critics who write mean-spirited hatchet jobs, and they're the parents who think that schools should teach nothing but the skills that will get their kids a job.

They don't always look like hardnuts, but they're easy enough to spot. They're the sort of people who tell you that modern art's a con, or orchestral conductors aren't really doing anything, or poetry's for poofs, or that a fourteen-year-old kid could never understand the *Eroica* Symphony.

Don't believe a word of it. Ignore them. Maybe they'll go away.

Turk Town

After hours of practice, wearing two pairs of socks in the draughty hallway, I was getting the hang of the piano. I was playing with and without music, improvising and jotting down ideas. Where did the ideas come from? I had no idea. They were just there. But I'd reached a point where my brain was running too far ahead of my fingers. I needed piano lessons. This was fine with my parents, but I'd have to wait until we moved.

We were moving to Gosport, on the other side of Portsmouth Harbor. Moving from Portsmouth to Gosport was like moving from London to Surbiton, or from Manhattan to Staten Island. Gosport had a naval submarine base and some sort of factory that made bombs and torpedoes. But as far as I could tell it was a social and cultural desert, inhabited only by sailors and old women. I didn't want to move. I was used to Paulsgrove, I was getting beaten up less, and my asthma attacks were still bad, but less frequent. I liked taking the bus downtown and rummaging in the junk shops, browsing in W. H. Smith's, or just walking around, observing the life of the city. I had a couple of musical allies at school, and my strange voyeuristic friendship with Tom, the teenage Don Juan. Generally, things were OK, or at least, I knew where I stood. But my dad was building houses in Gosport as part of a "self-build" cooperative, and we were to get the second completed house. We would own our own house! Wasn't that great? No, I thought, not if it's in bloody Gosport. But the house was finished, and I was dragged kicking and screaming to Turk Town.

Gosport got its nickname in some distant historical war, when Turkish prisoners had been incarcerated there, and it served them right. The local pronunciation was more like "Turk Teyn," and at this point a note on the Pompey dialect might be in order.

The accent of the Portsmouth and Gosport area is a peculiar mix of West Country and cockney. It combines the burred "r's" of the west with the harsher tone of the working-class southeast. Like the west, it turns "i" sounds into "oi," but also into a lazier "aw," sometimes in the same sentence, as in "aw rode twenny mawl on me boik" (I rode twenty miles on my bike).

The conjugation of verbs can be odd: "I goes," "they goes," "I doos," "you doos," etc. The most distinctive feature of Pompey-speak, though, is its way of turning "ow" sounds (as in town, round, brown) into something like "ay," but less broad: "ey," I think, is better. People in Pompey go "reynd the corner," or "deyn the pub." Men are commonly addressed as "mush," which usually comes out more like "mish," and the universal Pompey greeting is still "Orroight Mish?!"

Naval slang is much less common now, but I remember it being rampant. "Roight ship, wrong mess," for instance, meant that something was more or less right, but wrong in some crucial respect; and on winter mornings "ocky doysters" would be found on the streets and doorsteps of the town. This was backslang for "docky oysters," frozen mementos left by chain-smoking workers spitting on their way to their early shifts at Her Majesty's Dockyard.

My mother, naturally, had a Pompey accent, but my father never quite lost the accent of Staffordshire or Derbyshire. I never realized until much later how hard it must have been for him to settle in a strange city, at a time when people really didn't, very much. For him, the move to Gosport might not have made much difference.

As it turned out, we were to live in Bridgemary, officially in Gosport, but closer to the shopping center and bus station of Fareham, to the north. This was small comfort to me. Our new house smelled of cement and felt empty. It seemed to me that it had no soul. Our road had been prettily named Meadow Walk, but for the most part it was still a muddy building site. Pete thought it was all great fun and took an interest in the building process. He looked like he might someday follow in father's footsteps. Chris wasn't saying anything. But I hated the house. I also hated our only neighbors, a pair of lugubrious little trolls called Peggy and Den, whom my mother called Pig and Dig.

Twenty years later, I got my hair cut by a man in Melbourne, Australia who claimed not only to know nothing about music, but to actually dislike it. This sticks in my mind because of its sheer novelty—everyone, if you think about it, likes *some* kind of music, some of the time. It was so unusual that it took me back to the last time someone had made that claim: my next-door neighbor at Meadow Walk, Bridgemary, Gosport. Den, or Dig, hated music. Of course, he was the kind of person who would have found a reason to hate food, drink, or sunshine. As soon as we moved in, he started complaining about every sound that emanated from our house, but especially about my piano.

My dad stuck a large sheet of Formica on the back of the piano, so there would be a barrier between it and the wall that separated us from the trolls. No good. Then he hauled the piano out into the hallway, which, unlike the hallway back at Paulsgrove, was at least heated. But the piano had to stand right up against the radiator; it was the only possible place for it. The worst possible place. From then on my nerves were jangled by practicing on an instrument that never stayed in tune for more than a few days at a time. And Dig still came grumbling and threatening to our door, often in his string vest, from which tufts of thick black chest and back hair protruded. I seethed with righteous anger. Why couldn't he see that I was pursuing a noble calling? What gave him the right to complain? I didn't complain about his bloody TV.

Despite the move, it was decided, by some mysterious cabal of parents and teachers, that Chris and I should not interrupt our studies at the Tec. Pete would start secondary school in Gosport. But Chris and I would go to school by two buses, changing at Fareham. Since the Tec was at the northern end of Portsmouth, this would be slightly quicker than taking the harbor ferry, which is the usual connection between Turk Town and Pompey. It was still a long journey, but I was, somewhat to my own surprise, relieved. I could keep my connection to the city I preferred, where I was becoming a big fish in the small pond of Reggie Wassell's music department. Not only that, but I was soon to join the Portsmouth Schools Symphony Orchestra.

The Schools Orchestra was a lot better than the Tec's school orchestra, consisting as it did of the best players in the area. It rehearsed after hours at a school in Fratton, not too far from the Tec, and its conductor was a Mr. Metcalfe, a pudgy, myopic tortoise of a man with several chins. More importantly, the orchestra was about sixty percent female. At last I had a way to meet girls, if only I could overcome my chronic shyness.

I experienced my first crush. Her name was Rachel, an elfin violinist with a pretty, intelligent face, short dark hair, and round rimless glasses. We joined the orchestra on the same day, and I was convinced that our destinies were somehow linked. We did become friends, although not in quite the way that I hoped.

Hormones raged, but music-making would have to stand in for other forms of gratification for a while yet. I'd experienced the thrill of playing in a large ensemble once before, when I'd played the oboe in a church concert of Christmas music. I didn't actually play very much; I was still a beginner and spent most of the time fussing with split or bent reeds. But being in the center of this orgiastic sound—the massed choirs and orchestras of several schools, along with the church organ—was a high that would prove to be addictive.

Churches puzzled me. I'd only gone intermittently to church as a child, and religion was another of the many things that simply weren't talked about in our house. I had no religious feelings that I was aware of, and yet here I was playing religious music in St. Mary's, the biggest church in town, and I was thrilled by it. But I felt not so much that I was playing music to praise God, but that God's church existed to honor the music. Was this blasphemy? Or was I on to something? Who created music, after all? Religion suddenly seemed a lot like sex: huge and seductive, dark and hidden.

By the time I joined the Portsmouth Schools Orchestra, I'd given up on the oboe and was losing interest in the violin. I joined as occasional pianist and second percussionist. This meant that I crashed a cymbal or pinged a triangle here and there while a stuck-up sixth-former called Robert took care of my speciality, the timpani.

Robert had an appalling, contrived upper-class accent—a rarity in Portsmouth—and spent entire rehearsals moaning languorously about how *aaawful* the orchestra was, what *boooring* pieces we were doing, and what a terrible pair of drums he was forced to play. His favorite word was "grotty," which he applied to virtually everything, and every so often he would let out an exasperated "Donna Alvia!"—a curse I'd never heard before and have never heard since. He was arrogant and pretentious, but he was a character, and he taught me a lot of percussion technique, and I appreciated him on both counts.

After a while, Robert left for some "grotty" university or other, and I became a full-time timpanist. In fact, I was the whole percussion section. This gave me an idea. With a bit of planning, I could actually play most of the percussion parts myself. I arranged the battery around me so that, with an occasional dramatic lunge, I could reach everything, and I laid out all the charts across three music stands. Except where the parts overlapped too much, I was able to do the work of three players, sometimes playing the timpani with one hand and the triangle with the other, or using a suspended cymbal for crashes whilst playing the snare drum. This was great fun. It even raised a chin-wobbling smile from the dour Mr. Metcalfe.

It was around this time that I discovered jazz. Reading a book on twentieth-century music, I learned that jazz, whatever it was, was apparently taken quite seriously, and that someone called Duke Ellington could even be considered one of the great composers of the century. I managed to find a couple of secondhand jazz records and some piano music—Dave Brubeck, George Shearing, and some ragtime—in Waites's music shop on Fratton Road. Another musical world was opening up.

So many musical worlds opened up in my teens that it's hard to remember how, or in what order. I soon found a piano teacher in Gosport, a Mr. William Nield. He chain-smoked No. 10s during my lessons and had some kind of strange dark cyst, or growth, on the top of his bald head. But he was a pretty good teacher, and I progressed with a speed that startled both of us. The piano seemed easy after wrestling with that medieval torture device, the violin. I was soon playing Mozart sonatas and the easy volumes of Bartók's *Mikrokosmos,* as well as finding my way around blues scales and teaching myself to read jazz chord symbols. I practiced scales and arpeggios with grim, almost masochistic determination. But I also improvised more and more, and made some tentative efforts at composing: fragments of piano pieces and string quartets.

I started to order cheap secondhand LPs from a mail-order company. Often they came in plain white paper sleeves. I got lucky with a recording of Beethoven's Violin Concerto, a glowing, soulful performance by Wolfgang Schneiderhan which is still my favorite. (I never knew until Deutsche Grammophon rereleased this recording on CD, decades later, that Herr Schneiderhan bore a startling resemblance to Henry Kissinger). But more and more, I ordered "modern" classics: Debussy's *La Mer*, Stravinsky's *Petroushka*, Bartók's *Concerto for Orchestra*.

I hadn't thought about rock music for a long time, but it was starting to reappear on my horizon. I couldn't help but be aware that my peers were into Cream and Traffic and Jimi Hendrix. They had the names written all over their satchels and exercise books. Maybe there was something to this childish pop stuff. After all, no one went around with "Prokofiev Rules" written on anything.

Pretty soon I couldn't help but be aware, acutely aware, of all the music around me. "What are your influences?" has always struck me as a difficult question. Where do I start? It all goes in the pot and gets cooked. I've heard music I didn't even like, and yet one element has stuck in my mind, and been gradually transformed into an ingredient of something new. You'd never know where it came from, and I'm not telling. I may not even remember.

And so, since I'd never really known what "my" music was, I began to think that it could be whatever I wanted it to be, even if it was Sibelius one day and Miles Davis the next.

During my first year as resident of a building site in Gosport, I also went into my first pub. It was just down the road, a thoroughly average, characterless place called the Hoeford Inn. My father, in his strange solitary way, rarely went to pubs. All the more reason to try it. I entered nervously on a Saturday afternoon. I may have been fifteen or sixteen; either way, I was underage, and I was convinced I'd be laughed at and thrown out. Instead, I was served a Light Ale (the first thing that had caught my eye) and then ignored.

I was so self-conscious, I'd brought a pack of cards with me, and sat at a corner table playing solitaire. Gradually, I realized that no one was interested in me. The beer tasted good, and I felt luxuriously comfortable. Here was a neutral space, neither home nor school—or, for the adults, neither home nor work. It was an oasis, both public and private. It was sociable, if that's what you wanted; otherwise you could just mind your own business, and other people would mind theirs. What a great idea. A beautiful thing, in fact.

I was going to like pubs.

Howl, Howl, Howl

ADOLESCENCE is a state of excitement and terror and confusion, but above all, it seems to me, a state of frustration. Being an adolescent is like suddenly finding yourself in a big flashy grown-up nightclub, but at six in the evening, before the music starts.

I was sixteen and hoping to stay on at school for A-levels, but work was one of many exciting, terrifying, and frustrating things that I was just going to have to get to grips with. I took a series of Saturday jobs. Up until then, the only jobs I'd ever done were for a bob, during my brief stint in the Cub Scouts. Bob-a-jobbing around Paulsgrove was no fun. People told you to bugger off, offered to give you a bob to wipe their arses, or some such drollery, or else gave you the worst possible job they could find. Cleaning up their back gardens with your bare hands, picking fag-packets out of the mud. Cleaning out a filthy car with a tiny moth-eaten brush. I suspected that "a Job" was actually an institutionalized form of sadism, and my Saturday jobs did nothing to change my opinion.

The first was stacking shelves in a Fareham supermarket, and after a few weeks I was sacked without explanation.

Then came a bathroom showroom, where my duties were never clearly defined. The place was unnervingly quiet, a silent graveyard of toilets, washbasins, and coffinesque tubs. Once or twice a day, someone would come in and ask the price of something, I would look it up in a catalog, and they would thank me and leave. The woman I worked with told me to look busy. If the boss saw me just standing around there'd be hell to pay.

"But there's nothing to do!" I said.

"It don't matter, just look busy!" said the woman.

The boss was a thuggish, piggy-eyed man with greasy black hair. Most of the hair was held in place by Brylcreem; a few strands escaped to hang over a flushed and bloated face. He looked as though his head had been boiled. He also had that way of looking at you that seems to dare you to do something wrong, just so he can show you what would happen. So I marched in and out of the storeroom, taking things off shelves and putting them back again, thinking that surely this was all some sort of hoax. I was sacked anyway, again without an explanation. This time I went to the boss and asked for one.

"Well," he smirked, as though it would have been obvious to anyone, "every time I see you, you're not doing anything."

I left, completely baffled, and got a job delivering leaflets. This was a lot better. I was by myself, at least, and getting some exercise. Every so often I would hear an "Oi!" behind me and turn round to see an irate old geezer clutching his leaflet in a shaking fist, demanding to know what this bloody rubbish was and what made me think everyone wanted to be bombarded with it all the bloody time. That was OK: nothing to do with me, mate. After a while I started to amuse myself by folding the leaflets into paper airplanes. I would peer through letter boxes and see how far into the houses I could get them to fly. Sometimes they'd soar through an open kitchen door and all the way into the back garden. This was fun for a while, but, I had to admit, pretty pathetic.

Unfortunately, these were just the sort of jobs that were waiting for me if I couldn't find some way to make a living out of music.

Strange as it might have seemed to any rational person, I didn't see any reason why I *shouldn't* make a living out of music. It had dawned on me, over the last couple of years, that I had no desire to be rich. What would I do with heaps of money? Cars, houses, clothes—there were no material things that particularly interested me. And the thought of playing even the worst possible music in the worst possible places was infinitely more appealing than the prospect of working for sadists with boiled heads, or hammering rivets or whatever they did in the dockyard. By now I could play a bit of jazz and a bit of ragtime, and I'd picked up a couple of buskers' books, each of which had the melodies of fifty or so standards, with the chord symbols above.

For hours I tried out different interpretations of those symbols: waltzes, "walking bass," but mostly "stride" style, alternating bass notes (on the first and third beat of the bar) with chords (on two and four). This was as challenging as anything in the Beethoven sonatas. To keep both hands going, without either playing bum notes all over the place or losing the steady rhythmic feel, demands a kind of split consciousness, each hand independent but still under a centered, Zenlike control. The great practitioners of the style, like James P. Johnson and Art Tatum, were extraordinary artists, who seemed to turn the piano into an orchestra. Such heights were as far above me as the virtuosic displays of Rachmaninoff or Liszt, but I was able to accompany myself convincingly enough. I was close to a standard that, if nothing else, might get me some solo gigs in pubs or restaurants.

I was also acquiring a kind of determination that people sometimes mistook for confidence. Maybe it *was* confidence, of a sort, but it didn't feel like it. Self-assurance, poise, optimism about my prospects—these were not things I innately possessed, and neither had anyone tried very hard to instill them in me. I don't think they knew how.

But determination I seemed to have. I started to organize musicians at school and in the Schools Orchestra to play chamber music. Then I was invited to play trio sonatas at the home of a violinist who was universally known as Horse-face, with his similarly unattractive sister on cello.

It was the first time I'd been in a "cultured" middle-class home. The delighted Mrs. Horse-face fussed around and made us sandwiches with strawberry jam and cream, which was like champagne and caviar to me at the time. At home, we had something called "Red Jam," and we certainly didn't have cream with it. Nevertheless I felt ill at ease, eating off a willow-pattern plate and wondering what to do with an embroidered napkin. I was out of my depth in the teatime conversations of a family who actually talked to each other, and talked, what's more, about the theater and the ballet. Something was beginning to trouble me: There seemed to be invisible barriers everywhere, which had to do not only with art and music but with social class. And all these barriers seemed to cross each other at various angles that I didn't understand.

I found a drummer and a bassist at school and made a first attempt at forming a jazz trio. The drummer, with a kit that looked like it had been made by Tupperware, was particularly bad, but we managed to knock a couple of pieces into some sort of shape—a Brubeck tune and a blues number—and performed them at a school assembly.

Before the performance I felt as though my bowels had turned into tepid blancmange. Once the music started, though, I felt good. A difficult feeling to describe: hot and cool, calm and excited at the same time. As far as I can remember, this was my first piano performance in front of an audience, and it was received with polite, if slightly bemused, applause. I've been nervous before every performance, ever since.

As exam time approached, I dropped out of mathematics for good. A young student teacher tried to talk me into an enthusiasm for the subject, on the grounds that it was closely related to music. A lot of people believe this, and I can see why, up to a point. You can argue that music and maths are both art forms built on abstract logic. But I've never been moved to tears by an equation.

"Look at Bach!" said the student teacher. "His fugues are all based on mathematical formulas!"

"No they're not," I said, "they're just so perfectly structured that they can be interpreted that way by people who don't appreciate music."

The class tittered and the student teacher gave up.

"Look," he said, "if ycu don't want to learn maths, you might as well not come to my class. It's all the same to me."

I got up and walked out, and spent maths periods from then on practicing the piano. I struggled through Bach fugues, too, but with mixed emotions. Bach was never my favorite composer—I preferred the more human, fallible Beethoven, with his struggles and rages—but Bach has grown on me over the years, and there are times when he inspires in me a sense of what I can only call religious awe. Anyone who's tried to write a fugue, for instance, knows how hard it is to weave three or four distinct melodic lines together throughout a piece, and make it sound reasonably musical. But to build a fugue into a cathedral of sound as Bach does requires a genius bordering on the inhuman—or the divine. Beethoven, I've always thought, is the Shakespeare of music: profoundly human, tragic, comic, and wise. But if Beethoven is Shakespeare, Bach is Moses or Jesus or Buddha. He scared me then, and I'm still a bit nervous around him now.

Reggie Wassell sometimes talked about the "Three Bs," the third being, of course, Johannes Brahms. As far as I was concerned, Brahms wasn't in the same league. Even now he sounds, despite many beautiful moments, like duff Beethoven to me. Beethoven (if I can indulge in one more analogy) is like one of those inspired chefs who can just throw a tomato and an onion and a couple of herbs into a pan and somehow manage to produce, in a few minutes, something both original and utterly delicious. Brahms, by comparison, is the musical equivalent of jam-sweetened porridge.

Communing with such giants, if only in my mind, it's hardly surprising that I had very little respect for my teachers. I was more openly rebellious, or what the Paulsgrove kids would have called "stroppy." Some time after walking out of maths, I was called to the office of Mr. Vine, the careers master, who was called Croak because he'd had throat cancer and spoke in a sinister, rasping whisper. He demanded to know why I wasn't taking any exam in maths, even the supposedly painless CSE.

"There's no point, sir. I'm so bad at maths I would only fail."

"Jackson, are you aware that you need qualifications to get a *job?*"

There was that word again.

"Sir, if by some miracle I get a 'pass,' it will be a Grade 5 and I don't think that's much of a qualification for anything."

"Very well, it's not compulsory," said Croak, "but don't come crying to me if you need the qualifications."

"Are you joking, sir?"

"Jackson …"

"Yes sir."

"Get out of my sight."

And so it went. I may have been the weird kid who played the piano, but when it came to sullen defiance of authority, with occasional outbreaks of sheer cheek, I was at one with the masses. I was given detention for minor offences—like telling a teacher that I was wearing nonregulation flared trousers because I had flared legs—and it was worth it. I may have had a different agenda from most of my peers, but I was starting to be more accepted.

I coped with the exams reasonably well. I was either good at a subject or I wasn't, and when I wasn't, I simply gave up. I got a third of the way through the chemistry paper, until I came to the question: *How would you prevent an aluminum dustbin from rusting?* This was just too ridiculous.

I wrote: *Throw away, buy plastic dustbin,* and left the rest of the paper blank. I still ended up with four O-level passes, and, thank God, I wouldn't have to work for a living just yet. I'd go on to the sixth form, two more years, taking A-levels in music and English.

Literature was the only thing I loved almost as much as music, and I enjoyed every book we studied, which were predictable but solid choices: *Sons and Lovers, Lord of the Flies, 1984, Macbeth,* and English poetry: John Donne, Wilfred Owen, or Ted Hughes.

Apart from Reggie Wassell, the only teacher I respected—although I wasn't sure I liked him—was the neatly bearded, vaguely Satanic-looking Mr. Thorpe, who taught drama. He was an eccentric who would, for instance, sit cross-legged like some Indian swami on his desk during lessons. He did a decent job of making Shakespeare interesting, sometimes by extreme measures. There was, for instance, a classroom reading of *King Lear* in which the climax of the play, the death of Cordelia, fell dismally flat as the boy reading Lear intoned flatly, "Howl. Howl. Howl."

Thorpe flew into a rage.

"For Chrissakes, boy," he shouted, "the man's just lost his DAUGHTER. She's BLOODY DEAD!"

Thorpe stormed out of the classroom. Puzzled silence. Then a voice from the end of the corridor, first moaning eerily, gradually rising, then screaming in agony.

Stunned silence. Then Thorpe reappeared, wild-eyed.

"That's King Lear!" he shouted.

Thorpe was also obsessed with sex, and tried to interpret everything in a play from a sexual point of view. On one occasion he talked at length about the historical background of *Anthony and Cleopatra,* but then digressed into an analysis of what he considered the chief motivation behind the whole play: "sheer unbridled lust." This segued into vivid descriptions of what the protagonists' lovemaking might have been like.

"Imagine them," said Thorpe, "unable to resist the heat of each others' bodies; over and over again, rutting like animals!"

"Please sir!"

"Well, what is it?"

"What else would they do, sir?"

"Oh, one imagines them licking each other all over, licking the sweat from each others' thighs . . ."

Meanwhile a classful of sixteen-year-old boys smirked, squirmed, and clamped hands over mouths.

We may not have been able to relate to Lear's tragedy, but we certainly related to sexual obsession, and howling too, for that matter. By now I was playing duets with Rachel, but that was about as far as it went. I became friendly with several girls in the Portsmouth Schools Orchestra, and decided that I liked girls a lot. On the whole they stirred more sexual feelings than boys. The bad news was that for some reason girls seemed to regard me as a safe alternative to other boys, the normal boys, the ruffians who were always trying to get into their knickers. At some point I would attempt some bumbling overture, only to be laughed off, or told about their boyfriends, or worse still, asked for advice about their boyfriends. They seemed to assume I was gay, or perhaps asexual. As much as I liked girls, I began to wonder if I *was* gay. People were always calling me a poof or a queer. I was somewhat effeminate, but not a pretty boy. Rather, I was awkwardly androgynous, and open to just about anything, short of sexual congress with beasts of the field. I wouldn't have minded being a poof, if it meant I could be a sexual being.

It was hard, though, to see how I was ever going to lose my virginity when I was too shy to impose myself, and too odd-looking—which for a lot of people is the same thing as ugly—to be an object of desire. And male beauty, as I realized later, is an even bigger deal to gay males than it is to teenage girls. The only males who took a sexual interest in me as a teenager were an old man who tried to "give me a wank" in a public toilet and an oily middle-aged businessman I hitched a lift from one evening. He put his hand on my knee, I asked him to please stop, and nothing more was said until he dropped me off. I felt rather sorry for both of us.

Somewhere in the "primitive" world, there must be a tribe that encourages the civilized custom of teenagers, of both sexes, being initiated by an older partner, as a matter of course, for the psychological health of the whole community. Why not? Unfortunately, I, a benighted British savage, had to make do with Becky.

Becky was another violinist who started inviting me to her home, a council flat on the edge of Paulsgrove, when her parents were out. She would play loud music, dance around in a short skirt, sit on my lap, and then slap my hand away when I touched her. I would give up, but then at the next orchestra rehearsal she would invite me again, on the condition that I "behaved myself." This was said with a wink. What did the wink mean? I don't think she knew any better than I did. She was not a malicious tease, but the type who simply doesn't know what she wants. What she *needed*, perhaps, was a boy who knew what he was doing. In other words, not me. But I kept going back for more torture, maybe getting a kiss, or maybe ten seconds of my hand resting on her thigh before being swatted away. And as if this weren't bad enough, she would play Marc Bolan records the whole time. I would go back to Gosport on the bus with "Telegram Sam" ringing in my ears, and aching balls.

As a musician and as a man, I felt stranded at the edge of the real world. I had no sentimental attachment to the so-called innocence of childhood, and have never had since. I wanted the adult world, but it didn't seem to want me.

I made the leap forward first as a musician. I was sixteen when I did my first Gig.

Solo

THE PIANO is the second-most useful instrument you can play. Musically, it can do just about anything, but the guitar just about trumps it by being portable. The great thing about both is that they can be played solo. Of course, this doesn't mean that anyone else appreciates it.

A *Playboy* cartoon I once saw sums it up, one of those lavish full-page color things. There is an opulent dining room, all velvet drapes and champagne and chandeliers, and it's full of glamorous starlets in feather boas and rich swells smoking cigars, and in the corner is a droopy sad-faced little man playing the piano. And if we look closely, we can see the title on the music in front of him:

GERSHWIN'S "CHOKE, YOU BASTARDS."

Playing solo piano, at its best, is a great and underrated craft, and enormously satisfying to do. At its worst, you're on about the same level as the busboy, but with fewer tips. I confess that, like most people, I've found myself being serenaded in a restaurant and thought: I really like this, *in theory.* In *practice,* I wish he'd shut the hell up.

Still, I feel a vaguely sentimental sympathy for pianists I come across in hotel bars. I've bought them drinks and, once or twice, even played duets with them. On the other hand, there have been times when I've had to be restrained from strangling them with their own bow ties.

Lounge pianists typically suffer from a couple of unique afflictions. One is Arpeggi-itis: the compulsion to play flashy arpeggios up and down the keyboard every couple of bars. Another is a sort of rhythmic Aphasia. Not being constrained by a bassist or drummer, the pianist simply forgets to play in time. One bar has four beats, the next five, the next four and a half. So what? he seems to be saying. I'm playing (mostly) the right notes, aren't I? What more do you want?

But it's quite possible to get a groove going as a solo player—in fact I saw it as a prerequisite, as part of the job. Even the lowliest forgotten boogie-woogie and stride pianists have done it. Dr. John and Elton John and Jerry Lee Lewis have done it, and they're not exactly virtuosos. At sixteen or seventeen, I was no Horowitz either, but playing rhythmically was always my strong point. By this time I had a pretty good repertoire of jazz standards, ragtime, Beatles songs, and pub sing-alongs, padded out here and there with some awkward improvisation. But it all swung, or so I thought. So when I saw an advertisement in the *Evening News* for a pub pianist, I pounced.

The Wicor Mill was a nondescript pub in Portchester, which lay between Fareham and Portsmouth, along my school bus route. The first thing I had to do, when I got there, was ask what the foul smell was that hung around the place.

"That's the glue factory, luv," said the landlady.

"What glue factory?"

"The Wicor, next door."

"Why does it stink so much?"

"Well, it's from all the horses' hoofs and bones they grawnds up to make the glue. We're used to it boy ney, don't hardly notice it really."

The pay was "four peynd a noight." Four pounds! I was a professional! I showed up for the gig wearing a waistcoat I'd picked up in an Oxfam shop. For some reason, I felt that pub pianists should wear waistcoats. The place was almost empty, and I started with "When I'm Sixty-four." What happened after that, I have no idea, except that my repertoire didn't last as long as I'd expected, and I had to play a few tunes twice, but no one seemed to mind.

In fact, a couple of the locals—who were friendly enough, considering that they lived in the shadow of the glue factory—bought me pints. The pint sitting on top of the piano definitely completed the picture. My mistake was to actually drink it, and then to drink another three. By the end of the evening a sort of swirling fog started to overtake my brain, and more dangerously, my fingers. I loved pubs—I'd started going in one with some older kids after orchestra rehearsals—but I was still an inexperienced drinker.

So I learned at least one lesson on my first gig. Nevertheless I was deemed to have been a success, and as I reeled out into the night, I bought a bag of chips and felt pretty pleased with myself.

After this I played percussion in a Schools Orchestra concert, once again at St. Mary's church. During the quietest string passage of the slow movement of a Mozart symphony, I dropped a cymbal. The crash was deafening: People gasped as it echoed around the stone walls forever and ever, driving bats from belfries, waking dozing pensioners with a start—World War III had arrived! Please God, I thought, strike me down, but don't let anyone have a heart attack.

Undaunted, I worked hard at expanding my solo repertoire, and played several more weekends at the Wicor Mill. I always took the bus there and hitched a lift home, or, occasionally, ended up walking all the way. I learned to pace myself with the beer, the atmosphere was pleasant, there was a sexy barmaid, and every now and then a couple of old crones in the corner would sing along with me. It was almost too easy.

The high point was Christmas Eve, for which I even got a pound or two extra. The night ended in general disorder, the sexy barmaid sitting on top of the piano singing, or rather, shrieking, while I ogled her legs through an alcoholic haze and pounded out twenty or thirty choruses of "What Shall We Do with A Drunken Sailor." After this, the landlady decided she'd had enough piano-bashing in her pub for a while, and I returned to amateur status.

But the Wicor Mill had boosted my confidence. I was going to be the Fats Waller of Pompey. All I had to do was find more gigs. Then another pub, the Seagull, also in Porchester, advertised for a Sunday lunchtime organist.

I thought I could handle this. There was a Hammond organ in the school assembly hall, used for morning hymns, and I'd fooled around on that a bit. It was usually locked during the afternoon, but my brother Chris had found a way of taking the back off and starting it up with a hairpin. As sober and responsible as Chris appeared, he had an unsuspected talent for petty larceny. When the assembly hall was locked, he managed to steal a key, and when the grand piano was locked, he mysteriously produced the key for that, too.

The organ at the Seagull was completely different from the Tec's. The place was busy as I sat down to play—and realized I didn't even know how to turn the instrument on. And when I finally managed to get a sound out of it, it was still painfully obvious I hadn't a clue what I was doing. I pressed buttons randomly, desperately, and the organ would produce horrible whining tones, or one keyboard would suddenly sound ten times louder than the other, or all the sound would suddenly disappear in the middle of a tune, and I wished I was dead. Finally I stayed with one keyboard, and one tone setting, and quietly dirged my way through half an hour or so, hoping no one would notice me. I was given a couple of pounds out of pity and sent on my way.

Shortly afterwards, a local band advertised for an organist. I've got to keep going, I told myself; don't admit defeat. I took a deep breath and dialed the number, and a friendly voice invited me over for a cup of tea. The voice turned out to belong to a charming, energetic young guy called Ray who had a cozy little house on the outskirts of Fareham and a gorgeous girlfriend who was also the band's singer. We all chatted merrily about music for nearly an hour, and although they were five or maybe ten years older than me, they seemed to take me quite seriously. This is it, I thought. I'm on my way. Then Ray asked, casually, "So what kind of organ have you got?"

There was an awkward silence. God only knows why I hadn't anticipated this obvious question. But I hadn't.

"I was hoping," I mumbled, "that maybe you had one."

There was no reply.

"I thought, maybe, you know, the band might own one."

Ray looked at the ceiling.

"Or else, maybe out of the money I'd earn, you could, you know, help me buy one, or I could pay you back, or we could rent one, or . . ."

Endless, excruciating silence. Then Ray said, "I'm afraid we can't really help you, mate."

"I don't think you can help us, either," said the gorgeous girlfriend.

More silence. It's amazing how quiet everything gets when one stands alone like this, naked, as it were, before one's fellow man, revealed as a total asshole.

"Well, I'll be off then," I said and rushed out.

"Drop in any time," called Ray. Yeah, sure, I thought, fuck you, damn you to hell, but of course I was mad at myself.

I'd taken one step forward and two steps back. I tried to work off some of my anger and frustration by walking all the way home. It was a chilly night, but clear. I could see the Milky Way. Oscar Wilde said that we are all in the gutter, but some of us are looking at the stars. I thought I knew what he meant. I was burning to escape from this dismal world, but I couldn't find the connection, the stairway, between the one and the other. I felt as though my feet were stuck in the gutter, and my head was floating in the stars, like a balloon, attached by just the thinnest string.

The Pub and the Pier

IT'S A DARK and rainy day in Manhattan, and of course I think of England. The Yanks think I'm joking when they ask me what I miss about England and I say, "the climate." But, pervert though I am, it's true. There's something about the gloom that softens the hard edges of things, and is soothing to my soul.

I'm thinking of dark and rainy Manchester. I once sat in a pub there, looking out of the window at the rain, when I overheard a deadpan Mancunian conversation at the bar:

"You know why it rains so mooch in Manchester, don't yer?"

"No, why?"

"Coz we *deserve* it."

I decide to listen to the sound of Manchester, and I put on a CD by Oasis. They sound like the Beatles retooled for the '90s, and the songs are pretty good. I like the Fuck You attitude in the singer's voice, like John Lennon filtered through Johnny Rotten. Every song ends in an extended howl of amp feedback, as though they're anxious for us to know that they're real rock 'n' roll bad boys, and not a bunch of poofs just because their songs have tunes to them. Suddenly I feel a bit sad. Everyone is so much more self-conscious than they were in the freewheeling glory days of the '60s. But how would it look to me if I were sixteen now?

Everyone has their own personal history of rock 'n' roll, but your sense of perspective, of how things line up, depends to a great extent simply on when you were born. For instance, a guy ten years younger than me once told me that he thought of the year 1976 as "Year Zero." And 1976 meant punk. What was my Year Zero? Maybe '64 or '65, and the Beatles. But my quirk was that I missed out a big chunk after that, working my way through Beethoven, Stravinsky, and Ellington. I was drawn back towards the rock world around 1971 or 1972. So maybe one of those can go down in my personal rock history as Year One.

In Year One, the hippest thing in rock was (don't laugh) something called Progressive. The Summer of Love had come and gone, pretty much unnoticed by me, but one of its legacies was a general feeling that electric guitars and drums could be used to create music that was, at least to some degree, grown-up and serious. Not that your parents were supposed to like it. But W. H. Smith's even had a "progressive" section in the record racks. Plain "pop" or "rock 'n' roll" had become naive, outdated categories.

Progressive rock is one of the least respected subgenres, failing to become retro-hip even after the revival of flared pants. Rock musicians can be embarrassing when they strain too much in the pursuit of high artistic goals. But the reason is not, as a lot of people assume, that there's something wrong with high artistic goals. The problem is that they're not always good enough to pull it off.

This isn't just a question of "technique." Quite a few prog-rockers could play tricky riffs and fast scales up and down the fretboard. But being a good musician is only partly about technique. About twenty-five percent, I'd say. The rest is divided between imagination, good taste, and that indefinable something called "soul."

Of course a lot of progressive music was absolute crap, but then, a lot of everything is crap. Whatever its faults, progressive got me back into rock. I liked the idea that rock was developing into something more like a real art form. I was a musician, and the more the music stimulated me with jazzier chords, or odd time signatures, or extended structures, the more I pricked up my ears. It wasn't that I didn't appreciate a good, simple tune. And I respected anyone who had the balls to get up on a stage and do something—anything. I liked the standards and Beatles tunes I'd played at the Wicor Mill. But I didn't yet fully appreciate the art of the three-minute pop song, which is a trickier business than it looks. Nor did I fully understand the symbolic power of rock. Image and attitude seemed to me much less important than music. I struggled to understand why, for so many of my peers, it was the other way round.

Although I, a Beethoven fanatic, was not a snob, a lot of progressive rock fans were. They were contemptuous of anything simple and tuneful. The skinheads I was starting to notice around town were snobs, too. Only ska music would do, something that still puzzles me, given the skins' racist, nationalist attitudes. You'd think they'd be into something irrefutably white and British: Gilbert and Sullivan, perhaps. Anyway, one of the biggest, dumbest myths of the pop music world is that there's no snobbery there; that snobbery or elitism are things that only come couched in posh accents and the strains of string quartets. In reality, "classical" musicians are often refreshingly unpretentious, since all they really care about is the music.

I started to listen to John Peel's radio show. His droning Liverpudlian voice was somehow beyond fashion, and he played music that was heroically obscure but often fascinating. Soon my favorite band was the Soft Machine. They were heavily jazz-influenced, and pretty good players: Their long, open-ended compositions were atmospheric and full of intriguing passages in 5/4 or 7/8 time. I also liked King Crimson, especially for Robert Fripp's guitar playing. Then there were less well-remembered combos such as Caravan, Van Der Graf Generator, and Egg. And from the other side of the Atlantic, Captain Beefheart and Frank Zappa. Zappa's *Hot Rats* was a favorite, jazzy instrumentals being more to my taste at the time than the more song-oriented Mothers of Invention. Another favorite was *King Kong*, the album on which the jazz violinist Jean-Luc Ponty performed Zappa's compositions.

As a sixth-former, sitting with some satisfaction on the top of the Technical High School heap, I was in much smaller classes and made more friends. I fell in with a bunch of guys who liked the current music, lent each other LPs, didn't smoke pot yet but knew people who did, and tried desperately to grow their hair long. Along with the detested school uniform, short hair was mandatory at the Tec, and I doubt that even the most sadistic teachers really understood the shame and humiliation we felt outside of school.

We grew our hair as long as we could, stuffed it behind our ears, slicked it down, and prayed we'd get through another week without being spotted. We tried to make our hair invisible by sheer will power. Complex,

POW-camp strategies were devised for avoiding Mr. Slade, who was the chief enforcer of the dress code, a blatant despiser of all things "artistic," and an all-around bastard. The most dedicated of the group was John Grant, who combed his hair back behind his ears, curled it up again underneath itself, and stuck it down with some sort of wax. Every so often we would be sitting in the library and Slade would pass by, pause, walk back, and examine Grant from several different angles. He would do this very slowly and deliberately, for the sake of maximum suspense. Finally he'd take a ruler and carefully dislodge a greasy strand of hair, letting it spill onto the shoulder of Grant's blazer. Another pause for effect, and then:

"What is *this*, Grant?"

"Hair, sir," Grant would say, whereupon he would be dispatched to the barber, get an inch or two cut off, and try again.

I started to go drinking with Grant and the Three P's, John Pike, Tony Pratt, and Tony Prout, who'd been friends ever since a junior school class had forced them together in alphabetical order. Every weekend we would meet at a dingy place called the Shaftesbury Arms, where we would eat cheese-and-onion crisps and drink Double Diamond. Why this mediocre dive? It must have been chosen for its very anonymity and the fact that no one cared that we were underage. We all wore dark crewneck sweaters, jeans (flared, but not too much), and denim or imitation-leather jackets. In the winter we wore army-surplus greatcoats. Corduroy jeans were more or less accepted. Why did it have to be so drab? Secretly, I liked the idea of dressing with a bit of style, but in this, as in so many things, I had no role models.

Instead, I had a new sensation: For the first time, I felt like one of the boys. We drank, smoked, and played darts, and I liked it. I actually belonged. I didn't want to be like Gilda, the outrageous queen who occasionally dropped in to the Shaftesbury. Gilda was an infamous Pompey character, a half-crazy, hideously ugly but flamboyant gay boy whose parents gave him money to stay as far away from them as possible. He would flounce into the pub and pirouette around the pool table in a flurry of bangles and beads, basking in the jeering attention. He didn't seem especially happy, though, underneath the camp bravado, and often there would be a black eye underneath the mascara.

At chucking-out time, I would take a bus to Fareham with John Pike and then take another bus or walk to Bridgemary, trying to keep my head down and steer clear of drunken sailors. Occasionally, walking the last stretch back to my building-site home, I would hear a pair or a trio of footsteps behind me. Then I'd hear a voice: "Hey pal, got a light?"

Here we go again, I'd think. There'd be a scuffle, but the sailors were usually too drunk and uncoordinated to do much serious damage. I would wake up the next morning with a fat lip or a black eye, and they would wake up with monster hangovers.

One night at the bus stop I was confronted by a lone skinhead.

"Oi! Wanna fight?" he asked. A polite request, almost like an invitation to dance.

"No thanks," I said.

"Go on."

"No!"

"Why not?"

"What do you mean, why not? Why do you want to fight?"

He looked at me with a sort of sneering disbelief, as though I was the stupidest creature he'd ever laid eyes on.

"Because," he explained calmly, "I'm a skin and you're an 'airy!"

We stared at each other for a moment in mutual incomprehension. Then he shook his head and walked off.

I acquired a more-or-less steady girlfriend, or thought so, anyway. She was yet another violinist, a hippie-ish blonde named Helen, who lived in a big rambling house in Southsea with what seemed like dozens of brothers and sisters. We went to concerts together, beginning with my first ever rock concert, a band called Curved Air, who featured an electric violinist and some rather clumsy "classical" flourishes.

After that came a series of now-legendary shows on South Parade Pier. They always featured three or four bands, and were a magnet for everyone who was anyone in the long-haired, dope-smoking, patchouli-scented Portsmouth "scene." On the Pier I saw Fairport Convention, Steeleye Span, Hawkwind, Argent (playing their hit, "Hold Your Head Up" five times in one show), Stone the Crows, Chicken Shack, Ten Years After, Genesis as the support act for Supertramp, and, later on, the newly formed Roxy Music supporting Rory Gallagher. At the Guildhall, I saw Soft Machine, Traffic, Gentle Giant, the Moody Blues, and Pink Floyd playing with the first quadraphonic sound system, which had everyone spinning around open-mouthed in their seats.

After a while I just went to every concert I could afford. Every penny I had went on concerts, although at the Pier I quite often managed to sneak in without paying. The shows didn't have to be progressive. I was starting to get off on the same things as everyone else: the visceral impact of a big PA system, the lights, the atmosphere, the release from boredom, the chance to mingle with lots of other young people. Drugs were part of the picture, too, and I was curious, but the archetypal dope peddler outside the school gates failed to materialize, and no one in my circle knew where to get the stuff.

Helen talked all the time about acid trips and pot-smoking with what I assumed to be her seriously hip friends. When I told her I thought Hawkwind was a boring band, she said, in a soft and deeply meaningful voice, that you had to be in the right *frame of mind* to appreciate them. So why wasn't I invited? How the hell did I know? Why wasn't I invited into her bed? Eventually, after our strange on-and-off relationship had drifted on more-or-less platonically for a year, she suddenly told me she was pregnant, by a guy twice my age who had apparently been her real boyfriend all along. Every relationship I attempted with a girl seemed to leave me furious at my own naivete.

I looked in the mirror. I had big ears and a few spots, but I wasn't dumb enough to think that if the spots went away, girls would come running from miles around. What was wrong with me?

I asked my mother.

"There's nothing wrong with you," she smiled reassuringly. "you've got lots of nice features."

"Like what?"

"Lots." She thought for a minute. "You've got nice hands."

"Hands?!" I looked at my hands. What the hell was the woman talking about? I stormed out of the room and went to the piano. The piano didn't care. The piano always accepted me just the way I was.

Later, Ken Russell, during the filming of *Tommy* with the Who, burned down South Parade Pier. It was rebuilt, but there were no more concerts there. I never did drop acid, and nostalgia, as someone once said, ain't what it used to be.

Musically, at least, I was becoming shamelessly promiscuous. It was obvious by now that I had no loyalty to any one genre. I respect such loyalty, in a way, but I don't relate to it. At the more obsessive level, it strikes me as bizarrely funny, like some quaint and harmless sexual fetish. There are people who can attain musical ecstasy only with the aid of pre-1960 rhythm-and-blues recorded in St. Louis on the AceTone label, or Monteverdi played on sixteenth-century instruments. Good luck to them, but musical obsessions seem to me to be more about obsession than about music. After all, if you're really moved by melody and harmony and rhythm, wouldn't you still respond to it, on some level, no matter what outward form it took?

I went to a lot of rock shows partly because classical concerts were much rarer in Portsmouth, and jazz was almost nonexistent. But I was still practicing both Bach and Brubeck and composing more and more adventurous pieces, mostly either for piano or small combinations of musicians who were available at school, some of whom were pretty good by now. A couple of these pieces were even rehearsed.

The musicians complained that their parts were too difficult, and I had to learn another important lesson: that a composer needs to know at least a little bit about a lot of instruments. You can't just assume that an idea you come up with on the keyboard is going to work on a cello or a French horn. Everything needs to sound right, and feel right, on the instrument you're writing for; it needs to sound like it couldn't have been played on any other instrument; and it sounds better when the player actually enjoys playing it.

I also learned that there's no point in writing virtuoso parts unless you have virtuoso players. But as I studied more and more scores by masters of orchestration like Mahler and Ravel, I saw that strong and original effects can be produced by very simple means. Good music can be simple or complex, but the best ideas, the ones that make us laugh with pleasure, are often simple ones that just hadn't been thought of before.

What about the style of my own compositions? They were strongly influenced by Stravinsky and Bartók, with a lot of jazzy inflections. In other words, I didn't really have a style yet. Which, under the circumstances, was hardly surprising.

2 + 2 = 5

IN BETWEEN concerts at the Pier, pints of Double Diamond, and orchestra rehearsals, I managed to meet my first real musical collaborator. He was a guy about my age, and we even looked alike: tall and skinny, hair already starting to recede. His name was Martin Keel, and he had a keen intelligence and a great appreciation of the absurdity of life. Martin was a saxophonist, although the word doesn't do him justice. He played all four saxophone sizes, plus clarinet, flute, bassoon, and trombone, as well as various recorders, pennywhistles, kazoos, and anything else that could be blown to produce some kind of sound. Not satisfied even with this arsenal of instruments, he invented new ones by joining bits of different instruments together, unholy Frankenstein creations like the clariosaxatrombophone.

Martin and I jammed together a couple of times at his parents' house. Unusually for a saxophonist, he was more blues- than jazz-influenced. On the other hand, he was, like me, open to just about anything. One of our sessions, while his parents were away, took place under the influence of two or three joints, and was recorded for posterity on a cheap reel-to-reel tape machine.

By now I'd smoked hash a couple of times. The first was at the home of a neighbor of one of my school drinking-mates, John Pike. The neighbor, a few years older than us, was the son of a local furniture-store magnate, by the name of Mendel. He was not only the first pot-smoker, but the first rich person and the first Jew I ever met. The drug seemed to have no effect on me, except to give me a ravenous desire for the frozen cheesecake I'd spotted in the fridge. Mendel Junior, on the other hand, got more and more paranoid, sweating, staring wildly, and asking more and more questions, until I was paranoid too. I was convinced he was an undercover narcotics agent, and he was probably thinking the same about me. I slipped out of the house without saying good-bye.

The pot-fuelled jam session with Martin was different. Every note seemed to take on a mystical significance, and Martin and I became telepathically linked. We were one great oceanic brain, navigating through endless musical possibilities with languid ease. We played until there were no more notes to play, until every musical question had been answered, and only a deep, satisfied silence remained. And sleep.

The next day, we played the tape. It was bloody awful.

Undeterred, we made plans: the band we were going to form, the gigs we were going to play, the worlds we were going to conquer. We lived in a musical Garden of Eden. No one was judging us, no one had any expectations of us, no one even knew we existed. We were completely free, and, with or without dope, the possibilities *were* endless.

Ironically, success can tend to shrink, rather than expand, your horizons. The freedoms you once took for granted—to experiment, to write or play exactly what you want, to scrap everything and start all over again—now have to be fought for, and fought for in the glare of the spotlight.

For Martin and me, those problems were distant luxuries. For now, we could be what we were by nature: musical eclectics. It never even occurred to us that we should pick one specific genre, learn its rules, and swear a tribal allegiance to it. Music wasn't something that came in a choice of colors. It was a mosaic.

Some people are scornful of eclecticism, and sometimes I don't blame them. But we should try not to mistake stylistic purity for "authenticity." Artists who are easy to define are quite often the more calculating ones, the ones who've just picked a style, as it were, from the menu. The real artists are back in the kitchen, creating new dishes.

We live, more and more, in an eclectic world. So why are we so suspicious of eclectic artists?

One reason, I think, is that our culture is so dominated by marketing and advertising that we're all more and more likely to think like marketeers than, for instance, like artists. We tend to fall for marketing myths: for instance, the theory that if something doesn't fit neatly into one category or another, there must be no audience for it. We go along with the tendency to "dumb down" everything until every idiot and his dog can understand it, since we don't want to be considered snobs. Or we think not in terms of works of art finding an audience, but in terms of products being aimed at a certain "demographic." I was once actually asked in an interview what "target group" my latest record was "aimed" at. I told the journalist that I was writing music for anyone and everyone, and I had the distinct impression that he wasn't impressed.

Another reason for distrusting eclecticism is harder to argue with. It is that we're saturated with information and overwhelmed by choices. We want to know where we stand with artists, just as we want to know, in the face of the overwhelming cornucopia at our local supermarkets and megastores, exactly what product does what.

I'm not idealistic enough to propose that all categories be abolished. Clearly definable genres obviously exist, and I have my preferences, like anyone else: I love salsa and Irish Traditional, for instance, but have never had a particularly strong feeling for country or blues. The longing to know what's what is understandable, but when it comes to art, we shouldn't protest too much. Art is all about opening up new worlds, surprising us, and making connections between things we never knew could be connected: making two and two equal five. If we keep insisting that the number should always be four, we're going to miss out on some of the best stuff.

It wasn't that I didn't know, at seventeen, that my tastes were broader than those of my peers. I just didn't care. After all, my musical heroes were eclectic, and I think I grasped the essential fact that in being so, they were being true to themselves. I'd become fascinated by Gershwin. In his lifetime, people were always saying that he had "one foot in Tin Pan Alley and one foot in Carnegie Hall." This was meant as criticism, but it was no more than a statement of fact: Gershwin *was* a man with a foot in both camps. His special gift was to be tuned in to both sides, and to be able to make a bridge between them.

My biggest musical hero, Beethoven, was a radical eclectic. We file him rather smugly under "classical," and yet he broke all the rules of the Viennese classical style. He was inspired by the French Revolution, and highly influenced by the French and Italian composers of his day—people like Gossec and Cimarosa, who are mostly forgotten now—and much of his music would have sounded jarringly French or Italianate to his contemporaries. When he used trombones in the orchestra for the first time, in the Fifth Symphony, people said it was a terrible racket and trombones should stay in military bands, where they belonged. And when he brought a bass drum and cymbals into the finale of the Ninth, people would have assumed he was starting up a Turkish march. Like Gershwin, he used the popular dance rhythms of his time, and there are Russian themes in the Rasumovsky Quartets, and the list goes on and on.

To say that something is eclectic is not, or shouldn't be, a value judgment. It's neither a good nor a bad *idea* to write (for instance) a jazz concerto for piano and dance band, as Gershwin did with *Rhapsody in Blue.* On second thoughts, the *concept* is terrible. But what's important—more important even than the fact that Gershwin was building a bridge—is that the music is beautiful and fresh and alive. The proof of the pudding, as my grandma would have said, is in the eating.

Eclecticism has its own pitfalls, too, but as I schemed and dreamed with Martin, I was blissfully unaware of them. My biggest worry was not philosophical, but practical: How the hell was I going to get my hands on a keyboard?

I knew that I wasn't going to get much further until I could somehow find enough money to buy an electronic keyboard, which at the time meant either a cheap and nasty organ or a primitive electric piano. To rely on the availability of a real piano—let alone a good one—was limiting in the extreme. Besides, I wanted to play with other people. The solo act was all very well, but I wanted to be in a band, and I knew that as soon as a guitarist or drummer got going, I'd be wasting my time, pounding the keys inaudibly.

All those pub pianos, going to waste in the electric age. Standing in corners like silent tombstones, used as pieces of furniture to put drinks on, or as ashtrays, or urinals.

But the urge, the need, to play music could hardly be put on hold. I wasn't done with pub pianos just yet.

The Admiral Drake

IN THE ABSENCE of an electronic keyboard, I dared to hope that a jazz trio could still work, if the drummer wasn't too loud. It had worked, sort of, in the school assembly hall a couple of years before. Somehow I connected with two "jazzers," much older than me, whose names I've forgotten. They organized rehearsals, and we'd worked up an hour or so of material when the drummer found us a gig.

"It's at the Irish Club," he said, "but don't worry, it won't be all Irish people."

The bassist and I exchanged suspicious glances.

"Honestly, it'll be fine," said the drummer. "They use the club for all sorts of things, rock, jazz, folk, you name it. The guvnor told me we should have a good crowd."

The following Friday, I arrived at the Portsmouth Irish Club, a dark, stale-beer-smelling place, and took the front off the upright piano. The drummer would play lightly, mostly with brushes, and the bassist would keep his amp set low. I looked around for clues to the kind of audience we could expect. There were none, but I had a queasy feeling, a vague premonition of being beaten to death with shillelaghs.

"Does anyone know the Irish national anthem?" I asked.

The bassist shook his head.

"Look, we're a jazz trio, alright?!" said the drummer. "We're not playing the national anthem of anywhere! We'll be fine, and anyway, if they don't like it, they can just piss off, can't they?"

I was not reassured by this. But the drummer was right about one thing. The crowd that trickled in as we started our first set was not Irish. They were all skinheads. Even the girls were skinheads, hard as nails in cheap two-tone suits. One or two of them laughed derisively at us. The boys just stood and stared. They didn't understand. This soft tinkling piano and swish of brushes made no sense to them. It wasn't ska. It wasn't even music. Their brains labored visibly, trying out other categories. Was it a joke? Were they being insulted? Who was in the wrong place, us or them?

My skin started to leak. There was no doubt in my mind: It was we who were in the wrong place. Pretty soon, the collective skinhead consciousness would come to the same conclusion, and we'd be done for. Meanwhile, caught on a knife-edge between stunned incomprehension and incipient violence, we started a long, nervous blues improvisation, not looking at anyone, not even each other. After a couple of choruses, an empty cigarette packet landed on the piano keyboard. Then a fag-end flew, still smoking, over my head. I glanced over to the bassist and saw him sitting on his amp, his back to the audience, apparently in tears. Then came a few flying pennies, another fag-end, a couple of peanuts. We played on, and on, until the missiles stopped coming, and as I finally looked out at the audience, I saw the last couple of skins giving us the finger before disappearing. We were to be spared. Not out of kindness, and certainly not out of respect. As far as I could make out, we were to be spared because there were better places to go, and we just weren't worth the time or the trouble of being murdered.

There must be one decent gig in this godforsaken town, I thought. I started to do a strange kind of pub crawl; I walked into pubs just to see if they had a piano, usually walking straight out again. Eventually I found myself in the Admiral Drake, a rough pub at the wrong end of Commercial Road.

The pub not only had a piano, but, as Charlie, the landlord, informed me in a nasal Brummie accent, "a 1902 Bechstein." He'd be delighted to have someone perform on this fine instrument, which had lain dormant, like a volcano, for many years. It wasn't a bad piano, at that, but after playing it for a couple of minutes I knew its whole sad life story: years of drunken abuse interspersed with years of neglect, and a few fag-burnt keys for good measure. I asked Charlie if I could bring a couple of mates in, as guest musicians.

"I can't pay yow any more," he shrugged.

"That's all right. Pay us as much as you can and we'll split it between us."

"In that case," said Charlie, "yow can bring the fooking London Philharmonic in for all I care."

I called Martin Keel. He would be glad to combine his two great loves—music and drinking—in this way. The Admiral Drake was offering a residency, a regular two nights a week, and we were going to knock 'em dead. We pooled our resources, our buskers' books and other sheet music, and made lists of songs. What would go down well in a pub? The old-time sing-alongs, of course: "Underneath the Arches," "Shine On Harvest Moon," "Me and My Gal." We wanted to play some jazz, too, but we stuck to the more "honky tonk" end of the spectrum: "Won't You Come Home Bill Bailey," "Ain't Misbehavin'," "When The Saints Go Marchin' In," "Is You Is Or Is You Ain't My Baby," and so on. This kind of thing formed the cornerstone of our repertoire; it was, more or less, what used to be called trad jazz, with a large dollop of the kind of boozy tongue-in-cheekiness popularized by the Bonzo Dog Band and the Temperance Seven. We also played ragtime, blues, waltzes, and well-known standards: "Strangers in the Night," "The Lady Is a Tramp," "Fly Me to the Moon." I splurged on a Gershwin songbook and a Beatles songbook, and Martin would bring in moldering sheet music from antique shops, forgotten gems like "In a Little Gypsy Tea Room," "Oh, Arthur," or "How Ya Gonna Keep 'Em Down on the Farm (Now That They've Seen Paree)."

On our first night, the landlady made a dramatic entrance. She was a ravaged ex-tart with unnaturally jet black hair and eyebrows that looked as though they'd been drawn on with a felt-tip pen. She wore low-cut blouses, chain-smoked, and had a ragged husky voice and a dirty Sid James laugh. She'd probably been, at one time, a sexy girl. But, whereas a beautiful girl can mature into a beautiful woman, the landlady had turned into something harsh and unsettling to behold. Nevertheless she was popular with the locals, who probably didn't look too closely, and in any case wouldn't have won too many beauty prizes themselves.

The Admiral Drake had a vaguely seedy, red-light ambience. In the Ladies' toilet was a kitsch poster of Adam wearing only a fig leaf, and the fig leaf was a flap, which, of course, cried out to be lifted up. And underneath the flap was a tiny notice that read: A BELL HAS JUST RUNG IN THE BAR. Which, in fact, it had, and locals would line up outside the Ladies' to jeer whoever came out. This was considered great sport.

The key to our success, we soon realized, was the Royal Marines Field Gun Crew. The Admiral Drake was their watering hole, and they were its unofficial social committee, and both its criminal element and its police force, depending on how the mood took them. These men were iron-hard, bullet-headed, tattooed from head to foot (one had "JOCK" tattooed across his neck). They made the Irish Club skinheads look like nuns. They drank astonishing amounts of beer, and—thank God—they liked us. They bellowed along with "We'll Meet Again" or "Hello Dolly," banged their glasses on the table and stamped their feet, bought us drinks, and steered dangerous drunks away from us. Martin and I exchanged satisfied smiles. We had a good gig.

Pretty soon, we started to expand. Martin's friend Phil "The Mouse" Mousley came down to play drums. I took every removable piece of wood off the piano, for maximum volume, but Phil had the right idea. He played softly, but in the right spirit, with wood-blocks, milk bottles, a toy Chinese cymbal that went *splat* and various other pots, pans, bells, and whistles. Martin's Frankenstein tendencies soon emerged anew. He played solos on a teapot with a trumpet mouthpiece and on a hosepipe. He improvised from a coat hanger a cigarette holder that stuck out of the side of his saxophone and played with a dummy Long John Silver parrot attached to his shoulder. Meanwhile, behind the bar, there was a real parrot, which would squawk "You bloody bastard!" or "Pint of Tankard!" every time we started to play.

We couldn't believe we could have so much fun and get away with it. After a couple more weeks, we became a quartet with the addition of Keith, the new violin teacher at the Tec, who was only a few years older than us. Recently arrived in Portsmouth, single, and friendless, he was happy to play anything, anywhere, with anyone. I started working overtime writing arrangements, trying different ways of combining the violin with Martin's various instruments. But much of the time we were loose and sloppy, and apart from making sure that we never strayed too long from a catchy tune, did just as we pleased.

Nothing was too silly. Martin would stand on a chair to take a solo, and get down again when he'd finished. Phil the Mouse, who was learning the trumpet, would play a couple of braying choruses whilst thumping the bass drum, with Martin playing the cymbals. We would play a duet on kazoos, accompanied by The Mouse on a biscuit tin. And Martin became the only musician ever, to my knowledge, to perform a toilet solo. He connected a trombone mouthpiece to a length of pipe and a toilet bowl salvaged from a demolition site. It sounded roughly how a French horn might sound, if a French horn could fart. The *pièce de résistance*, though, was the bluesy wa-wa effect Martin got by opening and closing the toilet lid.

One Friday evening my brother Chris, then fifteen years old, dabbling with the piano, and not yet the connoisseur of pubs he would later become, ventured into the Admiral Drake. The first thing he remembers is the parrot screeching "Pint of Tankard, pint of Tankard!"

"And what would yow loik?" asked Charlie.

"Errr … a pint of Tankard," said Chris, before turning his attention to the band, which was bashing its way through a slightly-less-than-sober version of "The Charleston," with a segue into the *Monty Python* theme. Then there were loud and persistent requests for "The Stripper," and the band eventually gave in. As The Mouse started a boom-boomba-boom on the tom-toms, one of the Field Gun Crew climbed up onto a table behind me and proceeded to strip. More and more choruses were called for as the noise of the crowd grew to near hysteria, and I turned around and saw a pair of naked hairy Royal Marine buttocks a few inches from my face. A deafening roar of approval was immediately followed by the deafening crash of the table collapsing. Beer sprayed everywhere, bodies sprawled and piled on top of each other, and the naked marine's legs waved in the air as his mates struggled to get to his clothes before he did. Time was called at the bar and the evening ended with a rousing rendition of "We'll Meet Again."

Chris came over to the piano, looking slightly shaken.

"Is it always like this?" he asked.

From then on, nights at the Admiral Drake went from the ridiculous to the sublimely ridiculous. Martin decided that Phil the Mouse should play a beer-glass solo. We bought eight pints of bitter and tuned them to the notes of a scale by drinking appropriate amounts of each one. They were then secured to a table with pieces of chewing gum. Unfortunately Phil's solo, inspired though it may have been, could barely be heard, and we were forced to drink the rest of the beer.

A couple of weeks later, my brother came by again, and heard, with a horrified sense of *déjà vu*, loud demands for "The Stripper." The band demurred but were bribed with large quantities of beer. Boom-boomba-boom, went the tom-toms, but this time the featured artiste was the landlady. The old Dragon herself. She stripped down to her black bra and panties, a more shocking sight even than a naked marine, and had to be restrained by her husband from going further.

"You bloody bastard! You bloody bastard!" squawked the parrot, and where could we possibly go from there?

The only way, of course, was down. The mood gradually soured in various small ways. Phil the Mouse was grumbling about the money—or rather, lack of money—and I was pounding the piano harder and harder, to less and less effect. Sometimes I could barely hear myself above the general din, and on one occasion I actually saw a hammer come flying out of the top of the piano. I suggested to Charlie that the time might have come to invest in a new instrument.

"That piano," he said, his pride hurt, "is a nointeen-ow-two Bechstein."

"I know," I pleaded, "it was a good piano, once, but now it's just knackered."

"Well if yow was born in nointeen-ow-two, yow'd be bloody knackered too!" snapped Charlie, and stormed off.

The following week, Martin was about to give me a lift home in his impressively eccentric car—a red and white three-seater Austin Metropolitan, with internal boot—when I had to run back into the pub to take a leak. I came back and got in the car, and off we went, completely forgetting that I'd left our whole collection of sheet music on the car roof.

The next morning I remembered. In a blind cursing panic I took the bus over to Portsmouth. All I found were a couple of crumpled pages in the dirt. A lot of the music was irreplaceable; the rest I couldn't afford to replace. The few pounds we made at the Admiral Drake had all been spent on beer.

Of course it couldn't last: If hard pounds-and-pennies practicalities didn't finish it, we probably found a way, out of hubris, to screw it up for ourselves. But we'd had more fun than I ever thought was possible playing music.

Immediately after our last night, my brother showed up at the pub again, this time with a school friend. I was out somewhere drinking with the Three P's, and hadn't mentioned to Chris that we'd lost the gig.

"Oi!" demanded a marine, "where's your brother?"

"I don't know," said Chris, genuinely taken aback.

"Never mind, you can play!" said another marine.

"No I can't!"

"Yes you can! Come on!"

Chris was dragged to the piano and forced to play a dozen choruses of the only tune he knew. He was rewarded by the Field Gun Crew with loud applause and free drinks for the rest of the evening.

No Guru

As my A-levels approached, my parents, understandably perhaps, wanted to know what I was planning to be when I grew up.

Wasn't it obvious? I was going to be a composer, and to make ends meet, I'd play the piano, for anyone who'd have me. I didn't see any conflict between the two. Bach had made a living as a church organist, Brahms had played in brothels, and Shostakovich had accompanied silent movies. I didn't necessarily want to spend the rest of my life banging out "Take the A Train" on an out-of-tune pub piano, but, as the Admiral Drake had showed, even that beat the hell out of any alternative that might have been available.

My mother was fixated on the idea that I should become a music teacher. Surely it was the only possible way to make money from music? I told her I'd rather be boiled in oil.

Then she had another brilliant idea. Over bowls of impossibly delicious rhubarb crumble, she asked if I'd ever thought of being a librarian.

"A *what*?"

"Well, you love books, don't you? And you could still do your music."

I wanted to scream. A librarian! I might as well be buried alive. That my parents were genuinely concerned about my future meant nothing. I was almost eighteen and infuriated that they didn't *understand*. They didn't see that if you're following a great passion, it doesn't matter if you're on the dole or on the street or eating from a soup kitchen. They didn't see, I thought, because they didn't have a passion. The only reason I needed money at all was to escape from them.

I didn't know which was worse: my mother's sympathetic wheedling or my father's mostly silent hostility. He and I communicated less than ever. He'd taken me to concerts, he'd driven me to piano lessons, but enough was enough. It was time to face reality. I couldn't have agreed more; I just had a very different idea of what reality might be.

My dad probably thought I was on the highway to hell, and he wasn't about to pave it with good intentions. Was it my imagination, or was he getting cranky? He picked fights with my mother, and he and I had the occasional confrontation, which usually ended with him telling me that something or other was so because he *said* so, or that I wasn't too big to get a good thrashing, or some such Dad-speak. It hadn't impressed me as a kid; what made him think it was going to make a difference now?

That he envied my youth, my talent, or my determination would never have occurred to me. Nor could I see that *he* was trying to be someone, too, even if it was only in his own home. Trying to hold on to the only kind of authority or prestige he'd ever have.

We managed to agree on one thing. If I could get a grant, and if I could pass the auditions, I would go on to music college. At least I'd come out of that with the qualifications to teach.

I practiced like a maniac. I wanted to study composition, but I would have to have a Second Study too, and I knew the competition would be tough in the piano department. I worked on a couple of Beethoven sonatas, Debussy's *Suite Bergamasque*, and the later, harder volumes of Bartók's *Mikrokosmos*. I even dipped a toe into the chilly waters of serialism, with Schoenberg's *Five Pieces*, op. 23.

I was now being excused from sports to practice on the other ancient Bechstein in my life, in the assembly hall, but for a few weeks, sports came and found me. The gym was being renovated, and the assembly hall was going to be used for indoor exercises. The P.E. teacher told me to carry on with my practice. So I played on, while all around me boys did calisthenics and jumped over wooden horses and skipped with ropes. With musical accompaniment, it was like some kind of surreal ballet. Quite often, at the end of a session, I'd get a round of applause.

There was no doubt about it: Some of my peers, at least, were impressed, even if they didn't know quite what to make of me. Sometimes I felt like a big shot. Other times I still felt very much alone.

When I couldn't get into the assembly hall, I practiced in what we used to call the Old Army Hut. This was the soon-to-be-demolished Old Assembly Hall, or OAH as it appeared on school schedules. It was a dusty, creaking old place with a battered upright piano. The piano was neglected and unloved. No one else played it, so I used it for sadistic experiments. I'd read about avant-garde composers like John Cage writing pieces for "prepared piano," in which various objects were stuffed into the instrument to modify the sound. I stuck pins in the hammers, which produced a metallic jangling sound, or hung a chain across the strings.

One day I was playing Bartók in the Old Army Hut when a hardnut walked in. A muscular skinhead, he marched purposefully over to the piano and sat down next to me. He stared at me and I carried on playing.

I finished a piece. He said nothing. So I started another. Any minute now, I thought, this bastard is going to slam the lid on my fingers. Why doesn't he get it over with?

I finished another piece. Still no comment. No, I thought, he's going to pull the stool out from underneath me, that's always a popular trick. But he didn't. Finally he spoke.

"Can't you play something . . ." he searched for the right word. "Can't you play something *fast?*"

I couldn't believe it. This wasn't a tormentor, but an audience. What on earth should I play? I turned the pages of *Mikrokosmos*. Here was a fast piece, one of the pieces based on Balkan folk-dances. I tore through it and then looked around for a reaction. There was none. I cursed myself. What should I have played? A jazz number? A Beatles tune?

The hardnut looked at me with an expression that contained no hostility, just complete and utter bafflement. Then he got up and walked out.

Another kid—a posh kid, a confident kid, a kid with parents like Orson Welles's—might have just dismissed the hardnut as an ignorant lout, and carried on regardless. But I felt that I'd failed. I was playing Bartók with a bloody chain inside the piano, and I'd let the side down. I felt more alone than ever.

I still enjoyed drinking with the Three P's, but I couldn't follow their talk about football, and I didn't know how to tell them about my main preoccupation: trying to find a compositional voice of my own. From about 1970 to 1973 I was a prolific composer of piano and chamber music, as well as a few attempts at setting poetry, some arrangements of English folk songs, and some exercises in orchestration. I still have some of these scores. Some of them aren't too bad: for instance, a Sonatina for Bassoon and Piano, written for a fellow pupil (a year above me) by the name of Colin Wilson. It's structurally sound, and it has some decent melodic ideas. But it sounds like the work of a student very much under the influence of Bartók, with a dash of Duke Ellington thrown in.

How do you find your own style, anyway?

That's one of the Big Questions.

I had no guru to help me make sense of my many influences. Reggie Wassell had retired to be replaced by a tweed-skirted young woman. Even before that, he seemed to have lost interest. When I tried to show him my compositions, he seemed embarrassed, made excuses, and said he'd look at them some other time. I was crushed. I felt my face turning red. Were they really that bad? Was being a composer, after all, just a childish fantasy?

I suddenly realized that Reggie had been my only mentor, and now he was gone. Perhaps I had outgrown him. But if I had, I didn't know where to turn next.

I didn't know that I was grappling with questions that have been hard enough even for some of the greatest artists of the twentieth century. What style to write in? Where to turn, now there are no certainties, no models, no traditions left? How to find your own voice in the clamor—so many different schools of thought, so much of everything, available to everyone, like never before?

In the past, a musician, like everyone else, would either have been educated or not. If you were educated, you would have entered into a local academic or church tradition—Viennese, Venetian, and so on. If you were not educated—and if you did anything creative at all—it would have been rooted in the local folk tradition. Either way, you would have known where you stood. And influences from abroad—or for that matter from the next town—would have reached you slowly, giving you time to adapt.

But all those old structures have broken down, and now anyone with a few quid to spend can simply walk into a record shop and choose from five centuries' worth of music from all over the world. And if something has been lost—something about the *specialness* of a musical performance—most of us think that more has been gained.

All very well for the "consumer," but how often do we consider how it affects the artist? Where does he start, when everything is transient and disconnected? How does he know who to be, when his roots are themselves rootless?

These days I think it comes down to two choices, and they're both forms of specialization. The first is just to choose from one of the hundreds of genres or subgenres, from ambient to zouk, that are multiplying like hyperactive amoebas even as we speak. A white kid from Boston or Bavaria can decide to play ska, and, like the court musicians of the eighteenth century, he'll know where he stands. He can say, with conviction, "I'm one of *those.*"

The second, harder option is to take specialization to the limit. Taking whatever bits seem appropriate from all the influences around you, you can create your own musical world. In the midst of chaos, you can create an island of order, in which everything makes sense—at least to you. But maybe that's the best place to start.

This way, you become a subgenre of one. To use another analogy: Anyone can buy a suit off the peg. Some people will look better in it than others. But if you want it tailor-made, you're exposing yourself—your ideas, your taste, your *own* opinion—and any time you do that, you can soar higher but also fail more miserably. At worst, it can be a nightmare, of the standing-naked-in-the-middle-of-Picadilly-Circus kind. You're more vulnerable to criticism, but at best, your successes are more real; they're *yours.*

Sometimes I think that categories are proliferating to such an extent that nearly *everyone*, eventually, will be a subgenre of one. Maybe then we'll appreciate content a bit more than style—or rediscover the true meaning of style. Isn't style supposed to be an expression of individuality? Shouldn't style, in other words, be the opposite of fashion?

How do you get to grips with all this at seventeen or eighteen? To tell the truth, I feel that I'm only really getting on the right track now. But that's another of music's mysteries. As I reflect on my musical apprenticeship, I can't say where the apprenticeship ended, or if it even *has* yet. That's okay. It's actually comforting to think that I'll always be traveling and may never arrive. Because if you ever "arrived," wouldn't it all be over?

I got my A-levels in English and music, and went on to take a scholarship S-level in music. I passed that too, with a better grade than I got in the A. I was the only student in my school ever to get an S-level pass in music, and one of the very few to get one in anything. No one seemed very impressed. Maths, metalwork, football—these were what the Tec was all about. Reggie Wassell aside, it had never, ever, been supportive of the arts. No one congratulated me. There wasn't even a mention in assembly. To hell with all of you, I thought. An 'S' level pass meant I was almost certain to get a grant. Music college was within reach.

I applied to both the Royal College of Music and the Royal Academy of Music. I submitted some of my compositions, and played Beethoven's E Major Sonata, op. 14, no. 1, in my auditions. I was accepted at both. I was stunned. I never imagined I'd have a choice. I chose the Academy, which seemed friendlier and a bit more freewheeling. It even had something called a Jazz Workshop.

Now I was nervous. I was going to be a smaller fish in a much bigger pond. And it was a strange feeling, leaving the Tec: weary and sad and triumphant, all at once. Part of me didn't want to leave. Familiarity doesn't only breed contempt. But in a burst of bravado I took my school tie out into the back garden and set fire to it, not knowing, of course, that skinny ties just like it would be hip in a few more years. I grew my hair as long as I could. I had thin hair and it looked terrible, but that wasn't the point. I was finally going to be a full-time musician, and I was finally going to have to find out what kind of musician I really was.

The Creech Cottage All-stars

WHEN MY grant check arrived, I went straight out and bought an electric piano. It was a question of priorities. I wanted to do more gigs, preferably in a band. That was more important, in the short term, than using the money for rent in London. In fact, much as I wanted to get out of my parents' house, I wasn't particularly attracted to London. I was meeting more and more musicians in the Portsmouth area, and I was sure it wouldn't be long before I would actually be in a band. In London, I would have been just another bug hitting the windscreen.

For my first year at the Academy, at least, I would commute and economize. Then I found out that if I commuted I could get a cheap train pass. So I bought an amplifier and speakers.

The electric piano was a Hohner Pianet. If it was good enough for Mike Ratledge of the Soft Machine, it was good enough for me. Martin Keel's dad made me a wooden case for it, and Martin and I decided to form a band, along with a guitarist and singer by the name of Mark Andrews.

Around this time, during my last year at the Tec and my first at the Academy, I met several musicians who would become collaborators and friends for many years. Mark Andrews was the first. Martin had met Mark at a Folk Night at the Black Dog in Havant, and told him that he should, like Dylan, seriously consider "going electric." Mark spent nine grueling months working at the Smiths Crisps factory, after which he could never touch a crisp again, but he was able to buy an electric guitar and a Vox AC30 amplifier—the amps the Beatles used.

Mark was a romantic figure: a "bad boy" who'd been expelled from school, had long reddish hair and a beard, wore a leather Stetson, and lived in uncompromising outlaw style somewhere out in the woods. I was mystified as Martin drove us over the back of Portsdown Hill, into what might as well have been the Siberian tundra to me, city kid that I was. Surely no one could live out here? In fact, hidden in the woods was a crumbling old mansion called Creech House, which was haunted by a Mrs. Baring, a crazy gin-soaked old lady with a smelly entourage of dogs and cats. Mark lived with his girlfriend on the outskirts of the lady's property in Creech Cottage, a sort of hippie crash-pad with rising damp. Dope was smoked, bottles of cheap cider were drunk, and jam sessions stretched into the night.

Several other musicians drifted in and out. There were at least three different drummers. There was a balding, bearded, permanently bloodshot-eyed bassist called Bob—we found the alliterations irresistible. Then there were the Barfield brothers, from Gosport, who are still good friends.

I met Dave Barfield first. He had advertised himself in the *Evening News* as a drummer available for just about anything. I called him, despite having just about nothing to offer, but we had similar musical tastes and arranged to meet anyway. He brought half of his kit round to my parents' house, a strikingly good-looking, self-confident young man, blond hair unfashionably but fittingly short. We fooled around with some of my first, awkward, jazz-rock compositions, and jammed in various odd time signatures, both being Soft Machine fans. We didn't know where to go from there. Dave came to Creech Cottage once, but Mark didn't like his style. Dave and I agreed to keep in touch.

Soon after, I met Dave's younger brother Drew. At first sight, Drew was very much the sensitive singer-songwriter, with long hair and a wispy, poetic goatee. But he turned out to be warm and down-to-earth, with a great sense of humor. He played guitar and bass, and had a beautiful high, almost feminine singing voice. He became a fixture at Creech Cottage. Keith, the violin teacher, also dropped in. Some sort of band was gradually taking shape, although no one was quite sure what sort of band it was.

In retrospect, it's amazing that we could agree on anything. I wanted to play some sort of progressive, experimental jazz-rock; Mark was into

Crosby, Stills, Nash, and Young; Drew was a diehard Beatles fan; and Martin just wanted to play the blues. After a while Martin quit, as he and I disagreed over questions of musical freedom. I was all for musical freedom, but long aimless jam sessions started to bore me. I was interested in structure, and I was becoming a passionate arranger and orchestrator. What would happen if the violin played this melody line with the alto sax a fourth below? Now what would happen if we switched them round? How about just the piano playing the chords here, and the guitar doubling the bass line in octaves? How about doubling the bass line in tenths?

This sort of thing got on Martin's nerves. He couldn't bear to be told what to play. He accused me of having a stick up my arse, and I didn't really know what he meant. But freedom, to him, was the whole point. We remained on good terms, but for one reason or another we never worked together again.

As for the rest of us, we coalesced into a band of sorts, and managed to play three gigs in all. Equipment was our first problem.

Equipment is everyone's first problem. Trying to get a band together with no money is a punishing labor of love. At Creech Cottage, we used all four channels on Mark's amp—for guitar, bass, Pianet, and vocal mike. This wasn't exactly hi-fi, but it just about sufficed for the living room. To play a gig, we'd have to rent or borrow more gear, as well as transportation. We had a roadie, an amiable doper called Ollie, who always seemed to be somewhere in the background at Creech Cottage. He had long dark greasy hair and dark circles under his eyes, actually addressed people as "man," and was always either rolling a joint, smoking a joint, or unconscious. Roadies—which is to say, people with nothing better to do—can always be found. Money and PA systems are a different story.

Drew managed to get an amplifier through his father's naval connections. It was a monstrous thing, made for the bulkhead of a ship, and all its control knobs had been smashed or fallen off. Volume and tone adjustments had to be made with a screwdriver. It would have to do.

Next Drew needed a speaker cabinet. He couldn't afford to buy one, so he joined forces with his dad to build one. They got a fifteen-inch speaker, and, knowing that a bass cabinet needed to be large, built a towering edifice that would have made a spacious wardrobe. Then—knowing that a bass cabinet needed to be solid and stable—Drew's dad poured almost a foot of concrete into the bottom. Finally, the whole thing was covered in bright orange vinyl. It was a damn impressive piece of work, but it weighed a ton. Still, it worked, and kept working for years. It became famous. Eventually, it became an embarrassment, but no one could be persuaded to take it away. No one could even *lift* it.

I splurged on equipment early on, and I was going to have to wing it financially, at least through my first year at the Academy. I bought an impressive H/H amplifier in Charing Cross Road (the only secondhand one in captivity, I was told) and a battered Marshall stack. As any heavy metal fan knows, a Marshall stack consists of two cabinets, with four twelve-inch speakers in each, stacked one on top of the other. It's a favorite setup of power-crazed guitarists. One Gosport guitarist, Denny Barnes, had a *purple* Marshall stack. Drew, among others, had gone along to jam sessions in Denny's living room just to look at it. People would stand outside his house in the hope of getting a look at it through the window. Of course, a Marshall stack wasn't really appropriate for keyboards, but I found one that was going cheap. I'd use one cabinet and have the incredible luxury of a spare. Alternatively, I could sell it if (or when) times got tough.

In the world of the struggling rock musician, equipment is a big deal, and a certain prestige—sometimes accompanied by arrogance—attaches itself to the guys with the good "gear." But for me, there was always something funny, sad, and endearing about the struggle itself. A friend of mine swears he once saw a desperate little band in which the drummer had one cymbal but no cymbal stand. He had a friend stand next to him with a fishing rod, from which the cymbal hung, like some kind of mutant flatfish just dredged out of the deep. The only flaw in this arrangement was that every other time the drummer actually hit the cymbal, it would fall crashing to the floor, and have to be rehooked. I was awestruck. This, I thought, was real dedication.

At the other end of the spectrum, a penniless guitarist named Simon, a friend of a friend, was glancing through the *Evening News* one day when he saw an advertisement that read: Fendercaster Guitar for Sale. He laughed, since, as even many nonguitarists would know, there is no such thing. Fender are famous guitar-makers, and their two classic models are the Telecaster and the Stratocaster.

Simon decided to go and have a look. The guitar turned out to be an exquisite 1958 Stratocaster, in perfect condition, in its original case. It had been found in the attic, and its provisional owner, who didn't seem too bright, hesitated when Simon asked him how much he wanted for it. He obviously hadn't decided.

"How about a fiver?" said Simon, more-or-less joking.

The guitar-owner hesitated again, then shrugged and said, "Yeah, orroight then."

Simon handed over the money, calmly carried the guitar as far away as he could, and then stopped in a side street to do a sort of crazed, leaping Red Indian war dance. Sometimes a crumb falls from God's table.

Meanwhile, in darkest Gosport, a young bassist had just cashed in the insurance policy his mother had been putting a shilling a week into on his behalf ever since he was born. He got fifty pounds, and bought a build-it-yourself amplifier kit from *Practical Electronics* magazine. Shortly afterwards, we met at Fareham bus station. He was skinny and wore incredibly thick glasses. People always compare thick glasses to Coke bottles, but these were jeroboams of champagne. He introduced himself, or so I thought, as "Bodger."

Although his eyes swam disconcertingly behind the great panes of glass, like tadpoles in the far distance, Bodger was obviously a very nice bloke. The sort of bloke who's so infallibly nice that you occasionally feel like punching him. Shortly afterwards, I invited him to Creech Cottage. By the time we made our way out there, via a succession of buses, I realized that his nickname was actually "Badger"—on account of his being as blind as one. But by then he was wearing contact lenses, and I got to know him by his real name, which was Graham Maby.

Graham played at the cottage a couple of times, but our long association didn't really begin until later. What's more, I didn't yet realize just how good a player he was.

Drew Barfield played bass on our first gigs. We had a strange repertoire: a couple of Mark's songs, which were "rockers"; Drew singing the Beatles' "Come Together"; a couple of vaguely jazzy instrumentals; and my first faltering attempts at songwriting. Not having a clue about writing lyrics, I'd taken the words from, of all things, poems by Lewis Carroll.

The first gig was at the Tec, in the school assembly hall, some kind of end-of-term dance. We called ourselves "Strewth," which, in the process of tickets being printed, somehow turned into "Struth." I still don't know the right spelling.

Some things regrettably slip from memory and some things are just so god-awful that they *have* to be repressed. What can I drag up, from the dustbin of the id, about that night? That I played the school organ, which had seemed so loud at assembly but became completely inaudible over the bass, guitar, and drums. That between the hall's strange acoustics, the deficiencies of our equipment, and our ignorance of how to set it up and position it, no one could hear anyone else properly. That we had trouble keeping even approximately in time with the drummer, who was disgusted with us. That we played Zappa's "King Kong" with Keith on badly amplified violin, also inaudible. And that people walked out in droves. It was an unmitigated disaster.

We changed our name to the Scratch Band, and then, in an effort to focus more attention on Mark as the front man, to Andrews' Scratch Band. Our next two gigs were only marginally better. They were both at the Tricorn, the concrete monstrosity in the center of Portsmouth's main shopping area, which was once voted the second ugliest building in Britain. It couldn't even manage the distinction of being the worst. For a while there was a music venue on the top floor. Mark had worked there as a barman, and used his connections to get us two gigs as support act, first for an up-and-coming local band called Smiling Hard, and later for a bona fide big-time rock act, the Sensational Alex Harvey Band.

We were stunned by the Alex Harvey Band. Not, at least in my case, so much by the songs—which were still too "poppy" for me at the time—but by their presence, their confidence, and another whole dimension that I hadn't really considered until now: their showmanship, and their ability to create excitement.

We felt like very small fry indeed. And for all my musical training, I felt like a hopeless amateur. Restless but demoralized, the Creech Cottage All-stars drifted apart.

For This I Wear the Hat

ONE SUMMER afternoon at Creech Cottage, we set up all our equipment outside and played in the woods, until Mrs. Baring came and complained. We dragged everything back inside, but just as we started playing again, Mrs. Baring, perhaps refreshed by a gin and tonic or two, came knocking: She'd changed her mind. So we hauled everything outside again. But this time, just as we started to play, it started to rain.

In retrospect, this seemed to sum up the whole experience. Trying to get a band off the ground, playing original material, was, and is, like pushing a boulder up the side of a mountain. There would never be enough money or enough gigs for us to get anywhere near to catching up with our ambitions. As we admitted defeat, or at least temporary defeat, we and every player we knew seemed to be facing the same dilemma: Do we stick to our guns, stay true to vaguely defined progressive-rock, counterculture ideals, and maybe do a couple of gigs a year, if we were lucky? Or do we clean up our act, play Top 40 hits, and get more regular gigs? The latter was called, with a certain disdain, "going commercial." But if it worked out, you could gain precious gigging experience, make a bit of money, and buy better gear.

I didn't see this dilemma in quite the same way as some of my peers. To me it was not prostitution to use your skills to make money. Then again, maybe that's exactly what prostitution is. Anyway, it didn't bother me. I was committed to being a full-time, professional musician, and I was prepared to take the rough with the smooth. What puzzled me was that the gap between art and commerce seemed so huge and unbridgeable. The Admiral Drake, which had absolutely nothing to do with artistic self-expression, had been great fun and steady work, albeit at a laughable wage. But trying to do your own thing was, by and large, a pain in the arse. Some more Big Questions seemed to hang in the air. Did it have to be either one or the other? Does an artist really have to suffer, like some sort of Monty Python medieval penitent, bashing himself over the head with a slab of wood with every few steps forward? Did I want to be an Artist or an Entertainer? What, really, is the difference? And if launching a rock band was this hard, what kind of masochist would I have to be to be a "serious" composer?

As our band struggled towards its demise, Mark Andrews and I both came down on the side of getting out there and getting the experience, whatever form it took. For a while, though, our very different abilities took us in different directions. I was about to start college, but I couldn't resist auditioning for a piano-and-drums residency at a Greek restaurant.

The restaurant, the Apollo, was in Commercial Road opposite the Tricorn. It was also around the corner from a pub called the Bell, which at one time boasted a legendary piano-and-drums duo of its own. The drummer, who was about seventy, would walk in every night with a snare drum in one hand, a hi-hat in the other, a pair of brushes in his pocket, a cigarette hanging from his lip, and two or three inches of ash hanging from the cigarette. No one knew if this minimalist kit was all he owned, or if it was an adaptation to the fact that he came to the gig by bus.

The pianist, who was about seventy-five, also had a distinctive style. He played convincing jazzy runs with his right hand, but his left hand was another matter. It played a jarring approximation of stride, hitting the bottom end on one and three, and chords on two and four, quite correctly, but leaving the actual notes themselves almost completely to chance. As someone or other observed, he had the right hand of Oscar Peterson and the left hand of Les Dawson. Which is to say, a left hand like a bunch of bananas.

At the Apollo Restaurant, the owner, one George Stylianou, motioned to the piano and told me to play something. What? I had a moment of panic, and launched into a rambling jazzy improvisation, immediately cursing myself for it. But Mr. Stylianou stopped me after about fifteen seconds and told me I'd got the job. He then served me a magnificent free meal of stuffed grape leaves and *stifado*. What was he, some kind of nut? Anyway, all I had to do was to find a drummer. I called Dave Barfield, and just a couple of days later, we started a four-nights-a-week residency.

The gig paid an unexpected, and more than welcome, seven pounds a night each. All we had to do, apparently, was play "dinner music"—standards, bossa novas, nothing too loud. But as we were getting ready for our first night, a Greek fisherman walked in wearing a naval peacoat and carrying a bouzouki.

At least, he looked like the sort of character you could have seen on every postcard in the tourist shops of Crete or Corfu. He was short but barrel-chested and hugely muscular, with a bushy mustache and the traditional fisherman's cap jammed permanently on his head. He introduced himself as Yannis Grapsas, and he was "the cabaret." In other words, at a certain point in the evening, when most of the patrons had finished their meals, a spotlight would come on and we would accompany Yannis in some Greek tunes. The climax of the show was "Zorba's Dance," in which a young Greek waiter would suddenly leap onto the dance floor and dance, first slowly, teasingly, then faster and faster until he was whirling like a dervish, and the audience was expected to throw plates. The ceremonial first plate was always thrown by Mr. Stylianou, but the audience didn't always catch on. Holidays in Greece were not so common then, at least not among Mr. Stylianou's clientele, and most nights they looked at him as though he'd just taken leave of his senses.

The show usually went down well, despite being undercut somewhat by Yannis's own enthusiasm. He just wanted to play, and right from the start, he would join in with everything Dave and I did, whether he knew the tune or not. Mostly he was a good busker, but Mr. Stylianou wasn't happy about this overexposure of his star attraction. Yannis simply couldn't be restrained. He seemed to think he was playing most of the evening under some sort of mystic cloak of invisibility. When the "cabaret" spotlight came on, he just grinned harder and played louder.

I liked the sound of the bouzouki—at least, for the first couple of weeks—and Dave and I got on well with Yannis, in spite of his limited English. He always, for instance, used "one" instead of the indefinite article—"Would you like to have one drink my fren?"—and confused b's with p's—"Ah, that is one peautiful song you blay." But he was a stranger in a strange land, and he seemed almost childishly happy to have this opportunity to communicate through music.

The Apollo looked like a pretty easy gig, but it soon revealed some quirks and tensions. Chief among these was the tension between Yannis and the boss. Apart from the young dancing waiter, who was a temporary worker and stayed out of the way, they were the only Greeks in Portsmouth, and they had a volatile love-hate relationship. They would never have been friends in Greece, Stylianou the austere, rather melancholy businessman in the sharp suit, and Grapsas the scruffy free-spirited peasant. At least once a week, the night would end with a furious row, and Yannis would storm out of the restaurant spitting, cursing in Greek, and yelling "I never work for heem again!" On one occasion, trembling with rage, he swept past Dave and me as we were packing up for the night, and for the one and only time, tore off the fisherman's cap, and jabbed with a middle finger at a hitherto unsuspected bald spot on the top of his head.

"For this I wear thee hat!" he screamed. "For THEEESS!"

Then he lurched out into the night, leaving us staring open-mouthed. The next day, he was back, and the night ended with Yannis and Mr. Stylianou singing, arms around each other, over a bottle of Metaxa.

This performance started to lose its charm after a while, as did other aspects of the gig. For instance, the meals we were served at the end of the night, as part of the deal, got worse and worse. Peter, the chef, was a huge, sullen, hairy man, and a vegetarian, despite the fact that every time we saw him he seemed to be hacking away at great mounds of bloody flesh with an enormous cleaver.

"How can you be a vegetarian?" I asked him one evening.

"Because I see the rubbish you poor bastards eat," he said, and *whump!* went the cleaver.

Shortly afterwards, I stopped eating meat, although I still eat fish and have never called myself a vegetarian. I just never really cared for the stuff, and I seem to feel better without it. Besides, I don't want to be called anything that ends with *-ian*, except "musician"; or for that matter, anything that ends with *-ist, -ite,* or *-ive.*

Peter the chef probably influenced my decision—if not by his philosophy, then by his cooking. From the heights of *stifado* and *dolmades* we soon descended to leftovers reheated with baked beans and curry powder, or rubbery beefburgers and greasy cold chips.

Dave was furious about this, as well as other indignities. For instance, we were often, on Wednesday nights, forced to play for an hour at a time to an empty room. We were being paid, so we had to play! The worst thing, though, for Dave, was having to play with chopsticks.

A piano-and-drums duo is a flawed concept to begin with, since any drummer younger and more virile than our old friend at the Bell will drown out the pianist with ease. Dave gritted his teeth and played as softly as he could, got sick of playing with brushes, and when the boss still complained, tried playing with knitting needles and finally plastic chopsticks. These produced some rather sad, pitter-pattering drum sounds, and weren't too reliable either. Several times a night I would hear a "Fuck!" or a "Shit!" and broken pieces of chopstick would fly over my head, sometimes landing on the tables of startled diners.

Playing at the Apollo was slowly driving Dave insane. He wanted to lobby for better treatment and more money. I wasn't enthusiastic, and Dave accused me of being too passive, which hurt me. I like to think that, over the years, I've proved him wrong. But the Apollo, I thought, was what it was, and wasn't about to turn into anything else.

The one major exception to routine was the Night of the Persians. The restaurant was fully booked, and there was an air of festive anticipation. Mr. Stylianou, pacing and rubbing his hands, explained that the place was being taken over for the night by a party of Persians. He meant, as I found out later, Iranians. The Iranian navy was training nearby at HMS *Daedalus*, and this was to be their big night out. A Greek restaurant wasn't exactly a taste of home, but it was the closest they were going to get in Portsmouth. In their honor, Mr. Stylianou had procured a belly dancer and extra supplies of plates.

At eight o'clock, the Apollo abruptly filled with Iranian naval personnel, and they partied like this was their only chance to party in a very, very long time, which may well have been the case. Politely sober when they arrived, they were all riotously drunk within an hour and kept up a nonstop barrage of plates and pound notes for the rest of the evening. Every piece of crockery in the place was smashed. Plates flew in all directions, ricocheted off the walls, and piled up on the floor to the point where they had to be cleared away, only to be thrown again and shattered into smaller pieces. The belly dancer drew roars of approval and showers of money.

Yannis was driven into a frenzy of primal greed. As the Persians threw pound notes at him, he stopped playing in the middle of tunes, jumped off the stage, and scooped them up. By the end of the evening, he was jumping around like a frog, slipping and sliding on broken plates, stuffing money into his pockets, down his shirt, into his shoes.

Dave and I didn't get a penny.

Towards the end of our residency at the Apollo, bored, we suggested to Mr. Stylianou that we become a trio with the addition of a certain wonderful singer and guitarist of our acquaintance. The boss, probably seeing an opportunity to get Yannis to shut up for five minutes, agreed to a trial period, so for the next couple of weeks Dave's brother Drew played acoustic guitar and sang.

Our repertoire as a trio was so limited that a lot of improvisation was called for. We would vamp endlessly on simple chord sequences, or play twelve-bar blues in a minor key over a bossa nova rhythm, and Drew would just sing anything that came into his head. Apparently, no one noticed, so he started to change the words to some of our better-known songs, just to see what would happen. "Raindrops keep falling on me bonce / but that's not the reason why I'm singing like a ponce / maybe just the once . . ." he would croon, with a straight face. Or "You can have me on a Monday, a Tuesday, a Wednesday, or any day you like / but you can't have me on a Sunday, a Sunday, 'cause Sunday's the day I fix me bike." Still, no one noticed.

Eventually, Yannis walked out for good, and Mr. Stylianou decided to close the Apollo and open a restaurant somewhere else. We saw Yannis one more time, though. He called me with a brainwave: Let's form a band! I would play electric piano, Dave would play drums—with drumsticks—Drew would play bass, and we needed another instrument—what did I suggest? I said I knew a violinist called Keith who seemed willing to play anything, anywhere, with anyone. Yannis thought this was a brilliant idea. Skeptical, but curious, I agreed to contact everyone, and we met a week later for a rehearsal in Yannis's tiny Southsea flat.

We started off playing songs we all knew, and some of the Greek tunes from the Apollo—"The White Rose of Athens," and so on. The blend of pianet, bouzouki, and Keith's violin was surprisingly attractive. Then Yannis started to show us some traditional Greek melodies, darker and more angular than we'd heard from him before. Some had odd rhythmic patterns, or extra beats in certain bars. Most of the tunes were rather sad, but one was fast and furious, a sort of demented polka, in which we all had to shout "hey!" in unison at the end of a phrase. Clueless about the musical tradition we were glimpsing, we all played whatever seemed right to us. Somehow it worked.

As we lingered into the evening, a warm glow seemed to fill the room. We were creating a kind of music that didn't officially exist, but it felt as though it had been around for ever. Nothing outside had changed, but in the magical realm of music, the pebbles of Southsea beach were washed by the warm waters of the Aegean, and seagulls perched on palm trees.

Dave asked Yannis what he thought. Yannis closed his eyes, and an expression of deep satisfaction came over his face.

"My frens," he said, "I hear one peautiful sound."

A week later, he went back to Greece. We never heard from him again.

Academia

And what about the Royal Academy of Music?

At first it was a thrill. To go somewhere to study music, and nothing else, was hardly believable. I knew I was highly privileged. I was even addressed by the teachers as "Mr. Jackson." It had a strange ring to it, but after the indignities of the Tec, I wasn't complaining.

As new students arrived, we were given a certain amount of flexibility to arrange our own schedules. I arranged mine so that as much as possible was crammed into as little time as possible. Without a place of my own in London, I didn't want to spend half my life on commuter trains. More importantly, I needed free time to cultivate my career as a gigging musician.

I managed to condense my schedule into three days a week, Monday to Wednesday. But I'd have to get up shockingly early on Monday mornings. People sometimes tell me how lucky I am, as a musician, not to have to get up early. They don't realize that the egg came before the chicken. In other words, my hatred of the early morning hours was a big factor in my choice of career in the first place.

It was freezing cold and still dark on the morning of my first full day. Somewhere between 5 and 6 A.M., I had to sleepwalk onto a bus down to the Gosport ferry terminal, and then take the ferry across to Portsmouth harbor station. The ferry was clogged with dockyard workers and their bicycles. They all wore black donkey jackets and woolly hats, with scarves

—also mostly black—knotted tightly around their necks. Their bikes—"treaders," they would have called them—were all black, too. In my barely conscious state I wondered what would happen to a dockie who showed up one morning on a red one.

As the ferry docked, the workers poured like a sluggish plague of locusts through the Dockyard Gate, and I boarded the London train. An hour and a half later I got out at Waterloo, and then took the tube to Baker Street. As a childhood Sherlock Holmes fan, I got a kick out of this. Then, a five-minute walk along Marylebone Road, past Madame Tussaud's and the Planetarium, to the Academy, a Victorian red-brick building that looked disappointingly small on the outside, but was somehow much bigger on the inside. I was exhausted already. How the hell was I going to do this every week? And my first lesson on Monday mornings was also the toughest: my one-hour composition lesson.

I was still in search of a mentor, someone who could help me focus my ideas and my ambitions. I was making some headway as a gigging musician, but as a composer, I still felt very much alone. I also needed, on a basic human level, some encouragement. But my composition teacher, John Gardner, was a hard-nosed technician. He was noncommittal about my compositions, and apparently thought that what I needed was a stern taskmaster to whip my theoretical skills into shape. His authoritarian style reminded me uncomfortably of my father at his worst.

Gardner was big on Bach, and on score-reading—the art of playing a piece on the piano reading from a multistaved score. He was a vigorous white-haired man, stocky, probably close to fifty, but with an aggressive energy that made him seem younger. He wasn't a pedant, but he was a bit of a bully. For instance, he would make me play Bach fugues, over and over again, from an open score—that is, four parts on four staves—with four different *clefs:* not just bass and treble, but alto and tenor, too. This was pure sadism.

"Look, I just can't do this," I pleaded.

"Of course you can. Just try it slower," said Gardner.

"No, you don't understand. That won't help. I really can't do it."

"Then you must try it even slower, until you *can* do it."

So I struggled on, at speeds so slow that the music ceased to be recognizable, as a Bach fugue or anything else. What was the point?

And what was the point of Figured Bass? Figured Bass is a system of notating chords in a sort of shorthand, with numbers above a bass line. Widely used in the time of Bach and Handel, it's of little use now, except to baroque music specialists and church organists. Besides, I'd already learned a system of shorthand for chords: the jazz chord symbols. "C" was a C-major chord, "Cm" a C-minor chord, "–5" a flattened fifth, and so on. A logical and practical system, which had the added advantage of helping me to get paying gigs. So why wasn't it being taught at the Academy?

I wanted to learn, and I was willing to work hard, but I couldn't help feeling that I wasn't quite getting what I wanted. It was all nuts and bolts, when what I wanted was some answers to the Big Questions.

It wasn't all bad news. My piano teacher was a charming, serene old lady, and I continued to make progress. We worked on Debussy's *Préludes*, and I probably reached my technical peak as a pianist with her. I was certainly a better player then than I am now.

And then there was the Jazz Workshop. This was really a big band, in which musicians—mostly brass players—who had no jazz experience could play alongside the relatively small number who had. It was directed by a bona fide British jazz star, John Dankworth, who brought in classic charts by Duke Ellington and Neal Hefti and Gil Evans. The Academy's talent pool was supplemented here and there by outside players, including some first-rate session drummers and bassists. I was the only pianist to show up who had played some jazz and could read chord symbols. A stroke of luck. The gig was all mine.

Dankworth did some remarkable things in the Jazz Workshop. For instance, he would have orchestral brass players, who had never played without music in their lives, playing Count Basie riffs by ear, and once the band was grooving, he would borrow a clarinet from someone and play a gorgeous solo over the top. The brass players loved it. Dankworth would also write extra parts, for French horn, for instance, on the spot. Clarinetists started to show up with newly purchased saxophones. It was the most fun to be had at the Academy, and it's hard to believe it was so unusual at the time.

I learned a lot about arranging in the Jazz Workshop. Orchestration was my strong suit. I had a good ear for tone color, and I usually knew immediately what combination of instruments I was hearing, or what a combination of instruments on paper was going to sound like. It seemed obvious to me, no more difficult than imagining what red would look like next to blue. With Dankworth, though, and at orchestral rehearsals, score in hand, I was constantly fine-tuning my ear. I loved the orchestration class and got high marks for an orchestration of the first movement of Beethoven's D Major Piano Sonata, op. 28. I never actually heard any of these exercises played, but I continued to study scores over the years. Much later, when I was finally commissioned to write a film score with an orchestra at my disposal, I was able to produce a score that sounded, in almost every detail, exactly as I'd heard it in my head.

After a long and often arduous Monday, I would catch a late afternoon train back to Portsmouth. Passing through the Surrey commuter belt, these trains were crammed with raucous chain-smoking alcoholics in pin-striped suits, spilling out of the buffet car and spilling gin and tonics over everyone. Their laughter seemed forced and overloud, as though this half-hour or hour on the train was their one precious window of release from the twin oppressions of work and home.

By the time I got back to Gosport, I was wiped out. Tuesdays and Wednesdays were not quite so bad, but I was soon thinking seriously about finding a place to crash in London, at least some nights. Besides, I was starting to like the feel of the big city. Often I would linger as long as I could before heading for Waterloo, checking out Marylebone pubs, jazz records in Covent Garden, book shops in Charing Cross Road, sex shops in Soho, or post-hippie fashion around Carnaby Street.

If I was going to keep up this ridiculous schedule, I was going to have to justify it by at least getting more gigs on the south coast.

Then, one day, in the middle of a thunderstorm, something appeared at the door of our house that looked like a low budget alien from *Dr. Who.* It turned out, under many layers of waterproof motorcycle gear, to be the bassist of a local pop group called the Misty Set. Their pianist had been hospitalized, and they wanted me to stand in for a while. They'd heard I was pretty good.

I was pleased to hear that I was acquiring a reputation. Once I started playing with the band, though, I wasn't so sure. The bassist, who seemed meek and tiny without his space suit, was one of the worst I'd ever heard. He played a big old semi-acoustic bass with strings that hadn't been changed in years. Every note was a dull thud, barely distinguishable from every other note. Between this and the anemic style of the drummer, I felt rather naked and alone with my Pianet. The singer didn't play anything.

He stood, holding a microphone in one hand, with a music stand in front of him, on which were books full of lyrics. With his free hand he turned the pages and sipped scotch and soda.

The Misty Set's repertoire consisted of all the wimpiest, most inoffensive pop tunes you could think of. The high point of the show, in terms of raw excitement, was probably "The Hokey Pokey." I was grimly fascinated. They were like some bland and smiling master-race of a dystopian future, genetically engineered to remove every last spark of passion or originality. The show started with—what else?—"Misty," but played as an up-tempo swing number, over which the singer would not sing, but *speak*, in a phony American accent: "Well, and good evening ladies and gentlemen . . . we're called the Misty Set . . . and we'd like to welcome each and every one of you here tonight . . . and it's really wonderful to be here . . ."

This was almost bad enough to be good, but the show was all downhill from there.

I suppose that experiences like this helped to keep my feet firmly on the ground. In contrast, some of my fellow students at the Academy seemed unbearably pretentious, and the composers were the worst of the lot. I may have been an idealist, but these guys, I thought, lived in cloud-cuckoo-land. They wrote epic pieces for huge orchestras and seemed quite convinced that they'd get them performed. They huddled intensely over large complex manuscripts, debating over fine points. Should this be a bar of 2/4 followed by a bar of 3/4, or should I make it one bar of 5/4? And here, you see how I invert the principal motif in the violas?

When I think of these characters, I'm reminded of a story about one of my favorite composers, Dmitri Shostakovich, who was once subjected to a long tirade from the apparently rather pompous Sergei Prokofiev. After holding forth at great length about his latest symphony, how he was developing this theme in one movement and having trouble with that theme in another movement, and so on, Prokofiev finally paused to allow his younger colleague to comment. Shostakovich said nothing for half a minute, and then asked laconically, "What's for lunch?"

The opera contingent were almost as pretentious as the composers, but more entertaining. Opera was not a specialty of the Academy, but the department tried to make up for its small numbers by cultivating a dramatic presence. There were two fat sopranos, for instance, who scuttled around the place with outstretched arms, blasting glass-shattering high C's at each other, and calling everyone "darling." Sometimes I would run into three or four singers practicing, say, a scene from *Don Giovanni* in a corridor, complete with the kind of hammy acting that has always made it hard for me to completely embrace the operatic medium. I would push past them with a smirk that was half embarrassment, half scorn.

Of course, there was more to some of my fellow students than met the eye, and I should have gotten to know them better. For instance, there was a girl in my year with a Scottish accent who carried a flute case. She has beautiful eyes, I thought, but she needs to do something about that hairstyle. Apart from the fact that my own hairstyle was no masterpiece, she had a lot more potential than I imagined. Her name was Annie Lennox.

What was my problem? I'd finally arrived among my true peers, only to find that it didn't *feel* like they were my peers at all. Most of these kids came from middle-class families in the Home Counties, and I didn't really relate to them. I was more comfortable with some of the down-to-earth trumpeters and trombonists, for instance, who'd paid their dues in the brass bands of Yorkshire or Durham, than I was with the composers.

During my first week I saw a man sweep into the Academy wearing a cape, a six-foot-long scarf coiled like a giant python around his shoulders, and a huge floppy hat. He looked like a character out of some Victorian melodrama.

"Who's that wanker?" I asked a cellist.

"That," said the cellist, "is Sir Anthony Lewis. He's the principal of the Academy."

I'd been trying to escape my parochial background for as long as I could remember, but now I began to realize that I was a product of it, like it or not. It came as something of a shock. The tables were turning; suddenly *I* was the yob, the oik, the Pompey hardnut.

In retrospect, much of the affectation I saw at the Academy seems harmless enough, even charming. I couldn't make a convincing argument now either for or against a six-foot scarf, as opposed to the scratchy rags favored by those Pompey dockies on their treaders. Youth can be amazingly unforgiving.

Schoolgirl Slaves of Soho

I MADE ONE friend at the Academy in my first year. He was a composer named Dave, and he had blond corkscrew hair and wore round glasses. He looked like a cross between John Lennon and Shirley Temple. Like me, he seemed slightly out of place, and he was a fan of what he called "weird rock." We went to what was probably my first London concert: Captain Beefheart at the Rainbow. We both loved it. Afterwards I slept on a sofa at the flat Dave shared with someone or other, somewhere in the uncharted regions of north London—Highgate? Stoke Newington? Anyway, it seemed like luxury. I was beginning to hate the train.

I stayed with Dave a few more times. Then, one day, he came into the Academy wearing a long orange robe and sandals. He'd become a follower of someone called Bhagwan, and from now on he was to be addressed not as Dave but as Krishna Chinmaya.

A week later, Dave lurched into the common room unshaven, glassy-eyed, his hair wet and dishevelled and his orange robe stained with something that looked like creosote.

I asked him how he was doing, this fine morning.

"Great!" said Krishna Chinmaya, shivering. "I slept on a roof last night. The stars were beautiful. Until it started raining. But it was great!"

Just my luck, I thought, I manage to make one friend and he turns out to be the biggest nutcase in the place.

Meanwhile, in south London, three young actors were putting the finishing touches on a show they'd written themselves. They called themselves the Cabot Clowns, "World Champions of the Underground." On the fringe of fringe theater, they had plenty of ideas but very little cash. So how were they going to find the pianist they needed to accompany their musical numbers? "I know," said one of them, "we could try advertising in one of the music colleges. Maybe we can find a piano student who's willing to try anything and doesn't want any money."

At least, that's how I imagine the events that led to the appearance of a certain postcard on the Academy notice board. I was intrigued. I went straight to the phone booth in the lobby. A deep American voice on the phone introduced itself as Russell. Could we meet this evening? Well, maybe, but I didn't have anywhere to stay the night. Russell said that was no problem—I could stay with him. What the hell, I thought, and later that day found myself hired as the musical director and one-man orchestra of the Cabot Clowns.

Apparently I'd been hired as soon as I picked up the phone, since I was the only person to respond to the advertisement. This amazed me. What was the matter with those stiffs at the Academy? This looked like fun. If nothing else, I thought, these were interesting people.

Russell was very tall, dark, and film-star handsome. Jude, his wife, was tiny next to him, but she had a dynamic energy that made her seem much bigger. She had short black hair and her big pale blue eyes were almost unnervingly intense. But she also had a ready smile and seemed able to find humor in just about any situation. I was shocked to notice that the underside of one of her arms seemed to be made of twisted pink candle wax. I later found out that she'd been badly burned in an accident. But she made no attempt to hide it, so I pretended not to notice.

Despite being almost physical opposites, Russell and Jude seemed very much on the same wavelength. Bursting with ideas, many of which were gleefully absurd, they seemed to be making up their lives as they went along, in a way I hadn't come across before. They were also extremely generous and immediately treated me as a friend.

The third Cabot Clown, Teresa, was very different. She was attractive, with long dark hair, and rather mysterious. Later I found out that she was the black sheep of an aristocratic family. Theoretically stinking rich, she had obviously rebelled, and yet she retained a certain snobbish reserve. I was intrigued, but didn't quite know how to relate to her. She, in turn, was superficially friendly but not easy to get to know.

Russell and Jude were the creative brains of the outfit, and they explained that they were about to launch a comic strip drag musical featuring song, dance, thrills, laughs, sex, suspense, outlandish costumes, acrobatics, masks, and—oh yes—they were shooting a movie, which would be part of the show, too. The show was to be called *Schoolgirl Slaves of Soho.*

I grinned inanely and said it sounded great. I hadn't a clue what they were talking about. I'd never met anyone like them in Portsmouth, nor, sad to say, at the Academy either. In an earlier age, they would have been called bohemians. They were avant-gardists with a sense of humor. Although they were only a few years older than me, in their midtwenties, they seemed to hold the key to all kinds of doors.

That night, somewhere south of the Thames, the Cabot Clowns took me to a wine bar with candles on the tables. We ate more-or-less-French food and drank wine and I felt very alive and very grown-up. I looked out the window, not knowing where we were, and London seemed to be throbbing with possibilities in the dark.

We were soon rehearsing the show, which didn't make a lot of sense. The plot, such as it was, revolved around schoolgirls being kidnapped and sold into pornographic slavery by an evil mad scientist called Master Vadman (played, in drag, by Teresa). The heroine of the piece was Games Captain Lilac (Jude, brandishing a hockey stick). Russell, among other things, played a schoolgirl, which was quite a sight. His six-foot-four-inch frame was squeezed into a white bodysuit, over which he wore a gym-slip and a huge white doll-like mask with pink cheeks. The Cabot Clowns were very much into masks. There was also a circuslike aspect to the proceedings, with Jude (who actually had some training as a trapeze artist) doing back-flips or playing the clarinet while standing on Russell's shoulders.

As far as I could tell, we were trying to create something like a live comic strip. It was campy and surreal, and it might turn out to be sheer genius or utter disaster; I couldn't tell. But at least we were enjoying ourselves. The music was a communal effort. Jude had lyrics and rough ideas, and I had to flesh them out. They were thrilled with my input. "Hey, this guy can play anything!" said Russell. I wasn't about to contradict him. This might not have been many people's idea of a dream gig, but I wanted to be indispensable.

Russell and Jude had a house somewhere between Brixton and Camberwell, or rather, they lived on the top floor of a house that no one owned. Russell had met the estate agent, who was waiting for the market to improve before trying to sell it again. In the meantime, he said—probably succumbing to Russell's considerable charm—someone might as well live there. There was a spare bedroom, with bare floorboards, in which I spent quite a few nights, sleeping under my overcoat. We lived on toast—nothing else that I can remember, except on one occasion when Russell invited the estate agent to dinner. This was a shrewd gesture, except that none of us could cook. Jude tried; she battled tragically with the kitchen, like Charlie Chaplin in the automated electric house that goes haywire, finally producing a fish dish that was totally inedible. We had to abandon it and do what we always did: eat at a local wine bar or pub.

One evening we screened the amateur film that would be part of the show. Jude had borrowed a troop of real schoolgirls from the school where her mother taught, and they were seen marching along Downing Street, with Russell in schoolgirl drag towering above them. They carried placards extolling free and equal access to pornography (*Schoolgirls Not Fool Girls* and *We May Look Innocent—But Watch Out!*) and actually presented a petition at No. 10. A couple of burly coppers looked on impassively.

All of this functioned both as a Dadaesque artistic statement and a publicity stunt. The *Daily Mirror* played along, surprisingly straight-faced, with a short piece entitled Girls Demand Porn At School. The *South London Press* was hilariously earnest, quoting a spokesman for the prime minister as saying that they were "unable to acknowledge the petition or take any action."

I've always been suspicious of people who reminisce, sighing, about "more innocent" times. But thinking back to the London of 1973, I can't help feeling a twinge of regret. It's hard to imagine anyone indulging in such foolery on Downing Street today without getting themselves arrested. For that matter, it's hard to imagine an estate agent lending someone a house, rent-free.

But back then, as London started to reveal itself, I found it both exciting and reasonably friendly. A bit more money, a bit more food, a bit more heat at night would all have been welcome. But I didn't feel like there was anything to be scared of. Why does London seem so much harsher now? Could it be that I needn't apologize for softheaded nostalgia, and that it actually *is*?

Schoolgirl Slaves of Soho opened at the Dark and Light Theatre in Knatchbull Road, Brixton, at the end of February. Off to one side, in front of the rather too-high stage, yours truly, the pianist, played wearing a pink Afro wig. The audience couldn't have numbered more than fifteen, and apart from friends and family they didn't seem quite sure what to make of it, although they laughed in a few places. One of my favorite parts of the show was when Jude and Teresa would appear as leather-clad dominatrices, for no particular reason. They were a sort of show within a show, adding cabaret to the list (was there anything these people wouldn't attempt?)

"We're the Sadista Sisters," announced Teresa, cracking a whip, "and we love you to DEATH!"

The Sadista Sisters performed a sort of sick S&M magic act. A member of the audience was brought onto the stage and had a couple of his fingers chopped off. But they didn't magically reappear, as expected. Blood spurted and the victim screamed in agony, eventually being hauled out of the theater, yelling threats and curses. Of course, it was a hoax—the victim was a friend of Jude.

The biggest laugh of the evening came when Teresa, as Master Vadman, was supposed to light a cigar, which (this being the theater of the absurd) was in fact a Tampax tampon. Gales of cackling laughter erupted in the house. The reaction was so loud and unexpected that both the whole audience and the whole cast turned to see where it was coming from. It was coming from a huge, coarse, scruffy woman, a cockney charlady straight off of a seaside postcard. She'd sat in bemused silence so far, but this—*this* was funny. She couldn't stop laughing. Tears rolled down her cheeks. Then the rest of the audience started to laugh. The show ground to a halt, and when it got going again, it seemed more surreal than ever. It was as though Brecht or Beckett had just collided with *Carry On Nurse.*

The next night, the audience was even smaller, and no one even noticed the tampon. We were rattled, but keeping our fingers crossed for the review, which was supposed to appear the next day. This was exciting. Having missed my chance to be immortalized in schoolgirl drag by a *Daily Mirror* photographer, this would be my first time; the first time something

I was involved in would be validated by the press. Being in the press meant you actually existed.

The review appeared the next day, as promised, in *Time Out*.

> 'World Champions of the Underground' is the title that the Cabot Clowns say they are prepared to defend. On the evidence of their first night, they won't need to since I seemed to be the only person in the tiny audience who was not a friend of the company. If anybody does go and see this show, though, I don't know what kind of defence they could possibly mount. It's a long-winded rambling piece supposedly about the pornographic exploitation of schoolgirls, performed by the company of three in full masks which soon become boring and expressionless. Their limited vocal range and vocabulary of movement does little to patch up the inadequacies of the 'comic-strip' text. At the end of all this there's a film which, after the rest, seems quite fun and professionally set up. But perhaps it's only by comparison. (Probably ends Sat., but check with theatre.)

I read the review over and over again. You bastard, I thought, you mean-spirited bastard, who do you think you are? What good does this do anyone? What good does it do to spend half the review talking about how small the audience was? What can we expect, if bastards like you won't give us a break? Your "review" isn't even well written. What does "in full masks" mean? And "long-winded *and* rambling"?! Could you do any better? We don't even know what you look like, do we? It must be nice to be so smugly anonymous. You couldn't take the kind of shit you dish out. You BASTARD!

On my way to the theater that night, I was still fuming, and sick in my stomach at the thought of finding the show canceled and the cast in tears.

Instead, there was a pleasant buzz in the theater. On the first night, we'd had about fifteen people, on the second, maybe ten. But tonight there must have been at least thirty.

I was completely thrown by this. I went backstage and ran into Teresa.

"Did you see the review?" I asked.

"Yeah." She gave a kind of sneering half-laugh.

"Well . . ." I fought for words. "Well, I mean . . . I don't *get* it!"

"Get what?"

"All these people!"

Teresa half-laughed again. "I suppose a bad review's better than none at all," she said.

This was all very strange, but I felt that if I let it sink in for a while, it might start to make sense. We had audiences of thirty or forty for the rest of the week, and they were appreciative, if not exactly enthralled. But at the end of the week—just as that clever critic had predicted!—*Schoolgirl Slaves* closed.

After the last show, I met Krishna Chinmaya at the stage door.

"That was brilliant!" he said.

"You know what's weird?" I said, still groping for some kind of logic. "There was this really shitty review in *Time Out*, but since then, we've been getting a lot more people."

"I suppose a bad review's better than none at all," he said.

The wisdom of Bhagwan. We walked the streets of Brixton, orange robe and army greatcoat, looking for a pint before closing time.

Take Me to the River

As THE Cabot Clowns tried to regroup, I brooded over the myriad headaches that seemed to go along with any effort to reach an audience. I suppose I'm still wrestling with them now.

Sometimes it feels as though I'm on one side of a river, and the audience is on the other. They're not so far away, but how do you get *across?* Everyone needs help: from agents, managers, publicists, promoters, and of course, from critics. And sometimes the critic is the kindly ferryman, and sometimes he's the shark who bites your leg off. And you have to keep on smiling and say it's just a scratch, because unwritten law dictates that artists must never complain about criticism, and we're only asking for more trouble if we do. Still, I don't see why the subject—or any other subject, for that matter—should be out of bounds.

After *Schoolgirl Slaves* closed, I thought about our *Time Out* review over and over, and added more clichés about critics to my list: they're envious, they're on a power trip, they're frustrated artists, they don't even spell people's names right. But clichés don't get us anywhere. There are plenty of clichés about artists, too, and they too are both true and false: we're vain, pretentious, greedy, petulant, or stark raving mad. So what?

It's better to admit, when you get a bad review, that you're just plain hurt, and that you're hurt because you're human. It's like being hauled out in front of the class and humiliated by a sadistic maths teacher. It's like being picked on by a bunch of hardnuts on the bus. It often surprises people to know that some very great artists have been devastated by criticism. Artists are very often less sure of themselves than they seem. Bizet was utterly destroyed—driven to his death, many believe—by the hostile reception to his opera *Carmen*. I bet his friends told him not to take it personally. But your work is your flesh and blood, and it *feels* personal, and what are you supposed to do with the hurt?

I got the message early on that criticism can help, too, if only by providing publicity. I wish I could say that this put things into a balanced perspective, but balanced perspectives don't happen overnight. In the meantime I plunged back into the safety of obscurity. I had two more gigs to do with the Misty Set, polite affairs at weddings and social clubs.

I asked if I could sing one song. I'd been singing backup for a while, with the Creech Cottage band, but I had no idea if I could carry a lead vocal. I couldn't think of a better time to find out. No matter how bad I was, it surely couldn't make the slightest bit of difference, in this context, to anyone. The Misty Set owned a spare microphone, but no stand, so we improvised one from a folding music stand and a couple of feet of gaffer tape.

I sang (don't ask me why) "When I'm Sixty-four." I started off trying to sound like Paul, more or less, but panicked halfway through and switched to Ringo. It ended up sounding vaguely cockney, like a bad Anthony Newley. The response was embarrassed silence, both from the audience and the rest of the band, who packed away the spare mike after the gig and never said a word.

I have no idea what became of the Misty Set. They have the dubious distinctions of featuring the first vocal performance by a future recording artist and of making *Schoolgirl Slaves of Soho* seem like the Big Time.

The Big Time, I was starting to see, was a place where you might become more, rather than less, vulnerable. I've known musicians who, on the verge of a career breakthrough, have run away. It's the critic that frightens them, and not necessarily the literal, human critic, but all kinds of old voices: parents, teachers, friends, and enemies; but most of all, the critic inside their own heads.

The Small Time has its good points, and a lot of people are more comfortable there. I could never have attempted that first lead vocal if I'd known the gig was being reviewed for the *Melody Maker.* But I knew that for me, music was both more than just a hobby and more than just a job.

I was in this for keeps, so no matter how vulnerable I might feel, the Small Time was simply not an option.

I was going to have to deal with critics, both outward and inward, real and imaginary. How have I done it? It's taken a long time, and it's not a case of ceasing to care what people say. Unfair reviews still hurt. But I've had enough reviews, good and bad, and met enough critics, that I'm no longer impressed by the mere fact of something appearing in print and being circulated around the globe. I know that critics are human beings, that they may or may not be smarter than me, and that everyone has an agenda. The bad review is simply the product of an agenda different from mine, and the good one is a case of two agendas happening to agree.

Besides, casting all critics in the role of villains just doesn't hold up. I was once utterly charmed by a woman who, I later found out, had written a scathing review of my record a year before. The guy who writes a rave might, in fact, be a complete asshole. Who knows, his review could even be wrong.

This is why even good press doesn't quite get me doing cartwheels across the floor. I'm always a bit suspicious, and the pleasure I take from a good review is vaguely tinged with something like guilt. I feel how a footballer might feel after winning by an own-goal. The point is that we *should* be suspicious of critics. We're free to react to them in any way we like, to smash up the furniture or sulk or crack open the champagne, but what we must never ever do is be guided by them.

Good critics are knowledgeable and passionate about their subjects, and motivated by a desire to help others enjoy them more. Bad ones are spiteful judges in their own little kangaroo courts. But one thing we cannot afford to let a critic be is a guiding light. An artist who lets critics make his decisions for him is doomed.

How can I be so sure? Because I've read more reviews than I could begin to count, and if there has been any kind of meaningful pattern, it has stubbornly refused to reveal itself. As an example, here are two excerpts from reviews I received on a recent tour.

> Joe Jackson demands to be taken seriously as an artist. He practically insists . . . stiff ... often pretentious . . . the only thing missing was a sign on the stage reading 'Quiet! Artist at work!'

Loose, spontaneous, friendly, even a bit silly, the pianist and his vibrantly sympathetic trio was anything but distant ... pretentious, *lui*? Not a chance.

These are two reviews of *the same show.*

Two different agendas, two different sets of expectations, two different tastes. You just can't afford to get emotionally attached to this stuff, or you'll end up so confused you won't be able to create *anything*.

In an ideal world, we wouldn't need critics. But the world in which we actually live has become a cultural smorgasbord, and we all live permanently on the verge of indigestion. We have to have some help in sifting through the endless choices. There must be a better way, but I don't know what it is.

All we can do, those of us on this side of the river, is try to keep our focus. We have to find a guiding light somewhere within ourselves; and the only way to find it is by persistence. In the meantime, remember that if a bad review spoils your breakfast, it's because you're only human. The trick is not to let it spoil lunch.

Joe 90

Persistence and determination. Persistence and determination. I repeated the mantra over and over to myself on the tube and the train and the ferry and the bus backwards and forwards between Marylebone and Gosport. I still didn't feel confident. Persistence and determination would have to do.

Bleary-eyed on Monday mornings, I squinted at Bach fugues, and John Gardner, utterly unsympathetic, insisted that I needed glasses. He said it often enough to make me wonder. I went to an optician, who told me that my eyes were fine, but that a certain type of lenses might sharpen my vision slightly, if I wanted. I decided I did. I got a pair of round, gold-rimmed glasses, which I wasn't sure were actually doing anything at all for my vision. But I imagined that they made me look intelligent and intriguing, or at any rate a bit different from how I'd looked the week before.

My social life was in a state of flux. My school drinking-mates were dispersing. They didn't seem comfortable with me any more, and besides, I was tired of wearing crewneck sweaters and greatcoats. I bought what I took to be a moddish secondhand striped jacket in Carnaby Street, but I was stopped one day on the stairs at the Academy by a shrieking toff who greeted me as "an old St. Pauline." Apparently I was wearing his old school blazer.

Back on the south coast, I was becoming estranged not only from the

Three P's but from my family, too. Chris was trying a succession of musical instruments on for size, and he would eventually settle on the guitar, but his approach to music was stolid and methodical, completely unlike mine. He would never dream of seeking a musical career. Pretty soon he would join a firm of jewelers, and he's still with them now.

The two school years between us were still a barrier, and we moved in different circles. I was starting to think we were much less alike than we actually were.

Pete and I, though, were from two different tribes. My hair was dirty-blond, his was black, and as a teenager, he wasn't so cute any more. He was spirited and irreverent, which I liked, but music and books didn't interest him. He looked more and more like my dad, and would bond with him more than Chris or I ever would, on a tangible, practical level. When I picture them together, they're always happily bashing down walls, drilling, sawing, or mixing cement. Pete was going to make his living as a carpenter, and I suppose that to him I must have always seemed a strange and ethereal creature.

Pete had become a Gosport kid, but I still resisted Turk Town and spent most of my time in London and Portsmouth. Like many eighteen-year-olds, I took my family for granted and believed that if they were all abducted by aliens, I wouldn't miss them. There were only two kinds of people I wanted to be with now: musicians and girls.

I had some fumbling success with a girl called Jane, who lived in Southsea, and with another girl to whom I was distantly related—my cousin's cousin, I think. Apparently, girls—or a few girls, anyway—did actually find me interesting, and I was probably becoming a more accomplished fumbler. But I was beginning to realize that I had a sexual problem, an embarrassing, physical problem. Too much friction was actually painful. What was going on?

I searched the Soho sex shops in vain for something educational. I couldn't possibly talk to my parents about it. They'd never even told me the "facts of life," and in their presence I felt ashamed of any sexual feelings I had. In anyone else's, I was ashamed of being still a virgin. If there were brothels in Pompey, I didn't know where they were, and the whores who chased the sailors were less appealing than abstinence. Young men in my position had been raw meat for the armed forces since time immemorial, but in the absence of a war to bolster my uncertain sense of manhood, all I had was a piano and—another, more time-honored helper—booze, and the occasional joint.

One night I found myself at a party in Southsea that went on until all the beer was gone and the handful of us who were still conscious moved on to a lethal mixture of homemade dandelion wine and cherry brandy. After throwing up outside, I passed out, and came to at about 4:30 A.M. to find myself actually lying in the gutter, something I thought only happened to cartoon tramps. I then had to wander, or stagger, the streets until the first ferry left for Gosport.

I started to admit to myself, finally, that Gosport was where I actually lived. Getting to Portsmouth and back just took too much time and effort. I found a pub near my home, the John Peel, which sometimes had live music, and I started to meet more local musicians. Eventually, I was wooed by a Gosport pop band called Edward Bear.

Despite their deplorable name, Edward Bear was a busy group. They had an agent and a steady two to four gigs a week. Terry, the bassist, and Jim, the guitarist, came to my house to make me an offer I couldn't refuse. Terry had long sideburns and wore nothing but blue denim, and Jim had a thick black mustache. They weren't exactly cool, but they showed no sign of caring one way or the other. They were a working pop group. This meant smart stage clothes, moderate volume, and songs people could dance to, or sing along with, or both. It also seemed to mean a certain attitude: laid back, friendly, diplomatic, not too serious about anything.

Terry and Jim were probably about ten years older than me; not exactly ancient, but they had the air of seasoned veterans. There was a kind of solidness about them, a calm authority, as though playing with Edward Bear was an age-old tradition, as though you could ask anyone, anywhere, about Edward Bear and be told they were Good Lads.

Along with Steve the drummer, Edward Bear were doing fine as a trio. But something was missing. They had a dream, and they were willing to take a bit less money to make it come true. The dream was a sound that Jim had in his head. That sound! If only they could find that sound! It was Gosport's very own *Glenn Miller Story*. Except that Jim knew exactly what the sound was. It was the magic combination of a twelve-string guitar and an electric piano. He had the guitar. What kind of piano did I have? A Hohner Pianet, I said, pleased with myself. Terry and Jim exchanged a wink and a sentimental smile, like two little old ladies who'd just seen the cutest kitten. This couldn't be better. Yes it's a great sound, yer Hohner Pianet. That'll do nicely.

Terry and Jim explained the upcoming schedule and the money I'd be making, which wasn't bad. I was hesitant, fearing a rerun of the Misty Set, but Terry and Jim assured me it would be nothing so insipid. Edward Bear Rocked. This was a bit like saying that Tufty the Squirrel Kicked Ass, but I decided that as long as they didn't want me to sign a contract in blood, I might as well go for it.

I soon met Steve the drummer, who was a sweet, shy sort, despite being, as I soon realized, a bit of a dim bulb. He mangled words in rehearsals, putting the emphasis on the second syllable of "Marshall," and saying "rift" instead of "riff" ("So, you play that rift four times and then I come in, roight?"). Terry and Jim winked at me and tried not to laugh. Steve also had a strange nervous tic in his playing. When he played a fill around the tom-toms, his head would swivel simultaneously upwards and sideways, and he would make a noise that sounded something like "Phwaaaayy!" I found this a bit unnerving. One of these days, I thought, he's going to go for a really big fill and have some kind of seizure. And what if he decides to add more tom-toms to his kit? Luckily this never happened. Steve's drumming stayed within fairly predictable limits.

I kept putting my new glasses on and taking them off, in the way that other people smoked cigarettes or bit their fingernails. At one rehearsal, while I was wearing them, Jim turned to Terry and said, "'Ere! You know who he reminds me of?"

"Who?"

"Joe 90!"

Edward Bear collapsed into laughter. They all agreed I looked exactly like Joe 90, boy scientist, eponymous hero of a sci-fi TV show done with puppets, and wearer of enormous glasses. I was more puzzled than embarrassed. I couldn't really see it.

Recently I happened to turn on a TV and found myself face to face, for the first time in twenty years, with my wooden—or plastic?—namesake. I *still* couldn't see it. Okay, we had both worn glasses, but his lenses were *square*. I can only assume that there was something about his earnest, boy-genius persona that I shared, quite unconsciously, at eighteen or nineteen. Whatever it was, it stuck, and I was soon being called "Joe" on a regular basis.

Edward Bear's repertoire overlapped with the Misty Set's, but it was, thankfully, a shade more red-blooded. Of course, there were a lot of songs that every semipro pop group in the world seemed to play as a matter of course, as if required by law: "Born to Be Wild," "Proud Mary," "I Can See Clearly Now," "Summertime Blues," and so on. But the twelve-string guitar was used to good effect on a couple of numbers by the Byrds, which were new to me, but which I liked very much. "Classy pop" was Terry and Jim's ideal. They loved slick vocal groups like the Association and tried to recreate their harmonies, with me providing the third voice. It didn't sound too bad, although there were to be more than a few gigs where we could barely hear ourselves, and God only knows what it sounded like then. How did I manage to do so many gigs for so many years without the aid of a monitor system?

A lot of people, even those who are quite well informed about music, are not really sure what a monitor system is, and why so many bands they see in concert seem to be having so much trouble with theirs. Basically, the sound from a musician's standpoint can be very different from what the audience is hearing. On stage, we can hear the guitar amps—at least, if we're in front of them. But it's hard to balance your volume with, say, a bassist who's on the other side of the stage and whose speaker cabinet is pointing not towards you, but straight outwards. Disconcerting echoes come back at you from every wall and ceiling. Vocals, especially, become garbled, distant, or inaudible, since they're coming out of the PA system, which is pointing out at the audience. Since we can't have the PA system behind us (the microphones would feed back), we compensate by having an additional system of smaller speakers—monitors—that are pointing back at us.

Monitor speakers are now being widely replaced by in-ear monitors, earpieces molded to fit the unique contours of each musician's ears, and plugged into a radio belt-pack. Either way, the idea is to hear exactly what each of us *wants* to hear, taking into account the size of the stage, the acoustics, and so on.

Acquiring a monitor system is a big step up for a pub-and-club band. And when you have a monitor engineer at the side of the stage, mixing your onstage sound for you, you know you've Arrived. Of course, your troubles haven't ended! Your band-mates will want everything turned up louder than everything else; the stage area will have acoustical anomalies that make the bass boom uncontrollably, or make everything feed back at a certain frequency; you'll spend hours in soundcheck getting the mix just right, and it will sound totally different when the house is full; your monitor engineer will be deaf or stoned or a secret sadist. The next time you see a rock 'n' roll guitarist finish a show by slamming his instrument onto the floor and walking off with a scowl, consider that it may not be an antiheroic pose. He may have just spent an hour and a half in Monitor Mix Hell, that infernal region where everything sounds like it's coming out of an Edison phonograph at the far end of a railway tunnel.

And the next time you hear an out-of-tune singer in a pub band, consider that the poor bastard probably has no monitors at all and can't hear himself. Or rather, he hears his voice, sounding a bit fuzzy and boomy and not really like him, echoing back at him from all over. You can get sort of used to this, though, and some monitorless singers—including Edward Bear's Jim—have done a decent job, most of the time. But please, spare them a drop of sympathy if it doesn't sound exactly like a record.

Within a couple of weeks I was gigging with Edward Bear, mostly all over Wessex and the Home Counties. The gigs fell into three or four broad categories. There were working-men's clubs and social clubs: these were a bit rough, and the audience would start off indifferent but generally, after a few drinks, have a good time. Naval and army bases were similar, but the indifference was stonier and the ensuing drunkenness more extreme—sometimes frighteningly so. Then there were discos and nightclubs, with a younger, trendier crowd who sometimes liked but often merely tolerated us (the DJ was what they were there for—Tamla Motown and real records by real groups). Lastly, there were private functions, mostly weddings. These were probably the most appreciative, but they weren't our favorite gigs, since we'd often spend the whole evening fending off requests—requests for dreadful songs we didn't know or didn't want to know, or requests to turn down, which drove us crazy, since our volume was not exactly heavy metal to begin with. But Terry and Jim, ever the professionals, would politely comply, smooth over disputes, placate drunks, and sometimes—but not always—stop fights. I had to admire their diplomatic skill. Meanwhile Steve just smiled his shy, crooked smile, and I pretended to be invisible. Don't shoot me, I'm only the piano player.

Terry and Jim's smooth professionalism was balanced by an endless stream of vulgar bantering, although even this was rather harmless and well-meaning, and tended to follow unvarying, almost classical forms. Every time someone farted, for instance, Terry would say "Brown's out!" and Jim would say "Next man in!" This got a laugh every time.

The first longish van journey I went on with Edward Bear quickly turned into an orgy of lechery, which in the coming weeks proved to be typical. Terry and Jim tried to outdo each other with protestations of lust towards every female we passed.

"Look at this one!"

"Nice legs."

"Yeah, nice tights, too. Important, that is."

"You're roight there mate. Can't stand women's legs without tights or stockings."

"Yeah, 'orrible pasty things."

"Look at the tits on that one!"

"Bugger me. You don't get many of them to the pound."

"I tell yer what mate, I'd get deyn on me knees and beg for some of that."

"I'd crawl on me hands and knees over broken glass mate."

"Right . . . er . . . I'd crawl ten miles, naked, over broken glass, *just to throw stones at her shit!*"

"Bloody hell mate, that's what I call true love. You can have her."

"Cheers."

"All right, what about this one?"

"Bit of an old boiler, but I'd stand in her way."

"I'd stand in her way" was Edward Bear code for "I'd block her passage," which in turn was a euphemism for—well, *you* know. Like "Brown's out," it got a laugh every time.

The irony of all this was that Jim was happily married and Terry happily engaged. Neither of them so much as talked to a woman at a gig. Their banter was just part of their image: Men of the World, confident enough to treat sex as a lighthearted game. Steve stayed out of it, except to occasionally attempt a feeble "Next man in!" and I just smiled, partly because it was sometimes funny, and partly because I didn't want to be thought a prude. Besides, Terry and Jim seemed so worldly-wise that I was afraid of giving away my own inexperience.

Steve, who was a genuinely well-meaning guy, tried to make me feel like a part of the band, although he was limited both by a shyness worse than my own, and a lack of imagination. "Well then Joe!" he'd say dramatically at the end of a gig, and there would be a pause as he seemed to forget something really interesting he'd been just about to say. Finally he'd say what he always said: "Another gig bites the dust, eh?"

Equally unvarying at the end of the night was Jim's ironic, mock-gloomy overview of the day as he took the wheel of the van: "What a life, eh. Get up, have a crap, cup of tea, read the paper, sarnie for lunch, drive to gig, do gig, pack up, drive home, fuck the wife, go to sleep."

One day in the van, there was hilarity as someone came upon a *Peanuts* cartoon in the *Daily Mail*, in which Snoopy assumed the character of a bar-room piano player called "Joe Piano." Apparently he looked just like me, too. I'd been compared to a puppet and now a cartoon beagle. I didn't really care, but it was strange that one way or another I seemed destined, at least in this band, to be called Joe.

After a couple of months of this, I decided I didn't actually mind being called Joe. I'd always been called Dave or Jacko, neither of which thrilled me. Every other guy I met seemed to be called Dave, and Jacko was a name fit only for a monkey. But Joe, I thought, was a good name—a piano player's name. Joe Jackson? That had a sort of ring to it, too.

Useless

I'M LISTENING to Sibelius—the Second Symphony—and marveling at the way this great composer, even in this fairly early work, can sweep me along on an irresistible tide of sheer musical logic. The music grows like a living thing, with a momentum that doesn't let up till the last bar. You can still hear the influence of Tchaikovsky in the Second, but Tchaikovsky's symphonies don't have this organic quality. There are great moments and beautiful melodies, but the different sections seem to be held together with Scotch tape. With Sibelius you can't see the joins.

The Second Symphony was my introduction to Sibelius, via a second-hand LP with a stunning winter landscape on the cover. For some reason I've always been drawn to northern places, and this picture of the composer's native Finland thrilled me almost as much as the music; they certainly became inseparable in my mind. Few composers have conveyed the power of nature so brilliantly, and, in the slow movement especially, I saw a bleak and beautiful world of rock, snow, forest, and icy winds as clearly as if I'd been watching a movie. Sibelius got better and better at this, and his Fourth is about as bleak and beautiful as anything I can imagine. Recordings of it really should be issued with a pair of woolen socks and a miniature of brandy.

Listening to Sibelius also reminds me of an argument I had with a fellow composition student at the Academy. He was sitting next to me one day in the common room saying that Sibelius was a minor composer, not really modern, a reactionary, and I found myself coming to the composer's defense as though he'd been a mate of mine. Which, in a way, he was. But I then had to defend both of us, and I didn't do a very good job of it, waffling about Finnish pine forests while my adversary sat with a face like he was chewing a wasp.

"Stravinsky," he finally said, "says that music is powerless to express anything other than itself."

But Stravinsky wasn't saying, exactly, that music couldn't or shouldn't make an emotional connection with the listener; or if he was, he didn't always practice what he preached. Besides, he also once described the music of Rachmaninoff as "warm treacle," which sounds like a pretty subjective, emotional response to me.

These arguments were confusing, but then there were many times, during my first two years at the Academy, when I had a feeling I can only describe as musical vertigo. I was a pub and restaurant pianist, and a keyboard player hovering somewhere on the border between jazz and rock. I was playing pop hits with Edward Bear to make money. I was trying, intermittently, to write songs in the rock idiom, and at the same time I was a student of "serious" composition. But the more I met student composers, looked at their scores and those they admired, and went to lectures and rehearsals of contemporary pieces, the more I felt like the proverbial bacon sandwich at a bar mitzvah.

Both students and teachers seemed to favor the avant-garde, the abstract, and the intellectual to a degree that seemed almost perverse. The further away a composition was from the tastes of the general public, apparently, the better it was. And the more I felt myself pulled in the opposite direction.

The heroes of the hour were Webern, Stockhausen, Boulez, Xenakis, Nono, Maderna. I appreciated some of this stuff—I enjoyed certain pieces by Edgard Varèse and Luciano Berio, for instance—and I could usually understand the theories behind it. But on the whole, it didn't move me, and moving people, I thought, was what music was for.

While I was playing weddings and working-men's clubs, most of my fellow composition students seemed to be producing what someone once aptly called "eye music." That is, music that is more intelligible, and much prettier, on paper than it is to the ear. They loved to change time signatures with almost every bar, group asymmetrical clusters of notes across the bar-lines, and even invent whole new systems of notation. If Stockhausen's scores could be prefaced by lengthy instructions on how to read them, why not theirs?

It's funny, the way radical ideas get turned into convention. This year's outrageous hairstyle in the big city is de rigueur next year in the sticks. Stravinsky's shockingly original *Rite of Spring,* Bartók's *Music for Strings, Percussion and Celesta,* Schoenberg's *Pierrot Lunaire,* and a few other seminal works by composers who were actually highly individualistic, became reference books or even bibles. There were certain things that, if you wanted to be a contemporary composer, you just had to do: asymmetrical rhythms, constant changes of meter, angular atonal melodic lines, bizarre combinations of instruments, the extensive use of percussion, and so on. Symphonies and concertos were out of favor—"Romantic" descriptive titles even more so. My fellow students labored over scores with titles like "*Extrapolations,* for Alto Flute, Harp, Bass Clarinet, and Percussion."

Admittedly, I indulged in some of this myself. Looking at my student scores now, I see places where I obviously wanted to use plain old major and minor chords, but went for something more dissonant instead, probably fearing that I wouldn't be taken seriously. There are also places where I could have gotten the same effects by simpler means, making them less attractive to the eye, but easier to read and perform. Nevertheless, I *was* interested in what the music would actually sound like, and what effect it might have on a listener. Sibelius is dull on the page, but in performance he comes thrillingly alive and is utterly distinctive. He, and other composers I admired, were not just writing academic exercises, and I didn't want to, either. I certainly didn't want to be a serialist.

Serialism, also known as the twelve-tone technique, is a compositional system developed by Arnold Schoenberg around 1923 in response to the breakdown (at least, as Schoenberg saw it) of the traditional system of tonality, that is, the twelve major and twelve minor keys, which are, in fact, still very much with us. Schoenberg, and his disciples Berg and Webern, thought not only that music didn't *have* to be in any particular key, but that it actually *shouldn't* be. Their alternative was to arrange all twelve possible notes into a specific order (a series) and to base the music exclusively on this series, which could also be played backwards and upside down. But you had to use the whole series before repeating a note. Otherwise, one note might be unduly emphasized, which might suggest that you were in one key or another.

One day in the Edward Bear van, I tried to explain serialism to Jim the guitarist. He thought I was joking, and then, when he realized I wasn't, looked more puzzled than ever. Surely this was just an intellectual parlor game, not music at all. Don't worry, Jim, even the academics are starting to come around to your way of thinking. Serial music endures in certain circles, but it has just about passed out of fashion. Admittedly, some of it was interesting. But "interesting" was the word of choice among my peers at the Academy, and I sometimes wished to God they'd stop using it and say whether or not they actually *liked* something.

It's not that I have a problem with the avant-garde. An avant-garde is necessary as a breeding ground for new ideas. The best ideas (the theory goes) become absorbed into the mainstream, and the rest fall by the wayside.

But even as a student, I could see that the theory no longer applied, because everything had become so fragmented that there was no *garde* to be *avant*. And after fifty years, Schoenberg had failed to become truly mainstream, except perhaps in music colleges. Most people, even musically educated ones, would rather have their teeth drilled than listen to serial music. And yet the methods of Schoenberg and his successors had been made into a new orthodoxy. That influential egghead, the composer/conductor Pierre Boulez, was much quoted as announcing with a straight face that "any composer who does not understand the necessity of the Serial language is *useless*."

Many years later I visited Boulez's brainchild, IRCAM, the institute for musical and acoustical teaching and research in Paris. It had the look and feel of a laboratory. I felt as though I should have been wearing a sterilized white coat. The place didn't *feel* as though it had anything to do with music at all. Since my Academy days, the preoccupation with serialism had given way to a preoccupation with computers and music technology. But the music I heard at IRCAM sounded very much the same.

I find this intellectual pose, this attempt to make art into science, deeply offensive. But I wonder if it isn't really just a reaction to the uncertainties of the age. Perhaps we have to have *some* sort of dogma, no matter how bad or how temporary. Maybe serialism was an attempt to impose control in chaotic times. Some of the later serialists have tried to extend the technique beyond pitch, to rhythm and timbre. How anal-retentive can you get? Then, of course, there have been people like John Cage experimenting with "aleatory" music, in which large elements are left to chance. But isn't that the opposite side of the same coin?

By the time I was nineteen, I saw that contemporary "classical" composition was dominated by an academic elite whose members wrote complex, intellectual music for each other, and seemed to despise anything popular. Only young composers who followed that path were being officially recognized. Meanwhile, the rest of the human race was listening to popular music or jazz.

Not that sheer numbers were the issue. If I'd been passionate about Stockhausen or Boulez, I would have followed them anyway, like Scott to the Antarctic, no matter what the consequences. But I was beginning to think that popular music and jazz had all the passion and relevance that "classical" music had lost—or abdicated.

As rock musicians I knew asked me what I was learning at the Academy, it was harder and harder to explain. Edward Bear's Terry asked me one day who were the great classical composers of the moment. I couldn't think of one name.

In fact, it was a very good question, but the wrong one. The real question was, and is: How would we recognize a great composer, even if he were right under our noses? What kind of composer would he be: tonal or atonal, eclectic or purist, complex or minimalist, academic or popular? In the absence of a broader consensus, most people just assumed that "classical" music was dead.

In the second half of the twentieth century, the only musical structure that most people have agreed on, that has given us some sort of a yardstick, is the popular song. The great composers of the age were probably Lennon and McCartney.

So is there an opportunity, in the new century, for a détente between "pop" and "classical"? Admittedly the question probably has more urgency for someone like me, who has bounced around between the two, than it would for most people. And there's still more than enough concrete-headed prejudice on both sides. But "classical" needs to learn from "pop" how to be relevant again, how to engage an audience, and how to get out there and connect with it without needing huge orchestras and huge subsidies. And "pop" could learn a thing or two from "classical" about skill, longevity, intelligence, and emotional depth. I think the best music of the future might come from somewhere in between.

In my second year at the Academy, though, I was becoming not just disenchanted with the place but claustrophobic. I had wanted it to open things up, great vistas in musical Cinemascope, but the opposite seemed to be happening. I started to see the Academy as a little box, a pocket mausoleum, remote from the real world.

Maybe I didn't want to be a composer when I grew up, after all.

Nineteen Forever

I DECIDED to make some changes in my second year at the Academy. I cut my schedule down—only the absolutely compulsory classes and Jazz Workshop—and squeezed it into two days a week. I asked for a different composition teacher, and got one who made so little impression on me that I've actually forgotten his name. At first it was refreshing to work with someone pleasant and undemanding, but after a while I realized I'd gone too far in the opposite direction. My new teacher wanted to do whatever I wanted to do, and since I didn't really know what I wanted to do, the lessons were vague and rambling. We studied scores and discussed symphonic structure, which was fine, but I wasn't composing much any more. I was trying to write pop songs, and I knew I wasn't going to get any help from the Academy in that department.

I also switched my Second Study from piano to percussion. I'm not quite sure why I did this. I think I wanted to play in one of the Academy's three orchestras, but it never happened. My teacher was an agreeable woman from the BBC Symphony Orchestra, and I enjoyed playing timpani again, and brushing up my xylophone and vibraphone technique.

I also got several lessons a year with the legendary percussionist James Blades. He was very old, and the most encouraging teacher I've ever come across. He would stop me and exclaim "Oh, very *good!*" after practically each hit of a drum or tap of a tambourine. He was so encouraging, in fact, that I started to wonder if he was senile. For all his vast experience, I learned very little from him.

With my second-year grant money, I bought a Fender Rhodes electric piano, secondhand, from the keyboard player of a band called Mungo Jerry. I was interested to meet someone from a real big-time recording outfit, but of course he turned out to be just a poor struggling slob like me. What's more, he didn't tell me that one of the Rhodes's legs was lame. It didn't screw in properly, so one corner of the instrument was always precariously propped up. But it sounded great—a big, rich, professional sound compared to what I was used to.

The Rhodes was a big expense. I tried to offset it slightly by pocketing the allowance I got for the train, and dodging the fares. I became an expert at hiding in the toilet when an inspector came through, and then slipping through the crowd at Waterloo. If I was stopped, I'd say that I'd gotten on at Clapham Junction, and please, kind sir, where could I pay my fare? This was pretty pathetic, of course, petty crime at its most petty, but I needed to make the most of every penny, and I was shameless. Although money in itself didn't seem to interest me, I didn't want to be anything but a musician, and I was painfully aware that there'd be no guarantees.

I still felt that I should take every gig I could get, as long as I didn't actually lose money on it. Briefly, I went back into solo mode, and used my Rhodes for the first time at a Portsmouth pub called the Royal Standard. My dad, in one of his periodic flashes of kindness, gave me a lift there. I'd have to take a taxi back, which ought to leave me with a profit of a pound or two.

The Standard was quiet: a few dart-playing youths and an old degenerate at the bar who impressed me by chain-smoking Capstan Full Strength unfiltered cigarettes and chain-drinking Wood's Old Navy Rum—the liquid essence of Pompey. But after I'd played a couple of songs, someone put some coins in the jukebox, and I was drowned out. I played on, thinking there must have been some sort of mistake; surely someone would unplug the jukebox. They didn't. Eventually I stopped playing and waited for gaps between records. But every time I'd start playing again, more money would go into the jukebox. The landlord was vaguely sympathetic, but he didn't see how he could help. He was sorry, he said, but if his customers preferred to hear records, what could he do?

I was speechless. I battled on for another ten minutes, then gave up.

The landlord knocked a pound or two off my fee, but at that point I hardly cared. I just wanted to get out of the place. I would have broken even, if I hadn't bought a couple of Navy Rums.

One Saturday morning I was woken by a phone call from Russell. Could I meet him for lunch to discuss a new project?

This was more like it. I rushed to the station and a couple of hours later met him in a café in London, where he insisted on buying me a steak. I'd never had a steak in my life. The waiter asked if rare was all right. "Sure!" I said. I didn't even know what "rare" meant.

Russell explained that the Cabot Clowns were working on a new show, which was going to be "a sort of James Bond Scientology musical." He said this as though I should know what he meant, so I nodded my head and wrestled with my steak. Blood oozed everywhere and I resolved to give up meat for good.

There was something strange about this lunch. Where was Jude? As we talked, I gathered that this was Russell's project, and that he wanted to involve me, but Jude was looking to other musical directions, including possibly forming a band. The meeting ended inconclusively. On the way back down on the train, I felt as though I'd dreamed it.

It was shortly afterwards that I became possessed by the lunatic idea that I would go to Bristol, where Rachel the violinist, my first love, was now at the university, and try once and for all to win her heart. I tracked her down and we had dinner, during which she kept looking at me as though I were sprouting werewolf hair. After pleading to no avail for some sort of overnight accommodation, I found myself on a late train back to London.

As the almost empty train rattled through the night, I brooded over Rachel's lack of interest in boys, and her intense, secretive friendships with a couple of girls over the last few years, and something began to dawn on me. I'd always felt that Rachel liked me well enough, and that her sexual indifference was somehow *nothing personal*. I felt sick. Not because I had any problem with lesbianism. It was my own stupidity that had me cursing out loud all the way to Paddington.

In sore need of some friends, and a place to sleep, I headed for the Cabot Clowns' old Brixton headquarters. It was very late, but they were always up late. I pounded on the door for ages. It was finally answered by an enormous glowering Jamaican woman in a nightdress.

"Dem nah live here nah more," she snarled.

In fact, Russell and Jude had split up, Russell had gone back to the States, and Jude and Teresa were forming a theatrical rock band called the Sadista Sisters. The band included a guitarist called Dave Stewart, who later hooked up with a certain flute-playing Scotswoman from the Academy and formed the Tourists, who later became the Eurythmics and sold millions of records.

And Rachel's sexuality, like mine, turned out to be ambiguous. A few years later she would marry and have children.

But I didn't know any of these happy endings, as I walked the streets dejectedly and—right on cue—it started to rain. A policeman eyed me suspiciously. What do you do, I asked him, if you have nowhere to sleep and no money? You could stay in a doss-house, he said, to which he could direct me if I liked, but he assured me that I wouldn't like it. I could spend the night at the station if I wanted. I thought he meant in a cell, which might have been exciting. But I ended up spending the night propped up, in wet clothes, on a wooden chair in a drafty corner of the waiting area. I drifted with a stiff neck in half-sleep, and cursed everyone and everything. Bitter bile welled up inside me and I wanted to puke it all over the world.

The next day, I didn't feel too bad. I was nineteen, after all!

And, as one London contact disappeared, another opened up. Drew Barfield, from Gosport, was now a goatee-less art student at Goldsmiths College, and he had a flat in Camberwell. I started to stay there on a regular basis. I wasn't alone. It was a popular crash-pad, so much so that it sometimes resembled an army field hospital, with bodies stretched out all over the floor. Some nights were an insomniac's nightmare of farts, snores, and sweaty feet. But it was always good to see Drew, whose wheezing laugh was as infectious as ever. I had a real ally in London, who, what's more, was starting to meet musicians, which sooner or later had to lead to jam sessions and even gigs in the Big City.

Throughout all this, I was still a member of Edward Bear. Mostly, we worked from Thursday to Saturday, with occasional Sunday or Wednesday dates. I'd done well, I thought, arranging my schedule so that everything fitted in. The gigs rolled by and the set-lists and the banter were unchanging and eternal.

One night, at one of our smarter nightclub gigs, I finally met our agent. He pushed his way into the dressing room, a stocky, aggressive little man who obviously fancied himself as a wheeler and dealer. He was also very drunk.

"'Allo boys!" he slurred. "You one of my bands?"

Terry and Jim looked at each other in horror. He'd been their agent for three years.

The following week, a caretaker joined us onstage at a gig in a village hall somewhere in Surrey. He'd been told to start mopping the stage at midnight, but we'd started late, and as the witching hour struck, we were still playing, to quite a few dancers. The caretaker marched on to the stage and stood next to Jim, a stringy old geezer leaning on his mop and bucket, glaring at us and pointing at his watch. We played on for another fifteen minutes, gradually giving in to disabling laughter, but he folded his arms and wouldn't budge. Jim offered him his microphone, the audience joined in the laughter, but the caretaker stayed stone-faced to the end, the very embodiment of stoic and implacable Middle England.

For all its routine, I enjoyed Edward Bear. They were nice guys, and, playing so regularly, I gained confidence and learned to put bad gigs into perspective. One of the worst things about being in a struggling band at the lowest level is that gigs are so far apart that each one becomes a nerve-racking trial by fire. I wasn't exactly playing the music I wanted to play, but I was becoming a firm believer in the value of experience. Whatever didn't kill me, as Nietzsche said, would only make me stronger.

I played with Edward Bear for about six months. Towards the end, there was a distinct change of atmosphere. Terry and Jim started to speak nostalgically about the band, in the past tense. They sighed and shook their heads and smiled sentimentally. The banter dried up a bit. Finally they announced that they were breaking up the band. They'd had a good run and some good times, but Jim's missus wanted a baby and Terry was getting married and you had to settle down sometime, didn't you?

This may have been consistent with the lads' characters, but I found it bewildering. Where had I heard this before? I suddenly remembered my guitar-playing uncles. Apparently it was common knowledge that you could only be actively involved in making music for a finite period of time. It was certainly deemed to be incompatible with marriage. But why? Given a choice between playing music and "settling down," I thought I'd take music. Did that mean I was doomed to be a loner, a bachelor, and a misfit for the rest of my life?

What would I have done if I hadn't been a musician? People often ask me, but I haven't got a clue. Sometimes I look at assistants in shops or tellers in banks and I think: Who are these people? What tribe is this? Could I have ever joined it? Then I go out into the street and see some white dreadlocked urchin squatting on the pavement with a battered guitar and a mangy dog, begging for pennies, and I think: Well, this is more like it, this makes more sense to me. Sometimes I see myself in the sad bastards who mill around outside pubs at closing time, looking for a fight. Sometimes I think that music saved my life.

Terry and Jim started to take on the aura of battle-scarred veterans fading into the golden twilight of their lives. They couldn't have been more than thirty.

Where was I going to be at thirty? Why was I so driven, compared to other musicians I knew? I couldn't imagine "retiring" from music, even at sixty or seventy. To do what? For better or worse, I was going to have to stick to the path I'd chosen—or which had chosen me. Then I had an idea.

Terry and Jim may have been the founding fathers of Edward Bear, but they weren't the whole band. They were only half of it. What was to stop us from recruiting two new members and carrying on? I told them I knew a singer/guitarist who could handle the gig easily, and I was sure I could find a bassist, too. No one had any objections to this. Terry called the drunken agent, who said we could fulfil our existing bookings with whoever we liked, but he couldn't guarantee anything after that, not until he saw us. That was good enough for me.

I called Mark Andrews. He'd left Creech Cottage and his girlfriend, and was playing the odd gig here and there. But on the whole, he was bored to tears, and he jumped at the chance to play regularly.

Mark and I had agreed, after the failure of our first band, to go the "commercial" route and get as many gigs as we could. Now we had a chance to do it our own way. We agreed immediately on what needed to be done with the band. We would loosen it up, make it more fun, introduce some of what I'd come to think of as the Admiral Drake spirit. We'd keep it "commercial," but bring some more interesting material into the set, and, once we established ourselves, sneak in some songs of our own. And after that—who knows?

We both hated the band's name, but we agreed to keep it for the time being, in the hope that it would keep the gigs coming in. At some point, it would have to go.

The fourth member of the band was to be the balding bearded bloodshot bassist called Bob, but he didn't last long, for reasons that escape me. Pretty soon we switched to the man who, now that we thought about it, was the obvious choice: Graham "Badger" Maby.

Perhaps some of my Big Questions were starting to answer themselves. I was becoming an entertainer rather than an artist. What I hadn't quite realized, though, was that even as an entertainer I had a knack of making things difficult for myself by trying desperately to do them as brilliantly as possible. Maybe it was the artist in me.

Ten Doughnuts

As Mark and I launched the new improved Edward Bear, some priorities started to emerge out of my endless musical horizons. Mainly, these were: the art of winning over and entertaining an audience; and the art of the three-minute pop song.

Both contrasted starkly with what I was supposed to be doing at the Academy, but maybe that was the point. The academics were writing complex music for themselves. Okay, maybe I should write—or at least perform—simple music for the masses.

It wasn't quite *that* simple, of course. I couldn't unlearn everything I knew. It's probably significant that my favorite songwriters now were Walter Becker and Donald Fagen of Steely Dan. Their album *Countdown to Ecstasy,* which I'd been turned onto by Terry the bassist, was a revelation, and certainly one of the most influential albums of my life. It was a bridge between my earlier jazz-rock or progressive tastes and pure pop. Suddenly, it seemed possible to be hip and smart and sophisticated, and to have a high standard of musicianship, at the same time as working in an accessible pop format.

The next milestone was Stevie Wonder's gorgeous *Innervisions.* Steely Dan and Stevie Wonder took the place of Beethoven in my personal pantheon. But they were gods, and in between their albums, I started to appreciate the mere mortals of the UK pop scene: Elton John, for instance, or David Bowie.

Bowie, of course, had been on the cutting edge of British pop for at least a couple of years. I'd been aware of him, but it was his androgynous image, rather than the music, that had fascinated me. I was still sexually ambiguous. Sex seemed to me, and to a great extent still seems, an ocean of mysteries. In that ocean I was a plankton that could have as easily been straight or gay, male or female, animal, vegetable, or mineral.

One thing I *had* figured out was the nature of my Problem. It had a name: phimosis—a tight foreskin. The only cure was circumcision. Not a pleasant prospect, but if I ever wanted to have sex with anyone, I was going to have to get it over with. I went to see the local GP, and he arranged for me to have "the chop," as he called it, in a Gosport hospital. I would probably have to stay there for a few days afterwards. Damn. That meant I had to tell my parents.

I told my mother at the last possible moment. She said there was nothing to be embarrassed about, although we both obviously were.

"I mean, after all, it's only . . . er . . ."

"Only what?" I asked.

"Well, it's only *nature*, isn't it?"

I stared out of the window and thought: This is the same woman who, when I was about ten, caught me playing with myself in bed, turned on the light, pulled back the bedcovers, and slapped my legs.

"Lots of fellas have it done," she went on. "Uncle Tom had it done."

Uncle Tom? Another childhood memory floated up from the depths: Uncle Tom, with the balding head and deep voice, who had once whacked me for climbing on his sofa. I was convinced that he wasn't supposed to do that, but when I told my parents, they both agreed that if Uncle Tom had had to hit me, I must have been a very bad boy indeed.

I knew my mother cared about me, but I didn't want to talk, or think, about any of these things. And at that moment I wanted to be anywhere else in the world but in my parents' house.

"Go on, get dressed," said my mother, "and I'll take you to the hospital." And I was suddenly deeply relieved, and grateful, that I didn't have to go by myself.

A couple of hours later I was put under general anaesthetic. But something went wrong. I woke up before the surgery was over. In a few seconds of consciousness, which were like a Hieronymus Bosch vision of hell, I looked down and saw my poor beleaguered member covered in blood, and the bug-eyed face of the surgeon turning, in slow motion, towards me.

When I resurfaced, I was lying in bed, pumped full of Valium so that I would not panic but stay merely depressed. I'd been mutilated but I didn't care all that much. I was also given drugs to prevent sexual arousal, so that, when a pretty young nurse changed my dressing, I wouldn't tear the stitches.

I was visited by my mother and, on one occasion, Graham Maby.

"How do you feel?" he asked.

I had been disfigured for life and I would never have sex.

"How do you think I bloody feel?" I muttered.

Graham thought for a moment.

"Lighter?" he suggested.

None of this was ever discussed with my dad, although I vaguely remember a monosyllabic exchange when I came home from the hospital. ("Alright?" "Yeah, I'm alright." "Alright then.") Within a couple of weeks, though, I realized I'd done the right thing. I felt more than alright, not only more comfortable but more confident than before. Sex, or the possibility of it, became appealing again, and David Bowie once again stirred me in a mysterious way.

Bowie's records were getting more and more interesting, too.

Or perhaps it was me that was getting more interested. Our tastes are formed as much, if not more, by what we *want* to like as what we actually do like—or *would* like if our minds were really open.

My ambivalence toward the Academy was hardening into antipathy, and although I was drawn to the more sophisticated end of the rock spectrum, I was also more and more willing to see something good in the simplest, trashiest pop hits. Mark and I were both writing songs, but that wouldn't be our priority just yet. We made huge lists of songs we thought we could cover. We listened to the radio, bought singles, and transcribed the lyrics (sometimes getting them hilariously wrong). We followed the pop charts and, in my case, bought sheet music to songs that were harder to figure out. At first, as we took over the original Edward Bear's gigs, we were cautious. We replaced some of the old chestnuts in the set with songs we really liked, like Stevie Wonder's "Superstition," Bowie's "Suffragette City," and Kool and the Gang's "Funky Stuff" (which, with Steve's drumming, was not so funky). But we also tried hard not to offend.

We put together a ghastly band uniform of matching black-and-silver patterned sweaters and flares, and Mark toned down his wild appearance, cutting his hair shorter and trimming the beard down to a mustache. We also plunged gleefully into the campier end of the current scene and played songs by Alice Cooper, Gary Glitter, and the Sweet.

Depending on your point of view, this was either a hopeless mishmash of styles or a logical sampling of the pop scene at a particular moment. Not being a purist, I still find myself playing this game of shifting perspectives. It's like looking through a zoom lens. Up close, there might appear to be a million worlds of difference between, say, Aerosmith and the Pet Shop Boys. Zoom out, and they're both pop groups. Zoom out further, and it's all just music. What's the right perspective?

The new Edward Bear worked harder than the old. We rehearsed for hours and hours, building a large repertoire. But one of the real pleasures of rehearsing was finding myself, with each passing week, more and more in awe of Graham Maby's bass playing.

There was nothing Graham couldn't pick up in a few minutes. His ear was extraordinary, and his style was solid and tasteful, but fluid; he never *plodded*, like a lot of other bassists. His sound was full and yet clear. Rhythmically, he was spot-on, and I realized after a while that Steve the drummer was following him, rather than the other way round. There was nothing tentative about Graham's playing; every note was played with conviction; every note sounded *right*. He was also as modest and unassuming as he was talented. His ability was so natural and innate that he didn't even know he had it.

Good bass players are the unsung heroes of pop music. A listener may not even be consciously aware of what the bassist is doing, but anyone who's played in a band knows that a good bassist makes the whole band sound good. Graham is still making bands sound good now, and his style has barely changed. It didn't have to.

Steve wasn't in quite the same league. Whereas Graham was a born professional, Steve was the quintessential bumbling, well-intentioned amateur. He had the cheapest cymbals you could get, by Krut, which sounded like dustbin-lids. One day, as we gathered in his house for a rehearsal, he could barely contain his excitement; this was a special day: He had new cymbals! We were delighted, expecting them to be real cymbals like Zildjians or Paistes. Steve opened a box and held a cymbal triumphantly above his head, as though it were a trophy he'd just won. On it was the proud trademark: SUPER KRUT.

Steve was obviously the weak link in this new, punchier lineup, but we had too many things to think about without looking for a new drummer, too. For instance, we had to get a new van. So Mark and Graham went to look at a Bedford van that a friend of Mark's father was selling. Out on some desolate industrial estate, they were greeted by a sharp businesslike man in a sharp business suit, who chatted for a while, and then disappeared to get the van. Five minutes later, the man reappeared, driving the van, wearing greasy overalls, his hair messed up, looking slightly cross-eyed. He spoke quite differently, too, slowly and with a slight stammer, and he gave every appearance of being mentally retarded. He shuffled off, and after a while came back sharp-suited, hair neatly combed, to take the money. Or so it appeared. They were, of course, twin brothers.

Getting gigs turned out to be a bit trickier than we'd expected. The original drunken agent, for some reason, soon lost interest, and we had to beg, scrounge, and hustle for work. Some gigs we booked by ourselves, others came from a seedy assortment of small-time agents. Mostly, Mark dealt with these characters. He was a better hustler than me. But I remember some of them. There was one, for instance, who was famous for his toupee, which was so pathetically awful he looked like he was wearing a straw hat. I also remember vividly a phone conversation with a Portsmouth agent who was said to have some good gigs for the right sort of bands.

"What sort of band are you?" he asked. He sounded as though he was eating something as he talked, or chewing gum.

"Well, we're . . . er . . . a pop-rock band," I said. "We're commercial, though."

"Well what are you, pop or rock?"

"Both. I mean . . . we're really versatile."

"I don't want any original material."

"Oh no, of course not, none of that."

"I don't want any heavy metal, progressive rubbish, I want good pop music that people can dance to, and none of this long greasy hair and scruffy jeans and that."

"Well, we've got sort of long hair, but—"

"Look mate, I'm looking for professionals here. I want *smart* clothes, *neat* hair, and good pop music people can dance to. That's what people want, none of this bloody hippie stuff."

"Well, if you could get us a trial gig, then you can see—"

"The thing is, I get people ringing up here every day wasting my time." He was ranting now. What was his problem? "First you say you're a rock group, then you say you're a pop group . . . I'm only interested in smart, professional bands who do good pop music and know what they're doing and know what an audience wants, I mean, I'm talking about some smart clubs, know what I mean? *Smart* clubs that want *smart* bands who are *professional* . . ."

"Right, and good pop music—"

"Good pop music that people can dance to, *smart* clothes, and . . ."

As this tirade rose to a climax, the agent suddenly broke off in a storm of coughing and choking. It went on and on.

"Are you all right?" I asked.

"Oh my God (cough) oh fuckin' hell—"

More coughing and horrible retching.

"What's going on? Christ, are you all right? Shall I call a doctor?"

The choking gradually subsided. The agent took a deep breath and rasped: "I choked . . . on . . . on a FUCKIN' CHIP!"

He never did give us a gig. Mostly I was glad to leave this sort of thing to Mark, although he didn't have much more luck than I did. One agent, who was based somewhere in the notoriously rough housing estates of Leigh Park, got us a disastrous gig for something called the Eastney Crewing Association. We were made to play twice as long as originally agreed, for half the agreed fee, and as if that wasn't bad enough, Mark had his street clothes stolen while we were playing. He was furious. He'd heard that Chuck Berry got paid in advance for his shows, so he wrote to the Leigh Park agent, saying that any gigs we did for him in the future would have to be paid for in advance.

The agent replied with a politely worded but ice-cold letter, which contained the soon-to-become-legendary line:

> If you persist in this Prima Donna behaviour, I shall have great difficulty in placing you henceforth.

Prima donna behavior was actually the farthest thing from our minds. We aimed to please. Our repertoire expanded to the point where we could adapt ourselves to the requirements of any venue. We went down as well as, or better than, the original Edward Bear. We were also louder, which could be a problem.

Graham liked to tell the story of a gig he'd done with Boz, his former band. The local committee man, who had an impenetrable Welsh accent, came up to the stage after every couple of songs, waving his arms and crying, "Ten doughnuts! Ten doughnuts!"

This went on for some time, with the committee man growing more and more agitated. Finally the band, completely mystified, had to get him to spell out the words. What he'd been saying was "Turn down, lads."

We soon developed a sixth sense for which gigs were going to present volume problems. We'd be booked for a wedding, for instance, and the bride's family would start panicking as we brought our equipment in. We didn't have a lot of gear, but to them, we looked like Led Zeppelin. Or we'd be loading in to a working-men's club where a bingo session was already in progress, and fag-smoking grannies would turn round and tell us loudly to "Shussshhh!" We would exchange weary, knowing looks and someone would say, "Ten doughnuts."

Sometimes we tried to cut down the volume by playing with our speaker cabinets turned round to face the wall behind us, which sounded atrocious. But we didn't complain. We worked harder and harder to please the punters. We joined up-tempo songs together in medleys that got faster and faster, driving dancers into a frenzy. Then we'd throw in a slow song just as they started to wilt. With an older crowd, we'd play '50s rock 'n' roll numbers and ballads early on, to get them on our side. Pub crowds, which tended to be younger and longer-haired, would get songs by the Doobie Brothers or the Band. We also worked up a few "novelty" numbers: the infamous Scottish medley, a version of "Nutrocker" in which Mark and I both played my keyboards, and an a cappella version of Bobby Darin's "Things." God knows why we chose that song, but the a cappella setting was unusual enough to distract some pretty tough audiences from their beer and conversation for a few minutes. Mostly these musical baubles were enthusiastically received. Sometimes there were boos from people who found them silly. Better to be silly, we thought, than boring.

We were the human jukebox. Every now and again, though, I would look at the black-and-silver patterned sweater and wonder how long it could last.

Man of the People

ONE THING that Adolf Hitler and Joseph Stalin had in common was their attitude toward the arts.

In their respective visions of Utopia, artists were the servants of the people. An artist's duty was to produce work in a style that would be accessible to everyone, and his worth would be judged by his ability to appeal to the largest possible number of people. Individualism was not only undesirable, but actually dangerous—if not to the public, then certainly to the errant artist himself.

The great irony of this admittedly logical proposition is that it produced lousy art, which hasn't proved to be popular either.

You'd think we'd have learned some lessons from this. But similar attitudes to art persist throughout what we call our popular culture. I've come across many people whose beliefs about the "duty" of the artist seem to have come straight from the pages of *Mein Kampf.* They'd stop short of shooting the individualists, perhaps. But, they say, if the artist isn't trying to please the masses, he must be *self-indulgent;* just trying to please himself.

I think this attitude stems partly from good old Anglo-Saxon philistinism. "Arty" pursuits are basically suspect to begin with—art isn't a "proper job," is it?—but you can get away with it as long as you're doing something popular. That way you can be seen to be Serving the People. But otherwise . . . well, who do you think you *are?*

With the new improved Edward Bear I served the People with a smile.

In the old Edward Bear, I was just a hired gun. I kept the gig separate, in my mind, from my "real" work. But now it was my band and my choice. This *was* my real work.

Ironically, my people-pleasing was actually rebellious in spirit. I was rebelling against my earlier, earnest pursuit of excellence. I thought I'd been too idealistic, and too self-absorbed. And of course, by becoming a populist, I was rebelling against the Academy.

There was an element of class in all this, too. I'd grown up blissfully unaware of class distinctions. Later, having become a musician—a "classical" musician—I couldn't help feeling that I'd transgressed some unwritten law. Now I thought I had it figured out. "Classical" music was middle class; rock and pop were working class. And I was working class. So. Those posh twats at the Academy could all disappear up their own arses: I was going to be a Man of the People.

That I could have been so bloody-minded seems appalling to me now. Of course, there are plenty of hardnuts out there who would still applaud me for it. But what's their excuse? Mine is that I was only nineteen. And also that it was much less apparent, back then, that the British class system was breaking down, and the boundaries between high and low art, too. Of course, there's a long way to go. We constantly take one step forward and two steps back, and a working-class British kid who is drawn to art and culture still feels the pull of divided loyalties.

Nowhere is this volatile stew of confusion more evident than in rock 'n' roll. And nineteen-year-olds and rock 'n' roll go together like cigarettes and alcohol. Rock 'n' roll, personified, would *be* a nineteen-year-old. You can picture him: He's hedonistic, and craves sensation, but doesn't want to be thought of as shallow. He wants to be accepted as an adult, but also wants to rebel. He wants to be a star, but he wants to be one of the lads, too. He wants to be taken seriously, but can't help taking the piss. Tell him he is an artist and he laughs at you and tells you that art is a tool of the moribund Establishment. But tell him he's trash, and he'll argue with all the fury he can muster—which is quite a lot—that he's the equal of any man, and that his creative efforts are as valid as Mozart's and more relevant than Shakespeare's.

All these contradictions are part and parcel of rock. It could be argued that they're what rock is all about. The contradictions have multiplied, too, now that rock isn't nineteen anymore, but refuses to grow up. It keeps stuffing its spreading gut into the tight leather pants. Sometimes rock looks silly and predictable: a setup, like those fake wrestling matches we see on TV. We're about to give up on it, for the hundredth time, but then it delivers its knockout punch: that rush of sheer adrenaline that takes our breath away and reminds us of all the *good* things about being nineteen.

At nineteen, adrenaline was all I needed. I'd figure out the contradictions later. I certainly didn't realize that I was as close as I would ever come to musical Stalinism.

Some of the songs I was writing, though, were actually quite ambitious. They were heavily influenced by Steely Dan, but, of course, without quite managing Becker and Fagen's worldly sophistication. Still, they had "jazzy" chords and musical twists that sat uneasily alongside the glam-rock chart hits of the moment. Some had straight-ahead rock grooves. Others were more funky or had reggae or Latin leanings, despite the fact that I knew very little as yet about either genre. In some ways they were easy to write. With my training and my ear, I was able to come up with ideas in my head, without even needing a keyboard, which struck other people as clever, but which seemed simple to me. But that didn't mean the ideas were any good.

The hardest part was writing lyrics. I just didn't know where to start, and my early songs were full of clunky rhymes and cliches as I tried to write the kind of things I thought rock lyricists were supposed to write. You know the kind of thing: rhyming "girl" with "world," "dance" with "romance," "love" with "skies above," "down on my knees" with "beggin' you please," and inserting the word "baby" wherever possible (sometimes rhymed with "lady").

I had a bit more luck when I tried to be funny, or witty, although I probably wasn't either, not particularly. But the ballads I wrote tended towards the maudlin, which was worse.

The challenge of songwriting, I realize now, was in fitting words and music together into a package that was direct, to the point, and satisfying on a gut level. It had to *feel* right. It was good if the words made sense, but more important that they *sounded* right when someone sang them. Once again, I was working with mysterious, intangible elements. It was a kind of alchemy, searching for the right chemical reaction between word and melody. The thrilling moments in songwriting come when this suddenly starts to work. You hit the right combination, and sparks start to fly; suddenly you're Baron von Frankenstein, screaming, "It's alive!"

No amount of musical erudition was ever going to help me with this. I understood now why great songs have been, and still are, written by people with primitive musical skills. They just have a knack for that particular kind of alchemy. It may be all they can do, and it's quite often hit-or-miss. They may only be able to do it a few times in their lives, or even only once. Still, the important thing is there: the spark. Genius may be one percent inspiration and ninety-nine percent perspiration, but it's that one percent that is the important part. You can have a Ph.D. in music from every university in the world, but without that spark, you can write a hundred symphonies, and they'll all be dry as dust.

If I struggled to write songs, I struggled even more when it came to singing them. When I wrote something, I knew exactly how it should be sung. I tried to get my bandmates, Mark and Graham, to sing my songs, but that never quite worked. I wanted to sing them myself. I just wasn't sure that I could.

I hated my voice. It was thin and nasal. But then again, I told myself, so was Donald Fagen's. And what about Bob Dylan! Surely if you could look up "thin and nasal" in the dictionary, there'd be a picture of him. So I persevered, hoping there would turn out to be something about my voice that people would want to listen to.

Mark had been writing songs longer than me. They were simpler than mine, but tougher, and more convincing. Often they were "rockers" that reminded me of the Stones. And of course, Mark's vocal delivery was a hundred times stronger than mine.

For a while, Edward Bear performed two original songs—one of Mark's, one of mine. They were strategically placed, about three-quarters of the way through a set, with crowd-pleasing numbers on either side of them. No one threw garbage at us, and sometimes there was even applause.

On only one more occasion were the new Edward Bear accused of being prima donnas. We played a dismal "ten doughnuts" gig at Cosham Working Men's Club, where we were told to turn it down after almost every song. After a while our amps were practically off, and we were beginning to sound like a drum solo. Next, we turned the amps to the wall. Then we did a song without the guitar. Still not good enough. Finally we did the a cappella number, and *still* we were told to turn down. Something snapped. We looked at each other, shook our heads, and started to break our gear down. Petty officials buzzed around us like angry wasps, telling us we'd never work in this business again. I wish I had a pound for every time a small-time agent or club owner has said that! This time, we really didn't care. And really not caring is always the best way to get the upper hand. We told them to stuff their poxy club, loaded up the van in record time, and drove off to the nearest pub, where we got triumphantly drunk.

Maybe we needed to loosen up a bit. What were we doing this for, anyway?

We started to rehearse more original material. Maybe, we thought, we could please both the audience and ourselves.

Putting things into perspective, it's obvious now that for the vast majority of artists, from the lowliest struggling rock band to the intellectual giants of literature, it's not an either/or proposition.

It's stupid to say we must selflessly serve the masses, and it's stupid to castigate less popular, or populist, artists for being "just for themselves." There may be thousands of solitary poets, like Anthony Burgess's Enderby, writing on the toilet. If that's self-indulgent, at least it does no harm. Better to be self-indulgent with a pen than with a gun. But if the poet goes so far as to get his work published, we must assume that he wants to connect with whatever audience will have him. It's just that there's a crucial difference between, on the one hand, laboring to give "the audience" what you think—or have been told—that it wants; and on the other hand, trying to engage *an* audience by being yourself.

For the next few years, I'd be trying to find the right balance. At least, I thought, I seemed to have found the right vehicle. Now it just needed a tune-up.

Men Without Women

Edward Bear was loosening up, all right. We played more of our own songs. We also ditched the band uniform and became steadily more outrageous. Mark shaved off his mustache and started to wear glitter and makeup. There would be jeers and wolf-whistles as we walked on stage, which made me slightly nervous. In Paulsgrove I'd been regularly beaten up for less. But Mark was delighted. The whole idea, he said, was to get a reaction. He wanted to be not just the lead singer but the "front man." At one point he talked Graham into giving him his shoes, arguing that they were really front man's, not bass player's shoes. The shoes were bright green, with five-inch stack heels and silver stars on the toes.

Graham himself had shoulder-length hair and a beard by now, and favored post-hippie flares and wide lapels. I wore a succession of waistcoats and hats. But Steve, not having any better ideas, stuck with the black-and-silver sweater. He seemed, and probably felt, more and more out of place.

Mark found it hard to resist playing tricks on him. At one gig, he talked Steve into going on stage wearing a gorilla mask and starting a set all by himself. Steve was to start a shuffle beat and the rest of us would come on after a few bars, Mark said, all wearing masks. Of course, we let him play on and on, until he started to panic, and we finally entered—without masks.

Amazingly, Steve fell for this a second time. This time it was a skull mask, and we stayed at the side of the stage for a full ten minutes, falling about with laughter as Steve played on and on, and from somewhere inside the skull we heard strangled cries of "You bastards! You FUCKING BASTARDS!"

If the Beatles are the archetype of every band, Steve was our very own Pete Best. Fortunately, Ringo appeared at just the right time. When Steve took a vacation, we played for a couple of weeks with a stand-in by the name of Dave Cairns. The difference was astonishing. Dave played in a loose, almost sloppy style, but it worked; suddenly, there was a *groove*. His kit sounded great, and the funkier numbers actually felt funky. When Steve came back, it was pretty obvious what had to be done.

We drew lots to decide who would go and tell him, and the dirty deed fell to Mark. Apparently Steve took it quite well. At any rate, although I haven't seen him since, he's never come looking for me.

Every band has to sack someone sooner or later, but it feels terrible, like breaking up with a long-term girlfriend. I felt sorry for Steve. He was a nice guy and he'd done his best. But the band was finally a *band*, and a band with a killer rhythm section.

Dave Cairns was slightly older than the rest of us. He was married and had his own house in Gosport, and seemed very grown-up and very "together." He wore aviator glasses and his accent hinted at a more middle-class background than the rest of us. His musical tastes were quite sophisticated, too, and tended towards funk: the Crusaders, Sly Stone, the Meters, and so on—and he introduced me to a favorite band, Little Feat.

I'm going to go out on a limb here and say that Little Feat were the great band of the '70s. They were a rock band, sort of—but a funky, soulful, multiracial one. Very American, but in a deep and rootsy way, full of New Orleans spice and Memphis grease and a sweetness like Bourbon. And they were truly a *band:* all great players, but no one showed off. Instead they listened to each other and left spaces for each other, so the music had a rolling, snaky, organic quality that you don't hear much any more. These days we're more used to stiff, programmed dance beats, which is neither better nor worse. But one of these days a young band will start to play together like Little Feat did, and we'll all stand up and proclaim them as geniuses.

Compared to this, Edward Bear was pretty trashy, but Dave Cairns was enthusiastic about joining us. He loved working with Graham, as would any drummer in his right mind. Even better, he owned a Transit van, bigger and more comfortable than our old Bedford, which we could now sell and buy a better PA system.

We should have changed our name then, but it wasn't that simple. We were afraid that our fairly regular gigs would dry up and that we'd have to start from scratch. But probably more to the point was our inability to think of a new name. We each came up with long lists, which everyone else invariably hated.

You wouldn't think that naming a band would be so hard, especially since so many bands have made it big with the most fatuous names imaginable. But just try thinking of a name you really like, and then getting three or four other people to agree with you.

Mark tended to suggest names that were completely, deliberately, absurd. At one point he was obsessed for a week or two with changing our name to the Bakewell Tarts.

Graham didn't really care what we were called. His first band had been named for shock value: they were called Septic Bowels. They played only one gig, in Graham's living room, and the shock value was apparently lost on his mum, who sold the tickets. Shortly afterwards he was briefly in a Heavy Metal band who, after much deliberation, chose the Heaviest name they could think of: Iron Bomb. Maybe Graham was not going to be much use on this score.

I don't remember any of my suggestions, which were probably just as pathetic, but I've always liked puns or joke names, like One Hundred and One Crustaceans, or Rabble Without Applause. The trouble with this sort of thing is that it's only funny once, and then you have to live with it. I see so many ridiculous names listed every week at clubs like CBGB's or the Marquee, that I'm convinced there are actually only half a dozen bands in London or New York, but they change their name for every gig.

We couldn't even manage to change our name once. Tragically, we were to be stuck with Edward Bear for a while yet.

Meanwhile, in the winter of '74, the cast of characters in this musical soap opera was expanding. Picking Graham up one day from his parents' house, we were introduced to his sister Jill. Or rather, Jill insisted on introducing herself. She bounced into the room, a platinum blonde in a skintight stars-and-stripes T-shirt, showing off a superstructure that would have been impressive at any age, but at sixteen was a minor miracle. She was plainly impressed by me, or Mark, or both of us, and she positively fizzed with energy. Mark was obviously charmed, but I wasn't so sure. For one thing, hardly anything she said made any sense. Precociously sexy she may have been, but to me she was a cartoon: the archetypal dizzy blonde.

Graham's dad, Percy, meanwhile, sat as usual in his favorite armchair eating peanuts, farting, guffawing at the TV, and cracking outrageously awful jokes. Compared to his dad and his sister, Graham was actually quite sedate.

He soon moved out, though, and got married, to an odd, nervous girl called Julie, whom I liked but could never quite figure out. The obligatory booze-up took place the night before, at a Gosport pub. We all poured vodka and whiskey into Graham's beer when he wasn't looking, and then carried on into the small hours back at Dave Cairns's house. The last thing I remembered before passing out was stumbling into the bathroom and seeing Graham's naked arse in the air, trousers round ankles, head down the toilet.

Sister Jill started coming to our gigs to "do Mark's makeup."

"You don't mind if I come along, do you Joe?" she asked me. Everyone was calling me Joe now, although I'd stopped wearing the glasses. I rolled my eyes and said that I *supposed* not.

"Thanks," she squealed, "you're a bean!"

What the hell did that mean? Where, I wondered, could I get a large rubber stamp saying BIMBO, so I could slap it on her forehead? After a while we just scowled at each other.

Anyway, surely girls weren't allowed in band vans? I decided to put this to Mark one evening in the Public bar of a noisy and notorious Gosport sailors' pub, the Royal Arms.

"What do you see in that Jill?" I asked Mark, although I had a pretty good idea. Mark just shrugged.

"I wouldn't touch her with a ten-foot pole," I added.

Mark shrugged again.

"And apart from that," I shouted above the rising nautical din, "I don't think it's good to have wives and girlfriends traveling in the van with us and hanging around."

"Oh yeah? Why not?" asked Mark.

"I just don't think it's a good idea, that's all."

"Well, you haven't got a girlfriend, have you?" said Mark.

I didn't have an answer for this, so I changed the subject by suggesting we go through to the next-door Saloon bar where it might be quieter. It wasn't. A delirious drinking contest was underway, involving a disgusting cocktail of rough cider and orange juice. Barrels of cider and jugfuls of juice were set up on tables in the middle of the room. The combination had obviously been found by some mad scientist to be the fastest route to inebriation, and they'd been going at it for quite a while before we walked in. A thick cloud of fag-smoke and testosterone hung in the air: Men snarled and grunted and threatened each other, crashed into each other and sprawled on the floor, and fights seemed to start and then fizzle out every couple of minutes.

The full horror of men without women was all around us. Since no one seemed to be taking any notice of me or Mark, we stayed to see what would happen at closing time. Somehow, we had a feeling that a polite "Time, gentlemen, please," wasn't going to cut the mustard with these boys. We were right. At eleven o'clock the landlord appeared—a great lumbering ex-teddy boy with greased-back graying hair. As a colleague brought out a snarling behemoth of a dog, the landlord rang a deafening handbell, of the sort used to bring schoolboys in from the playground, and shouted "Roight you lot! FUCK OFF EYT OF IT!"

Mark and I were allies, but my envy of his sex life was not the only tension between us. For instance, I'd written a lot of songs by now, but Mark was often reluctant to play them. When we did try them out, he struggled with the guitar parts. I would bang out the parts impatiently on the keyboard, and then Mark would be affronted. As far as he was concerned, musicianship wasn't important; there were whole layers of what this band, any band, was all about, in which he was manifestly ahead of me. He was the one with the charm and the flash, and the one in the spotlight, while I felt trapped behind my keyboards. The keyboards, in fact, didn't particularly interest me. They were just an excuse to be on the stage.

I may have been the coleader, and a vastly more accomplished musician than Mark, but the fact was that the band *looked* like it was his. In many ways, we actually complemented each other. But we also each had more than enough ideas, and more than enough ego, to lead bands of our own.

Dave Cairns also had a healthy ego and a desire to be more than just the bloke at the back behind the drum kit. His input, though, was practical, financial, logistical. Always by far the most organized member of the group, he kept a diary of every gig we did. This is how I know that on

22 November, 1974, we played at the Southern Electricity Board Club in Cosham, and that we were paid £35; followed by the Bognor Regis British Legion Club, the Bordon Army Camp Sergeants' Mess, the Gosport Trades and Labour Club (£30), and something called the Pen and Parchment Club in Basingstoke.

At Penelope's in Paignton (£50) and the New Penny Disco, Watford (£40), we were booed and promptly cleared the dance floor as soon as we walked on stage. But then, at the Thorngate Hall, Gosport, we played for a drunkenly enthusiastic crowd of dancers, one of whom stripped naked towards the end of the evening.

What is it about the combination of live music and alcohol that compels some people to take off their clothes?! As the Gosport reveler got down to his socks, I must have flashed back to the horrific spectacles at the Admiral Drake, and Graham must have been reminded of a gig he's often described as the worst of his life. It was at the Coral Reef Bar on South Parade Pier in Southsea, with his old band, Boz, not long before he joined us. The audience consisted of exactly four people: a bored barman and three morose sailors. The sailors sat at a corner table, slumped over their beer, totally indifferent to anything except the usual task of getting monumentally drunk. Fifteen minutes or so before closing time, having each consumed a number of pints well into double figures, they were starting to slide under the table. The band, having exhausted most of their repertoire, started up a listless medium-swing instrumental version of "The Lady Is a Tramp." Suddenly, one of the sailors got up, leapt onto the dance floor, and started to "freak out," flailing wildly like a hippie at an acid-rock concert. The other two joined him as he started to tear his clothes off. By the time the first sailor was naked, the police had been called, and as the band packed up, their entire audience was hauled back to its ship, presumably to sleep it off in the brig.

Edward Bear's gigs weren't all bad. For instance, the Checquers Inn in Lytchett Matravers, Dorset, was not the sleepy rustic place it sounded, but a thriving music venue not far from Bournemouth. The crowd was young and welcoming, and we were actually encouraged to play our own songs. The place was managed by one Alan Matthews, who was also the manager of a famous Gosport band, Smiling Hard.

Smiling Hard was a big influence on us. They were like the slightly older brothers we resented, envied, and revered. They were great players—

they all seemed to be multi-instrumentalists, and most of them are still active in the business. (Andy Hamilton, saxophonist, has worked with Bob Geldof and George Michael, and keyboardist/trombonist Spike Edney was for many years a touring member of Queen.) Kevin Gilson, the youngest of a talented Gosport dynasty (his brothers Tony and Dave played bass and guitar), was a strong and versatile singer and played both guitar and saxophones, so Smiling Hard would be a guitar band on one song and then suddenly have a full horn section on the next. They also boasted at one time or another two of the best drummers in the area, Larry Tolfree and Dave Houghton, both of whom ended up some years later working for me. But that's another story.

Smiling Hard's show was slick, professional, energetic, and fun. They were more funk- and soul-oriented than us, and in my memory they're always playing Sly Stone's "Dance to the Music" and jumping around the stage like circus acrobats. Their original material, also funk-influenced, was strong, too, and they were always rumored to be on the verge of signing a recording contract. They had regular, well-paid gigs, and as if all this weren't enough, they seemed to attract nice-looking girls and rode around in a big van with aircraft seats.

Bastards!

We started to play the Checquers on a regular basis, and Alan Matthews seemed to be taking an interest in us. He watched us intently, and his wife (who for some reason was called Larry) made us toasted cheese-and-onion sandwiches between sets. This was exciting. We had visions of aircraft seats and fabulous riches. "The Hards" were said to make as much as a hundred pounds a show. We worked hard to impress. We were like girls done out to the nines, fluttering our eyelashes and hoping the bloke we fancied would ask us to dance. Apart from a decent name, a manager, we thought, was the only thing we were missing.

Beat That!

BY NOW I was in my third year at the Academy, and feeling like an impostor. People looked at me as though I might be concealing a bomb under my jacket. Percussion studies were the only thing I really worked at, as I'd decided to take my final exam in percussion. I might as well finish with a degree, and I thought I stood a better chance of getting it in percussion than in piano, where competition was fierce, or composition, which I really didn't have the heart for.

The Jazz Workshop had gone into a terminal decline with the departure of John Dankworth, but through it I managed to get myself an occasional place in the National Youth Jazz Orchestra. This sprawling conglomerate rehearsed every Saturday morning in a north London theater, and it was the last thing that diverted me from my mission to be a rock 'n' roll working-class hero.

Nyjo, as it was always called, consisted of the crème de la crème of British jazz players under thirty. Many of them are now well-known soloists or busy session players. The arrangements were challenging, and if the solos were not always quite first-rate, the ensemble playing was thrilling, if only for its sheer volume. Too many players invariably showed up, but they'd just keep doubling up the parts. Sometimes there would be ten or twelve trumpets, eight trombones, fifteen reeds, two drummers. Sure, one electric guitarist with a powerful amp can get just as loud—but it's a different *kind* of loud. Being in the middle of a band like this, like being in the middle of an orchestra, can come pretty close, at times, to a religious experience.

A pianist was at a disadvantage, though, in this freewheeling setup. Piano parts in jazz big bands are not completely set, but have large stretches of chord symbols, which the pianist has to interpret in his own way. Two or three people doing this at once would be superfluous, and a mess. So I had to take my turn on the coveted piano stool, sometimes with two or three other players looking over my shoulder.

Nyjo was directed by Bill Ashton, a tall, slightly eccentric jazz fanatic with a pretentious little King Tut beard and endless nervous energy. He waved his arms, clapped his hands, shook his fists, and also had a distinctive way of starting off a number. He would close his eyes in intense concentration, fix the tempo in his mind, and start snapping his fingers. The musicians watched like hawks, trying to pick up the tempo, but Bill's finger-snapping would invariably speed up, slow down, and speed up again, until he'd suddenly shout "a-one-two-three-four!" and the band would explode like racehorses out of the gate, all at slightly different speeds. After a few bars, though, they'd find a groove and swing like hell.

Everyone joked about Bill, in the way that English people so readily do about anyone so overtly enthusiastic. At the same time, I think, we all loved him, and were inspired by his dedication and sheer energy. I give Bill Ashton a lot of credit. He's still leading a new generation of Nyjo now, and he'll probably keep going until he dies of a heart attack at the age of 120.

Rehearsing with Nyjo reminded me that I loved jazz, but paradoxically it also confirmed in my mind that I'd never actually be a jazz musician. "Classical" and "pop" are fluid categories, diverse and open-ended. But jazz is a very particular thing, a fixed point somewhere in between. This is both its special appeal and its great limitation. As much as I enjoyed Nyjo, I decided that being a jazz musician was a serious business, like entering a priesthood. A beautiful thing, but not *my* thing.

Meanwhile I'd written a dozen or so songs, and I was feeling frustrated. Edward Bear wasn't getting enough of the kind of gigs where we could play our own material. And when we *could* play our own songs, at least half of them would be Mark's. As committed as I was to the band, I felt in danger of being overshadowed in it.

Just then, with perfect timing, another crumb fell from God's table, and my last year at the Academy produced one last happy connection. Someone knew someone who was doing a course in recording at Surrey University, for a "BA Tonmeister" degree. At the time it was the only such course available in the country. The university, in Guildford, had a fully equipped recording studio, and I could probably get in there for a day if I wanted.

I don't remember the name or the face of the student recording engineer in question, but it was an incredible stroke of luck. Whoever he was, he called me and said he'd be happy to give me a day of free studio time in exchange for nothing except the experience. I said I'd be there.

Why didn't I say "we"? I felt suddenly guilty and almost talked myself into calling Mark. Then I talked myself out of it again. This opportunity had fallen into *my* lap. The engineer in Guildford didn't even know that Edward Bear existed. I had a dozen songs, and for all I knew, this could be the only chance I'd ever get to put some of them on tape. Maybe I was selfish, but I wanted this opportunity for myself. Edward Bear demos would have to wait.

I rushed to finish off some unfinished songs. It's amazing how conducive to creativity a deadline can be. Then I put together a sprawling band, partly from Gosport and partly from London. Dave and Graham would be the rhythm section, and Drew Barfield would sing. There were also a couple of newer faces.

Foremost among these was a guitarist I'd recently met, by the name of Gary Sanford. He was a strikingly pretty, golden-haired Londoner whom Drew had met at college. When Gary played gigs, girls would actually gather around the stage and scream.

When he wasn't driving half the female population of south London into a frenzy, Gary smoked dope and dropped acid. Drew played some pub gigs with him, and I heard extraordinary stories. One night Gary became convinced, in his altered state, that he could communicate with a girlfriend in America over the microphone, and he started long meaningless conversations with her in the middle of songs. Then he would shout "Rock 'n' roll!" and start thrashing out high-speed riffs, regardless of what the rest of the band was doing at the time—they just had to stop whatever it was and follow him. This roller-coaster ride went on for a couple of hours, until finally Gary got off the stage, went over to the friend who was mixing the sound, said "I know what you're doing! You're controlling me with those knobs!" and punched him in the face. He was last seen dragging his guitar along the ground by its strap, heading towards Lewisham.

After hearing stories like this, I wasn't sure that I even wanted to meet Gary, let alone work with him. But he turned out to be a pleasant, laid-back character, improbably handsome, charming, and a fine player. He would be the lead guitarist for the Surrey Session.

Then there was Steve Tatler, who hailed from my old neighborhood, Paulsgrove. We'd met a year or two before, when Steve was playing a gig at Queen Alexandra Hospital in Portsmouth, but we didn't really become friends until he moved to London. He lived for a while in Woolwich, and I stayed overnight with him from time to time when I felt like I'd been abusing Drew's hospitality. Steve played guitar and sang in an unusual voice, hard-edged but resonant. I introduced Steve to Drew and they instantly became lifelong friends. Steve would play acoustic guitar and sing.

Lastly Drew's flatmate, an Irish drummer by the name of Tony Kelly, would come along for the ride and play percussion. Why not?

We rehearsed chaotically, by twos and threes: at Drew's flat, in a tatty rehearsal room in Portsmouth, and before or after Edward Bear rehearsals at the Stubbington Community Centre, near Fareham. Mark admitted to being envious, but he didn't protest. He didn't blame me. I was relieved. We were professionals after all: no hard feelings. Not yet.

Finally, Dave, Graham, and I drove up to Guildford in the Edward Bear van, and the rest of the ensemble drove down from London. There was electricity in the air. What little recording experience we had between us was mostly amateur stuff in garages. The university's studio was large and reasonably well equipped, and we felt like the Beatles at Abbey Road. We all set up in the middle of the room, with very few acoustic baffles to separate the instruments and amps. Everything would leak into everything else. We saw nothing wrong with that. Nor did we see any reason to spend more than an hour making sure that everything was working. As long as the drums sounded like drums, and the bass sounded like a bass, and everything was audible, we were ready to roll.

When I think of all the things that could have gone wrong that day, I can only conclude that the stars must all have been in the right place, or some kind of good Karma had built up in my favor, or some other benign force was keeping disaster away. Right from the beginning, the session was a breeze. Everything worked. There were no technical hitches. Everyone could hear everything perfectly, and everything sounded great. Everyone played well and the songs came together easily, despite being underrehearsed. Even the vocals, which were done in two or three takes at most, were in tune and not half bad. By midafternoon, it started to dawn on us that we were having the time of our lives. "If this is what recording is like, I don't want to do anything else!" said Dave, and Drew jumped up and down and whooped like a cowboy at a rodeo.

We worked at a feverish pace, partly because we were having such a good time, partly because I wanted to get a lot of songs down, but mostly —I can hardly believe it now—because Edward Bear had a gig that evening.

I still have the tape of this session, and it does sound a bit rushed, and not of the greatest sound quality. But everything is audible, and as a demo tape, especially for the time, it was pretty damn good. And what about the songs?

There's a rather generic up-tempo rocker called "New Brown Shoes" (as in "don't let them step on your . . .") and a funky midtempo song with lyrics poking fun at the pompous father of a girl I'd gone out with a couple of times, against his wishes. It has some nice syncopated riffs and Gary plays some impressive wa-wa guitar. There's a jokey cod-reggae number, two maudlin ballads, and one song with a frantic Latin feel and some clever chord changes. There's a jazzy, Steely Dan-ish tribute to Charlie Parker called "Bird Lives," and finally the honky-tonkish "Boogie Woogie Joe," a bit of personal mythmaking about a roguish barroom piano player.

Drew, Graham, Steve Tatler, and I shared the vocals, and my voice is one of the more embarrassing things on the tape. It's thin and nervous, although I have to say that it's in tune. My ear was helping me there, at least.

The other major cringe factor is the lyrics. Mostly, they're pretty lame. The two ballads have nice tunes, and I wanted to write slow, melodic songs, but I hadn't yet figured out that you have to mix a little bit of sour with the sweet if you don't want to turn peoples' stomachs. "Stony Ground" is particularly awful, struggling with the image of the sower sowing seed on stony ground as a metaphor for unrequited love. The other ballad, "Save Me," touchingly sung by Graham, is better, but there's nothing too original about a chorus that goes "Save me from myself / I ain't afraid of no one else."

On the whole, though, I'd taken a great leap forward. And the pleasures of the Surrey Session went way beyond the dubious merits of my songs. There was tremendous camaraderie—everyone involved still remembers the day vividly—and for me, the undreamt-of satisfaction of bringing together six people to play and record my own music, and seeing them all have a great time. It was more than just a confidence-boost, although that was precious enough. It was why I was doing this in the first place: the sheer joy of sharing music. When it's good, it's still hard for me to think of anything better. An energy fills the room that is impossible to describe. On some mystical level that I've never really figured out, I think it must be synonymous with love, with life force, with God.

And when it's bad, it stinks. There are few more depressing things than sitting in a recording studio, trying in vain to figure out why the glorious vision you had in your mind's ear is actually sounding—well, like shit. You've been in there for weeks, and the drummer still can't hear the bass properly, and something about the mix is making you sing out of tune without knowing it, and the groove on one song still doesn't feel right after twenty takes, and the engineer's just realized that the microphone on the bass drum hasn't been working all day, and the air-conditioning has broken down, and the guitarist is pissed off because he's been waiting to do his overdub for three days now, and you're behind schedule but they're booked up for six months after you, so if you can't get it finished . . .

But let's face it, if we wanted a safe job with no highs or lows, we'd all be working in a bank.

Ever since that first session, I've been a quick worker in the studio, and I tend to scoff at people who spend six months just getting the snare drum right. But I still don't know how we managed to do what we did in Guildford. Not only that, but three of us had to get to the Dilkusha Club on Hayling Island, and when we finally left the studio, at the last possible minute, the university's big iron front gate was locked.

We searched everywhere for someone who might have a key, but the place was deserted. It was a Saturday afternoon, the university was closed, and no one even knew we were there. There was no other way for a van to get out. We panicked for a few minutes, and then we did the only thing we could do: We heaved and strained like a team of navvies and lifted the gate off its hinges. We made it to Hayling Island just in time.

Eight tracks recorded (with overdubs!) and mixed, in one day, and a gig the same evening. Beat that!

Snobs

I'M SIPPING mushroom soup in a café in Durham, North Carolina. I'm here to see a dance performance, tonight, which has been choreographed to my music, and I'm feeling pretty pleased with myself. Not only because of this homage to my work, but because of the way my work, every now and again, has me jetting off to some place I'd never even thought of going. It's nice to travel without feeling like a tourist. I have a professional reason for being here, an honorable reason. In the days before tourism (I think as I taste a local microbrew beer, not bad) everyone must have traveled for a reason, honorable or not.

And then a pianist appears, a few tables away, and launches into a florid, sentimental version of Pachelbel's *Canon in D*. I can't *not* listen through a musician's ears. I can hardly remember, any more, a time when I wasn't a musician. By the time I was twenty, music was the element in which I lived, and I could no more have switched careers than a fish could have learned to breathe oxygen. If someone had asked me to describe myself in one word, I would have said "musician" sooner than I would have said "male" or "white" or "English."

It's taken me a long time to develop the survival mechanism of being able to shut music out. But live music is still harder to shut out than a recording. I can't help being irritated by the way this café pianist is turning a simple baroque piece—a piece that should be touching in its simplicity—

into something labored and cloying, almost neurotic, as he tries to squeeze every drop of cheap emotion out of every bar.

And when he finishes, several people stop eating and *applaud.*

More "light classical" pieces are then tortured to death, including the famous first movement of Beethoven's *Moonlight* Sonata. The triplet arpeggios on which the piece is built—*dah*-dee-dee, *dah*-dee-dee, *dah*-dee-dee—are torn apart by a wildly fluctuating tempo, so that the steady, hypnotic pulse the composer intended gives way to a series of hysterical spasms. The dynamics, instead of following the natural tension and release suggested by Beethoven's harmonies, go up and down like a roller coaster; dramatic (sort of), but devoid of either logic or taste. Every so often the pianist gets lost, too, and improvises clumsily for a while until he finds his place again, which is not necessarily where he left off. So the beauty and rightness of Beethoven's structure is lost, too. Lastly, like most bad pianists, he uses the sustain pedal too much. The pedal lends a kind of hazy coherence to the proceedings, but it also blurs notes and chords together. We hear, for instance, a C-sharp-minor chord and a G-sharp-major chord at the same time, just briefly, and then the G sharp gets blurred into something else.

And still people applaud.

This is starting to get on my nerves. I want to boo, I want to throw the remains of my bread roll at him, I want to stand up and shout, "Are you people nuts or what?!" But I also feel an old and familiar pang: I'm the odd one out. Everyone else thinks the music is just fine.

Are they bad, or stupid, people? Of course not. That white-haired lady on the next table could be my mother. My mother likes what she calls "nice music"—music that is simply pleasant to the half-attentive ear. She might well enjoy this.

And it strikes me that all these questions have been going round and round in my head for years: these issues of belonging versus standing out, of the general climate of opinion versus the personal vision.

Back in 1975—a year that started in a blaze of mediocrity for Edward Bear at the Newtown Social Club, Bognor Regis—my time at the Royal Academy of Music was not just running out but growing positively stale. On the other hand, my rock 'n' roll career was gathering momentum. Alan Matthews, of Checquers Inn and Smiling Hard fame, decided that the time was right for him to take on a second band. We were on our way.

I had chosen sides, and more and more I felt convinced, with a glowing satisfaction, that I'd made the right choice. It wasn't just about music, or about being on the road to success: It was about belonging. Being part of something everyone could agree on, and everyone could understand. No one was going to accuse *me* of being a snob.

Even now, sitting in this café, where I'd felt so comfortable a few minutes ago, I don't *want* to be the odd one out. Isn't it just "nice music"? No, that isn't going to work. I can't hear through anyone's ears but mine.

Then I can't help thinking of David Helfgott. After the success of the movie *Shine*, and the relaunch of this colorful Australian pianist's concert career, his name seemed to crop up in countless conversations. Hey Joe, you know a bit about this classical stuff, is he any good? And I'd have to answer honestly: No, not really. Whereupon I was lambasted for being an envious snob.

I was surprised at how vociferous the reactions were, and how *rehearsed* they sounded. It was as though people had always half-believed that this stuff they didn't really know about, this classical stuff, was actually some sort of scam foisted on them by elitists as part of some vaguely sinister agenda of social control. But now, emboldened by Helfgott's success, egged on by an ever more cynical and pandering media, they were going to have their say. Popularity is good, went the reasoning; the People have spoken, and you can't argue with that. He's popular and you're just *jealous.*

But I wasn't jealous, or envious, or particularly troubled by the Helfgott phenomenon. I'd always known that people I didn't respect as musicians could become stars for all kinds of reasons. I don't expect everyone to be musically educated and discerning. On the contrary, I know that real aficionados, of *anything,* are by definition a minority. The only thing that bothered me was being called a snob just because I knew the difference.

I knew the difference between Helfgott and Ashkenazy, or Horowitz, or Perahia, or Brendel. And I never for a moment thought that it made me "better" than anyone else. It made me, simply, more knowledgeable in a certain area. Millions of people tower above me in other areas, in everything from astrophysics to zoology, but I don't think that makes them "better" than me, and I don't assume that they think so, either.

As I leave the café and stroll back to my hotel, it strikes me once again that we all get so caught up in arguments about class and society and fashion and commerce, that we can't see the wood for the trees when it comes to art. Then I remember an interview I read recently, in which Brian Eno claimed to hate orchestral music because the orchestra was representative of an oppressive hierarchical social structure. And where was the antidote to be found? In Africa, where whole villages drummed and chanted together in communitarian bliss. No snobs there! I half-expected Eno to add that, by the way, those darkies have a wonderful sense of rhythm. The interview made me sick. Of course, maybe I've got it wrong, and Beethoven actually sat down with his quill pen and said, "Ha! Now I'm going to write one that'll really put the peasants in their place!" But if so, it didn't work, because the music cut through almost two centuries of sociopolitical claptrap and reached an ignorant kid in a council house in Paulsgrove. It went straight to my heart. And as for Africa, musicians become leaders and superstars there too, revered either for being the best musicians or—like David Helfgott—for being colorful characters, or both. And that's as it should be.

No doubt there are things to admire about Eno, but his comments in this case carry a strong whiff of a certain European intellectual pose that is actually another kind of snobbery. There are more kinds than we usually realize. This is the kind that denigrates its own cultural heritage while romanticizing—and patronizing—the Africans or Indians or Aborigines. And it might be a nice, self-deprecating touch at this point for me to say that I envy the North Carolinians in the café for being able to enjoy something that I can't, because I've become too sophisticated. But I get more out of music than they could probably imagine, and I don't envy them for a minute. Everyone should be sophisticated in *some* way. Mine could have been gardening or mountaineering or computers, but it turned out to be music. And if being so discerning is sometimes a burden, it much more often proves to be a gift.

So what is it, then, this *pang*? This pang of frustration, of loneliness, almost of shame? I can't imagine that an astrophysicist feels it. He must surely accept that hardly anyone shares his passion. Music, though, is all around us, and everyone knows a *bit* about it. And one side effect of the overwhelming ascendancy of pop—music that anyone can understand—is that the musically ignorant are given a license to be as smug and self-righteous as any stereotypical opera connoisseur of the past.

As for the performer, there's something seductive in knowing that if you keep it simple, and stay within the conventions that everyone knows, you can be accepted.

Very seductive indeed, for a working class twenty-year-old who'd grown up feeling like a misfit, who was sick of being the class weirdo, who wanted to belong. I'd chosen my side, and it was only much later that I could see how choosing sides usually involves some kind of betrayal. Practicing Beethoven on the school piano, instead of kicking a football, had been a betrayal of my tribe. I didn't feel like a snob, but I looked like one. I made up for it by joining the working-class rock 'n' roll world, even at the risk of betraying the goddess, the muse, of music—Music with a capital M—and becoming an inverted snob in the process.

I would soon wash my hands of the Academy, and stop playing jazz with Nyjo. From now on, I would ally myself exclusively with rockers—people who, while I'd been traveling the whole wide musical world, had chosen to stay in one country, even in one town. I wanted to live there, too.

Rock musicians knew where to *stop*. It didn't bother me that even those with tremendous talent were, and still are, often musical underachievers. Guitarists, for instance, like Mark Andrews, who learn just the chords they need to play the songs they want to play—and no more. Singers who develop a style of sorts, but won't expand their range, won't even learn some basic techniques which would allow them to sing night after night without losing their voices. Where's their curiosity, at least? What's holding them back?

I think it's the understandable fear that if you go beyond a certain point, you'll be lost in a limbo where you won't know what kind of music you're playing, and you won't know which crowd, which culture, which class you belong to. You'll be a traitor. For most people, it isn't worth it. They might love music, but not *that* much.

These days, I feel that it *is* worth it, and I *do* love music that much. So many other things have proven to be ephemeral, and fallen away. Someone with my diverse interests, who has a hard time sticking to the Pure Pop straight and narrow, will probably always look like a snob to some. I'll keep protesting, and keep pointing out, too, that there's as much snobbery in pop culture as anywhere else. But people are only going to see it if they want to. That pang, and the temptation to go out of my way to show that I'm just one of the Pompey lads, is still there. But it's an old itch I no longer need to scratch.

Back in 1975, starring at the Newtown Social Club, Bognor Regis, I was scratching furiously. I knew that some sort of narrowing of my horizons was taking place. But I didn't mind. It was, I thought, all going to be for the best.

For a while, it was.

Growing a Shell

ALAN MATTHEWS, Edward Bear's new manager, wasn't at all the stereotypical flashy hustler of pop myth. He was quiet and businesslike, with a sleek brown mustache and sensitive brown eyes, and resolutely unhip. He wore anoraks. There was nothing remotely impressive about him. But he was the only manager interested in managing us. He was also the only manager we knew.

We signed a typically verbose contract, in which Alan was guaranteed 15 percent of our earnings

> in respect of all activities of the Group throughout the world in the entertainment industry in every branch medium or form thereof including without prejudice to the generality of the foregoing vaudville (sic) music hall burlesque cinematograph films legitimate theatre television broadcasting and personal appearance of every medium and sort

and so on and so forth. We were uneasy about the duration of the contract—five years—but we were told this was "standard." We didn't know any better.

We didn't know, either, how hard it can be to make the leap from Small Time to Big Time, despite the fact that it always seemed to be happening to acts much less talented than us. Great local talent can thrive for years with an enthusiastic local following, but somehow never manage to "break out." Such would eventually turn out to be the case with Smiling Hard.

Success seemed to happen to people for arbitrary reasons, but we didn't want to believe it. We *had* to work on the assumption that if you were good enough, you just got bigger and bigger, all the way from the local British Legion club to Wembley Arena. We steeled ourselves and settled in for the long haul.

In the Small Time context, Alan Matthews wasn't the worst manager we could have found. The first thing he did was take over our bookings, effectively becoming our agent as well. I wasn't quite sure how this worked. I bumped into Dave Barfield one day and we discussed the situation. Why I thought he knew any more than I did, I can't imagine, but he gave the impression that he did.

"So what *is* the difference between a manager and an agent?" I asked him.

"Well, the agent gets you the gigs," said Dave.

"But doesn't a manager do that?"

"Not necessarily."

"Then what does he do?"

"He might negotiate with record companies."

"You mean an agent wouldn't?"

"Errr . . . well, he might, I suppose."

"Then what's the difference?"

"Managers don't usually book gigs."

"But this one does. Which means, we don't need an agent."

"Look, an agent gets you gigs, but a manager is responsible for everything, your whole career. He does things like . . . like getting you a better dressing room, for instance!"

"Oh." I thought this over. We'd changed in toilets, offices, storerooms, closets, beer cellars, and in the van, but it was pretty rare for us to get a dressing room at all. I'd have to watch Alan to see what he was going to do about that.

We did start to play some better venues. We still played "workies" clubs and naval bases, but there were a few more pub and club gigs where people actually wanted to hear our own songs, as well as more of the discos where they didn't.

It might seem strange that we played so many discos, when it was usually a dispiriting experience both for us and the audience. But at that time, the Musicians' Union had managed to get a ruling passed to the effect that nightclubs had to feature a certain amount of live music. So we were frequently booked by people who didn't actually want us at all.

For our part, we were desperate for gigs, and I think also that we prided ourselves on a heroic determination to play anywhere, anytime. If one person in the disco liked us, it was worth it. As we played more, we also started to earn a bit more money, but we seemed to keep less and less of it, as Alan took his percentage and the rest started to go into new equipment, clothes, roadies, or repairs to the van.

Alan encouraged us to think more about the band's image. He thought that everyone should have a definite "look" or character. He also thought that Mark was a natural "front man" and needed to take on more of a leadership role. Mark agreed, although he and Alan were both quick to point out that we'd still play my songs. Still feeling slightly guilty about my Surrey Session, I said that we'd work out some sort of balance and everything would be fine.

I was soon able to make amends by getting the band into the studio at Surrey University for two more sessions. Somehow these weren't as much fun as the first. They felt much more like a job of work. We recorded seven of Mark's songs and three of mine. This was only fair, I told myself, but I had an uneasy feeling that Mark was starting to think of this band as his, whether I liked it or not, and that Alan was going to back him up.

Still, Mark was a genuine talent. He also had a way of engaging an audience that was alien to me, the shy geek behind the keyboards. He would make wisecracks between songs, make fun of people in the audience and get people cheering and booing, or jump off the stage and dance around with some girl on the dance floor. He was more and more confident and more and more ambitious. The rest of us started to feel it, too. We were developing a sense of purpose and a sort of toughness.

Despite some tension between me and Mark, I was feeling good. I was the coleader of a band on the way up, we had a manager, and I even had a girlfriend.

On Christmas Eve, I'd been talked into going out carol-singing with Graham and his wife. At first I mocked the idea, Scroogelike, but Graham said he would play guitar, I would play accordion, we'd all sing in harmony, and we'd collect enough money for a couple of hours to have a good booze-up at the end of it. It turned out to be great fun, despite the unforeseen presence of Graham's bimbo sister. She'd broken up with Mark, and I thought I'd never have to see her again. But she seemed less annoying—or was it just the Christmas spirit? To my surprise, she played guitar passably and sang enthusiastically, and actually made me laugh a couple of times with outrageous quips and puns.

Later we went to the John Peel, the pub near my house that was becoming quite a musicians' hangout. As Graham and Julie immersed themselves in conversation, Jill and I were finally forced to get to know one another. Pretty soon I discovered that she wasn't a bimbo at all. She was no intellectual either, but she was honest and straightforward, and had a generous spirit. What I'd taken for silliness was partly a delight in absurdity and word-games, and partly her compulsion to make fun of me. She couldn't help it. I was just so *serious*.

"You know, I think I was wrong about you," she said, looking me straight in the eye. She had green eyes like me. "I thought you were a miserable old git."

"Old?!" I spluttered, "I'm only twenty!"

"You seem much older," said Jill. I was horrified. But Jill was only sixteen and more carefree than I would ever be.

My father once remarked that I'd never actually been a child. "You were born bloody forty years old," he said, and, God help me, I knew what he meant. Even as a child, I found childish things . . . well, childish. Childhood, for me, was no Paradise Lost. It was a time of sickness, loneliness, beatings, and humiliation, and a time of being too small and too ignorant to do anything about it. Life in the adult world was immeasurably better and getting better all the time. But now, for the first time, I took a step back and looked at myself. What kind of adult was I becoming?

Through Jill's eyes, I saw myself growing a shell, a shell of defensive pseudotoughness to protect my true self, which I thought was too sensitive for the world around me. I also realized that people found me almost unnervingly serious or intense. Partly, this was the work of nature. I just seem to have a serious face, and as a kid I was infuriated by aunties telling me to "cheer up" when I was perfectly happy. This sort of thing still happens now.

As for the perceived intensity, maybe it had something to do with my impatience with chitchat and triviality. There was also the burning desire

I'd always had to escape from the ordinary, and to excel in some way, which, somewhere in the back of my mind, was always rubbing uncomfortably against my desire to belong. It was like a dissonance inside me, like a C-major chord constantly clashing with an F sharp. The paradox was going to puzzle me on and off for many years to come.

What would I do if I could go back in time and meet my twenty-year-old self? Sometimes I think I'd want to shake him, knock some sense into him, save him a lot of trouble by telling him that it's not really a paradox at all. Because it's only by allowing yourself to be who you are that you can find a niche. It's only when you stop holding back parts of yourself that you start to make the right relationships, that you find the right place to be, find your true vocation, start to feel comfortable in your own skin.

But I have compassion, too, for my twenty-year-old self. And in fact I was rarely unhappy. I may have had (like my father, perhaps) a serious, even introspective nature, but I was an optimist. I've met quite a few apparently cheerful, funny, popular people who've turned out to be cynical, lost, or empty underneath. But deep down, I've always had a sense that life was fundamentally worthwhile, and I think I got that from my mother.

So life was a struggle, but I also saw it as an adventure, and hilarious in its sheer absurdity. Jill was more an accepter than a struggler, but she had a similar sense of humor. For her part, she was shocked to find out that I had a sense of humor at all. By the end of the evening, we decided we liked each other. Within a couple of weeks, we'd decided we liked each other a lot.

For years, I used to tell anyone who wanted to know that I lost my virginity at the age of nineteen. I think I'd actually convinced myself of this. Nineteen was bad enough, but I wanted to believe that I'd at least still been in my teens. Now that I look at the facts and the dates, it's obvious that I was actually twenty. But another great thing about looking back across a couple of decades is that I find so little to be embarrassed about. The important thing is that this sweet, sexy girl came into my life, better late than never, and with plenty of enthusiasm.

The much-awaited event itself was an anticlimax. It was nervous and short, which may have had something to do with the fact that my parents were downstairs underneath us watching TV at the time. I felt how girls are supposed to feel after the first time: "Is that all there is?" Jill wasn't discouraged. "I feel much more closer to you now," she said. She wasn't exactly a master of the English language. But she had other talents, and I soon found out that that wasn't all there was, not at all.

Jill was nothing like what I'd thought I wanted, but she constantly disarmed me with her uncomplicated warmth. She didn't stop me from growing a shell—circumstances in the years to come, and my own stupidity, would keep that in place. But if it hadn't been for Jill, the shell might have been a lot harder.

Grievous Bodily Harm

LOOKING AT Dave Cairns's diary, I sometimes wonder if he isn't just making it all up. Did we really play at the Flight Refuelling Limited Sports Club in Wimborne Minster? What was it like to play at the Berkshire College of Agriculture? Where is Enham Alamein, and is it still home to the Londale Wilson Institute?

We still played a lot of naval bases, where our hosts expressed their hospitality by plying us with drink. A favorite treat was to pour a double scotch into a pint of bitter; I'm told this is called a boilermaker, but the skates called it "a pint of bitter with a double scotch in it."

Another dubious treat was chatting with aspiring naval musicians. My favorite was Bernie, who hung around the stage all evening when we played at HMS *Sultan*. In between songs he asked us all kinds of not especially intelligent questions about our amps. When he finally moved off, a fellow rating, who'd been trying not to laugh the whole time, explained: Bernie had recently bought an electric guitar but been disappointed at the low volume level it produced. Almost inaudible, in fact. He didn't know that he was supposed to plug it into an amplifier. Instead, by a process of logical deduction, he figured out that since it was an *electric* guitar, it had to be plugged into the mains. Where was the cable? They must have left it out! So Bernie spliced a three-pin plug onto a guitar lead, plugged in, and hit a power chord that blasted him clean across the room. He was lucky to be alive.

When we weren't entertaining the navy, we were starting to go further afield for gigs. Because of Alan's Dorset connections, we played a lot of gigs in Bournemouth, Poole, or Dorchester. But there were also dates in Exmouth, Oxford, Coventry, and Southend.

Quite often, when I got home at 4 or 5 A.M., my dad would be sitting in the kitchen. He'd gotten fed up (so I was told) with the unpredictability of the building trade, and he'd started working for a local dairy, delivering milk, so he would have just gotten up. Bleary-eyed with sleep, he would grunt something unintelligible at me. Bleary-eyed with drink, I'd grunt something back, and then fall into bed as he went out to his milk float.

I didn't find out until many years later that layoffs over the harsh winter of '74/75 had brought my dad to the edge of financial disaster. He didn't complain. He just went out and got another job.

The stoicism was consistent, but otherwise my dad's personality was starting to change. The harsh, bullying side seemed to be wearing itself out, and something rather lonely, rather melancholy, was starting to take its place. But if he was ready to mellow, I was not. It would take me quite a long time to feel compassion for my father. For now he was just a bloke grunting in the kitchen.

Whether my dad saw it or not, I was working hard, too. Some of our gigs were a trial, to say the least.

For instance, we arrived one evening at a verminous club in Weymouth called the Music Box, to find a stage dimly lit in sickly shades of green and yellow. Mark asked the manager if we could do anything about the lights.

"What d'you mean, *do* anything about 'em?" sneered the manager.

"Well, can we change them at all?"

"Yeah, you can change them. You can have 'em *off*."

The place remained almost empty despite the added attraction, that night, of a stripper. The large-breasted blond lady in question, who spent the first part of the evening drinking at the bar, was the first woman I'd ever seen with tattoos. They were primitive, Popeye-style tattoos: an anchor on her left arm, and MOTHER on the right. Between our two sets, when the time came for her to perform, she left her cigarette burning in an ashtray on the bar, and just climbed onto the stage in her jeans and T-shirt as the taped music started. Within a few minutes it was obvious that she'd never done this before. After a few more minutes it was made even more obvious by the club manager calling out instructions from the side of the stage, and the stripper calling back, as though no one were watching.

"Take it off!"

"Wot?"

"Take it OFF!"

"Wot?"

"Take your top off!"

"Wot, now?"

"Yes, NOW, for fucksake!"

We watched open-mouthed from the bar, but the Music Box Club had yet more delights in store for us. At the end of the evening, while we broke down our gear, we were treated to an ugly scene between the manager and an obstreperous punter. The manager knocked the punter down and kicked him furiously in the stomach and ribs. Then, as the punter lay retching and moaning on the floor, the manager turned around, calmly picked up a table, and brought it down with all his strength on the punter's head. As the manager lifted the table above his head again, minions appeared and steered us away from the carnage and towards the stage door, out of which both we and our gear were encouraged to go, pronto.

As we lugged the first speaker cabinet outside, a huge skinhead was waiting for us. Now what? But he turned out to be an amiable simpleton who just wanted to help us with our gear. He wasn't good at much, he said, except lifting heavy things. This was OK with us, although we could have done without his life story as he did so. By the time we drove out of Weymouth, we'd heard enough about his being done for Grievous Bodily Harm, and his exploits in prison, to last us a lifetime. We'd had more than enough of the Music Box Club, too. As we drove home a sort of bilious silence descended on us, as we all wondered if we'd been witnesses to a murder.

We were heading into a time of exaggerated highs and lows. Some gigs were wildly successful, while others were like nightmare glimpses of Dante's Inferno. Then, suddenly, came a small glimpse of the Big Time.

Our demo tapes from Surrey University were heard by Andy Arthurs, himself a recent graduate of the BA Tonmeister course, now starting to make his way in the music business as a songwriter and producer. After graduating, he'd played some of his work for a representative of the Leeds publishing group, a division of MCA. The representative's name was Steve Stevenson, and he signed Andy to a publishing contract. A bit later, Steve formed his own production company, Glamswell Limited. His first release was a single, written, sung, and produced by Andy under the name of A. Raincoat, entitled "I Love You For Your Mind (Not Your Body)." The song was quite catchy and had the right campy, tongue-in-cheek attitude for the time, when people like Sparks and 10cc were having hits. It got good reviews and a bit of airplay.

After this, Andy and Steve looked for projects to work on together. It was a classic partnership: They were both—or hoped to be—discoverers and nurturers of talent, but each had his own speciality. Andy had long hair and musical and studio expertise. Steve had short hair, big ideas, and music biz experience, working out deals with record companies. It was Steve who heard in our demos something he liked: a song of Mark's called "Any More Wine."

I may not be very objective about this, but stories of how performers got their record deal, or their big break, always seem boring as hell to me. People expect something inspirational, but in nearly every case, the answer is a rambling chronicle of this person knowing that person who happened to bump into another person who just happened to be doing something or other at just the right time. Success stories are much less compelling, for some reason, than stories of struggle and failure.

Of course, not being anxious to struggle and fail, we were ecstatic when Andy and Steve called us to make a new demo with them. They booked an afternoon at a studio—a London studio!—called Tin Pan Alley, a seedy little place near Charing Cross, and with Andy engineering, we recorded two of Mark's songs: "Any More Wine," a honky-tonkish ode to the pleasures of drink, and a sort of trash-rock anthem called "Good Times."

It's difficult now to figure out whether our "discovery" by Andy and Steve came before or after we signed our contract with Alan Matthews. It's possible that Andy and Steve's interest came first, and helped to convince Alan that we were worth signing. Either way, he was happy to take the credit, and the percentage, and this is all pretty typical, too. Managers don't always have much to do with their clients' success. Quite often they're just along for the ride. They're in the right place at the right time, like everyone else. Smart, effective managers do exist, but they're rarer than you'd think, and it's amazing how many are actually cretins.

Just as failure is often more interesting than success, horrific events have a way of staying with us more than happy ones. The consolation prize is that they often become hilarious in retrospect. As Andy and Steve started to hawk our demo around the record companies, we carried on gigging, and that summer we embarked on what we jokingly referred to as our 1975 Tour of Wales. Alan booked us for two nights at the Valbonne Nite Spot in Swansea, followed by one at a rugby club in Resolven. This meant that we'd have to stay overnight somewhere, which was a first. We always drove home after gigs, no matter how late or how far. We couldn't afford hotels, but we decided to find the cheapest lodgings we could when we got there.

We set off for Wales with great excitement, and with an extra member, Clive "Buggsy" Bates, a guitarist friend of Graham's who had nothing better to do and agreed to help us out with the driving and the gear. Mark sat, as usual, in the back of the van, rolling joints. He was the unchallenged expert, and he rolled several different styles, of which the favorites were "the Slim Jim" and "the Funnel Freddie," and, the most impressive, a T-shaped structure that was lit on two sides and burned into the middle. Mark and Graham were the most enthusiastic dope smokers in the band, but I usually joined in, and the three of us were often in hysterics in the backseat while Dave fumed silently and drove.

This was the only time in my life when I smoked dope regularly and enjoyed it. At Creech Cottage, it had made me paranoid and slightly nauseous. I would sit, feeling as heavy as lead, absolutely convinced that my left eyelid was quivering and that everyone was studying it intently, and that there was nothing to be done, the eyelid would twitch and I wouldn't be able to move and everyone would know about it, forever and ever. Now the drug was relaxing me and making me giggle. After a couple of years, it got to work on the eyelid again, and I had to give it up.

On the way to Swansea, we heard a strange noise, on and off, from somewhere in the innards of the van. When we finally passed Bristol and stopped at the Severn Bridge for a cup of tea, the van refused to start again.

After poking around for nearly an hour, Dave pronounced the situation hopeless. At this point we were going to be late for the gig. We held a brief conference and decided to hire a van, anyway. But there was no van to be had within the next few hours. We'd have to blow the gig out.

It was seven in the evening and we were stranded, with very little money, at a service station by the Severn Bridge. We were going to have to eat chocolate bars for dinner and sleep in the van. To make matters worse, it was unseasonably cold and windy. But Mark had a lot of dope, and since it was the only thing we had in abundance, we indulged ourselves.

Late that evening, high as kites and sick of sitting in a crippled Transit van, we decided to walk across the Severn Bridge. I took the only blanket we had and wrapped it around me, and over my head, so that I looked like some kind of weird stoned Catholic nun from a Fellini movie, and we set off into the biting wind. After about ten minutes, I looked down, and started to hyperventilate. Initially, the dope had made me forget my usual vertigo, but now it was making it worse. Utterly terrified, I crawled on my hands and knees back to the van, and stayed there till morning.

Needless to say, no one slept very well, but we were eventually cheered up by the arrival of the sun and a big orange U-Haul van. We transferred our gear, and as our Transit was dragged off to be repaired, we headed into Wales.

We soon realized that we had hours and hours to kill. It was a glorious sunny day and we stopped in the country and smoked some more dope. Pretty soon we had the giggles, and there were *still* hours and hours to kill. But Clive Bates had a camera, so we passed the time by creating absurd and surreal tableaux. I still have the pictures. In one, Dave is swinging like Tarzan from a tree, naked except for a loincloth made of ferns. In another, I'm lying on the ground with my jacket pulled up over my head, and a fake head wearing a werewolf mask is lying a foot away. Dave poses holding a huge log, and it really does look like he's just hacked off my head with it. Then there's Mark posing as Eros. Wearing just a red hand-towel, he's balancing precariously on one foot on top of the van, which is in turn parked on a steep hillside. He's holding a bow and arrow made from twigs, and there is a strange and disturbing light in his eyes. (Mark was getting more and more reckless. Shortly afterwards he climbed out of the right-hand window of the van as we were driving through Portsmouth, crawled over the roof, and reentered through the left-hand window).

After a couple of hours of this infantile but hilarious activity, we collapsed into the van and drove into Swansea. Then, halfway through our sound check at the Valbonne Nite Spot, our PA died. The amplifier, like our van, simply stopped working. The music shops were closed, and there wasn't a PA amplifier to be hired or borrowed in all of Wales. We had to cancel the gig.

Mark tried to get some money out of the Valbonne for our pains, but he was threatened with physical violence. Now we were stranded in Swansea, with even less money, and no more hash. But no one could face another night in the van, so we found the cheapest bed-and-breakfast in town, which turned out to be a doss-house. We all slept in the same room, along with half a dozen assorted meths drinkers and down-and-outs. It was like being in some sordid Eastern European hospital ward. My bed was not a bed at all, but a hard, narrow couch next to a drafty window. I hardly slept. All night I listened to snoring, muttering, whimpering, bronchitic wheezing, and appalling, gut-wrenching coughs, and wondered if this was how I was going to end up. It didn't smell too good, either.

After breakfast (one greasy egg apiece, white bread, and margarine) we drove out into the valleys, to the Resolven Rugby Club, to beg for mercy. The DJ said we could plug our PA speakers into his amplifier. We must have gotten down on our knees and kissed his hands. The PA kept feeding back and sounded dreadful, and the sleepy Sunday crowd wasn't exactly thrilled by our rather anemic performance (we'd hardly eaten in three days), but at least we had forty pounds towards the van repairs.

That night, we drove all the way back to Gosport and, in the early morning light, unloaded all our gear into Dave's living room. Then, while I slept far into Monday afternoon, Dave and Graham had to drive the U-Haul van back to Bristol. They got there to find that our own van wasn't ready yet. They couldn't afford to get a train back, so they had to hitch their way home.

Still fancy a career in music?

I don't particularly like giving advice, but since I'm occasionally asked for it by budding musicians, I have two pieces to offer. The first is: Read the above, and imagine that this kind of thing will happen to you, over and over again, with no money and no guarantees of it ever getting better. Convince yourself, in fact, that the odds are overwhelmingly on the side of abject failure. Then ask yourself if you still want to do it. The answer has to be yes. If not, do yourself a favor: Go to law school.

The second piece of advice I'll get to later.

The Worst Job I Ever Had

After three years, my troubled relationship with the Royal Academy of Music came to an end. I took my final exam in percussion, which was a troubling experience in itself. In the Academy's concert hall, a panel of three professors sat at a table in front of me. Alone on the stage, surrounded by percussion instruments, I played a Bach violin piece on the xylophone and a Timpani sonata by some obscure dead Russian. I was sure I'd failed, and that I deserved to fail, since I wasn't even really a percussionist anyway. In fact I passed, and I was now entitled to use the letters L.R.A.M. (Licentiate of the Royal Academy of Music) after my name.

I didn't know how to feel about this. I was pleased but also somehow embarrassed, and I probably pretended to be scornful of the whole business. A struggling rock songwriter and keyboardist with a degree in percussion. It was too ridiculous.

After the percussion exam, I had another couple of months to go at the Academy, including a final yearly theory exam, which was not compulsory and didn't lead to any further qualifications. So, I thought, why stay? I didn't even have any friends there. All around me was a frantic buzz of fellow students talking about applying for a fourth year. They were all terrified at the thought of having to work for a living. I, on the other hand, took a last look around and walked out for good.

Not that I wasn't nervous about making a living. There would be no more grant money, no more rail passes, and precious little money from the band, either. And as much as I'd come to like London, it didn't look like I'd be spending much time there in the near future.

Ironically, I played my first London gigs around this time: my only gigs with the National Youth Jazz Orchestra. Two of them were at the theater where we rehearsed, and one in an enormous pub somewhere in the suburbs. Two of them I played on piano; on the third, I played vibes. It was the only gig on which I ever put my percussion skills to use. There were no charts for vibes. I doubled the written bits of the piano or guitar parts. It was enjoyably inconspicuous, until Bill Ashton suddenly pointed dramatically at me: I had to take a solo. Panicking, not really knowing the chords, I flailed wildly—my solo must have sounded like a dozen milk bottles falling down several flights of stairs.

Jill was in the audience, having come up to London for the day. London was like Disneyland to Jill, and her childlike excitement ("Oh my God! Is that the *real* Big Ben?") was sometimes sweet, sometimes embarrassing. I tried to imagine us living together in London, and somehow I couldn't. Did we have a future together, anywhere? I decided to think about it—in the future.

Back in Gosport, I weighed my options, which were few. I was broke; I was making only a few pounds a week from the band; but I was dedicated to the band, so I couldn't look for other gigs. I might be able to get a few pounds from Social Security. But I needed more, because I couldn't bear to stay with my parents any longer, especially now I wasn't going to be spending part of each week in London. Jill and I agreed: We should have our own place. We were tired of having sex in bushes or the back of the van. We looked at ads in the paper and estate agent windows. Flats were expensive. There was only one thing for it: I was going to have to get a job.

What kind of job could I possibly get? My bandmates Dave and Graham were working as groundsmen, Graham at a Fareham school and Dave at the technical college. They were lucky. They worked unsupervised and could leave work early for gigs. Mark, as far as I can remember, was on the dole. But I wasn't eligible for the dole, having never officially "worked," and even the thought of a "cushy" job like Dave's and Graham's was horrifying. I decided to try some temporary work, a little bit here and there, the minimum I could get by on.

I went to the Manpower office in Fareham. A polite but bored man took down some details, then asked me if I had any skills.

"Yes," I said, "I can play the piano!"

The bored man gave me a long look, completely, unnervingly devoid of expression. Then he turned back to his papers and wrote, with great deliberation: UNSKILLED.

A couple of days later I was sent out with two other guys in a van, delivering soft drinks to pubs and restaurants for Schweppes. We worked like madmen, lugging crates and sweating like pigs for hours on end without a break. I could barely keep up. This went on until about three o'clock, when the two guys drove the van down to Southsea seafront, changed into swimsuits, put knotted handkerchiefs on their heads, and flopped onto the beach. I hung around, not quite sure what was going on.

"How long are we going to break?" I asked.

The two guys laughed.

"We're done, mate," said one. "We always try to get it all done in one go, as fast as we can, then we come to the beach."

The following week, an electronics factory somewhere outside Fareham hired me and a few other people from Manpower to clean up the place for an impending inspection by the Big Boss. It was slave labor, without proper tools, scraping fag-ends and ring-pulls out of the dirt with our bare hands. It was also hot as hell and I got painful blisters and splinters in my hands.

Around this time, my dad's friend Uncle George, who'd helped to haul my first piano into the house at Paulsgrove, was killed in a freak accident. For some reason he was sitting in his car in a carbreakers' yard, when some monstrous machine picked up his car and crushed it, with him still in it. It was like a sick joke, the kind of thing you just couldn't force yourself to believe. My mother cried hysterically when we heard the news, and I went out for a long walk. When I finally got tired and sat down on the grass, I looked around and realized I was in a cemetery. It felt as though somebody wanted to make good and sure that I took this close encounter with death seriously.

My father, I think, took it very seriously indeed. George was probably his closest friend, and after his death, he didn't seem to make any more. Over the years, he became more and more isolated, disappearing into his own solitary world. He became more and more of a mystery to everyone around him, and probably even to himself.

And after Death: Insanity. Manpower came up with a job that I was told I could keep, if I wanted. It was at Knowle Hospital, a mental institution north of Fareham. Until then I'd only known of it from local folklore and schoolboy jokes.

"Don't worry," said the bored man, "you won't have to deal with the loonies." It was a nice clean job, he said. In the laundry room.

I caught the special bus that left Fareham bus station for Knowle every morning. When I found the laundry department, I was greeted—if that's the right word—by an old lobster called Fred, who wore overalls, red rubber boots, and a permanent scowl. My job was to help him sort out the dirty laundry and take it through to the next room to be washed.

The reason for Fred's scowl soon became obvious. Truckloads of dirty sheets and clothes arrived every couple of hours, to be thrown into a big, hot, stuffy barn of a room, where they piled up to the ceiling. Fred and I had to plough through them, in rubber gloves and boots, and no matter how hard we worked, there was always a mountain in front of us; we never caught up. This was bad enough, but the stuff we had to sort out made the job unbearable. There were sheets reeking of urine, towels that had been used to mop up blood and vomit, and pajamas with turds and used tampons lurking inside them. Fred cursed and grumbled the whole time. He'd been doing this for years, and he'd never gotten used to it.

When we stopped for a break, Fred would drink tea, smoke roll-ups, and grumble some more. I didn't blame him. Our one other coworker didn't help. He was a tall blond guy, about my age, who had the relatively luxurious job of receiving the sorted laundry from me and Fred and putting it in the washing machines, and he was the polar opposite of Fred. He was coping quite well with all this, and anything else the world might throw at him, by being a born-again Christian. He rode cheerily into work every morning on a bright yellow bicycle with THE JESUS BIKE painted on the side, along with a few decals of suns with smiling faces. Conversation with him was impossible. He had no opinion on anything unless Jesus had an opinion on it, in which case he'd be sure to tell us what Jesus's opinion was. Fred was possibly the most miserable man I've ever met, but somehow even he was better company than this smiling zombie.

The routine was broken now and again by mental patients who would wander in and try to talk to us as we worked. They twitched and drooled and blathered away in languages of their own invention. I was always relieved when men in white coats appeared and dragged them away.

At the end of the day, I had to fight my way through crowds of milling lunatics to the bus—where another lunatic would grab me by the elbow and insist on "helping me on." Finally, on the way back to Fareham, I had to listen to various nurses and orderlies giving accounts of the day, which at that point I could have done without.

Naming the Worst Gig I've Ever Done is a tough one, but this was without a doubt The Worst Job I Ever Had. I stuck it out for a week, although the job was apparently mine for life, if I wanted it. I could have inherited Fred's rubber boots. I could still be there now.

After this, I stopped returning Manpower's phone calls. I went on Social Security, and Jill started working at the Ultra electronics factory in Gosport, packing TV sets in boxes. This was slave labor, too, but she had more patience for slave labor than I had. Maybe *she* could be the breadwinner.

Soon after, I got home late from a gig and was astonished to find a note from my mother: Jill and I had a flat.

My mum had heard about a cheap place through a friend, and gone with Jill and Jill's mother, Millie, to check it out. Apparently it was as clear to my parents as it was to me that I had to go. Perhaps more surprisingly, Jill's parents felt the same way. Jill was only sixteen, but Millie told my mother that she had to let her go. If you don't let them go, she said, they'll never come back. These two self-effacing women, very much alike, had more wisdom than we gave them credit for.

The "flat," in Shaftesbury Road, Gosport, was actually the top floor of a terraced house belonging to a widow by the name of Mrs. Diffey. There was a tiny bedroom, a tiny living room, and a kitchen with a bathtub in the middle of it. We shared the downstairs toilet. The rent was £7.50 per week, which Jill paid. Whatever money I had went on food and drink. We had just enough for a couple of drinks at the local pub, and an occasional indulgence in a new passion: Indian food. Second-rate, greasy Gosport Indian food, but oh, so tasty.

I became a sort of part-time househusband. If I wasn't already on my way to Lytchett Matravers or Poole when Jill got home, exhausted, from the factory, I'd have a cup of tea and a bowl of hot water waiting for her, and she would soak her feet while watching *Crossroads*. I did the shopping. Sometimes, when money was particularly tight, I resorted once again to petty crime. I would slip half the groceries into my bag at the local Waitrose, and take the rest to the checkout, to avoid suspicion. A feeble ploy, but it actually worked every time.

I also cooked ghastly vegetarian meals—nut roasts and lentil pies. I was a terrible cook, but Jill was impossible. On the one occasion I remember her making dinner, she burned the toast and got all the beans stuck to the pan.

Quite often I wouldn't see Jill until two or three in the morning, when I got home from a gig. She would always wake up and we would make love until four or five. It was as though we were making up for lost time, or trying to make the most of whatever time we were going to have.

Jill and I lived together in blissful squalor for nine months. We had only just enough money to get by, but it was one of the best times of my life. I can't say that I've experienced either out-and-out destitution or fabulous wealth. But I've gone from having barely enough to being quite comfortable, and I know for a fact that money doesn't buy love, or happiness, or friends, or a good laugh, and it certainly can't bring back the dead.

People don't like to hear this from successful people (or people who look successful to them). It's comforting to blame your troubles on whatever you don't have. It's only when you *get* it, whatever "it" is, and find yourself miserable, that you start to realize there might be a bit more to it.

It must be one of God's little jokes. The world is full of people who worship money and slave joylessly, year after year, trying to make it—but never do. And then there's me, who hardly even thought about it, doing very nicely, thank you. But if I've been lucky, it's not so much because I made money, as because life seemed pretty rich to me without it.

What Does it Mean?

THE SUN IS setting prettily over Portsmouth Harbor, and I'm listening to a string quartet by Shostakovich: his Second. I bought a little place here a while back. I'd gone too long without a UK base, and my resistance to the idea of reestablishing myself in my home town finally crumbled. I never quite managed to become a one hundred percent, year-round New Yorker, and nowadays I like to say I'm bicoastal. Not New York and (probably the only place I truly detest) LA—but New York and Pompey.

Right now, though, listening to Shostakovich, I'm thinking of Russia. In 1996 I finally went there, and after soaking up some of the atmosphere of that troubled country—tragic, exhilarating, and surreal—this fascinating composer moves me even more.

The people I met in Moscow, the precarious way they lived, people in their thirties and forties, reminded me of how I lived with Jill in Gosport at twenty, in Shaftesbury Road, with the bathtub in the kitchen. Some of them were well-established literary and theater types, whose Western counterparts might have lived comfortably in Hampstead or Greenwich Village—but these Russian "intellectuals" lived in the same filthy communal apartment buildings as everyone else, eating sour cucumbers and drinking vodka out of ring-pull cans.

They were all passionate about art and poetry and music. In the West we tend to think of art as a pleasant accessory, something to add to our lives once we've achieved a decent standard of living. In Russia I saw the opposite. In a harsh and uncertain world, art was vitally important. It was like a flame that had to be kept burning, no matter what. In a metro station I saw a shabbily dressed string octet playing with a passion and commitment you don't often see at Carnegie Hall. In a gray and smoky café I saw a gypsy violinist playing like a man possessed, as though the Devil himself were behind him, jabbing with his pitchfork. The music, I sensed, was more real to them than "real life" was, and I could relate to that.

The Russians are a slobbish and disorganized lot, but when they make up their minds to do something, they really go for it. Drinking is another of their talents, and another thing about my Russian visit that reminded me of Portsmouth. If drinking was an Olympic event, the Russians would win the gold and silver every time. But a team of Pompey sailors could probably give them a run for their money for the bronze.

Sailors were everywhere in Portsmouth and Gosport. They were a distinct and separate species, though, at a time when just about everyone else over sixteen was either a "hairy" or a skinhead. They had their own style, and I saw echoes of that in Moscow, too: baggy trousers with enormous waistbands, shirts with enormous collars, tank tops and tattoos. I observed sailors like a baffled anthropologist. What made them tick? What did they believe in?

For that matter, what did I believe in? I think we're all, whether we admit it or not, looking for something that will give our life some *meaning*. The half-hearted Anglicanism of my childhood had failed to make much of an impression, and at twenty I considered myself a heathen. In fact I was a pilgrim, dedicated to the service of something larger than myself, something that transcended the mundane material world, something that could still fill me with awe. Music was my Christ on the cross, my Wailing Wall, my Mecca. A universe in which music existed could not be evil.

It wasn't until I experienced the atmosphere of an Orthodox church in Moscow, that I could imagine any of these feelings arising out of religious faith. In Russia, the faith was so intense that people either had to banish it with great force—as the communists did—or just throw themselves into it, for better or worse.

Shostakovich claimed to be an atheist, but possibly only a Russian atheist could be so deeply spiritual and still deny it. I once had a vivid dream about him. He was smoking a *papiros*—a nasty cheap Russian cigarette—and beckoning me to follow him, somewhere.

What does it mean?

I think dreams always have meaning. Sometimes the meaning is obvious; sometimes it eludes us; and sometimes we get it, intuitively, but we can't really put it into words.

The same can be said of music, which, more often than not, follows the logic of dreams. A Mozart concerto can be meaningful without telling a literal story, or making a political statement, or expounding on a particular philosophy. It has meaning on its own abstract terms, a meaning that we grasp more by feeling and intuition than by rational thought, and the experience can be profoundly satisfying, even healing. I think this was what Stravinsky was getting at in his famous comment about music being powerless to express anything *other than itself.*

On the other hand, there *are* composers whose music is full of philosophical ideas, coded messages, and symbolism. Rather than clinging to some preconception of what music can or can't, should or shouldn't do, I say we may as well at least try to meet them on their own terms. Mahler is a good example of this type of composer, and Shostakovich is another. Both used words and voices to convey specific ideas. But even in their instrumental music, they're always trying to tell us something.

Which brings me back to Shostakovich's Second Quartet, the second movement of which is called "Recitative and Romance." A recitative is a piece of sung narration, not quite a full-blown song, which comes in between arias and choruses in an opera, or especially, in an oratorio. You can hear quite a few recitatives in Handel's *Messiah,* for instance. They're punctuated now and again by characteristic chords: in harmonic terms, simple cadences—tonic seventh to subdominant, dominant seventh, tonic.

This is exactly what Shostakovich does in this movement. The second violin, viola, and cello create a backdrop that could have come straight out of a Handel oratorio or a Bach cantata. But the "recitative" itself, "sung"—or rather, declaimed—by the first violin, sounds distinctly Jewish. Proud, passionate, but melancholy, it's explicitly based on traditional Jewish scales.

Bach would never have thought of this. Shostakovich has put a cantor in the cathedral, and he's challenging us to ask why. Does it work, or doesn't it? Can there be a rapport, a solidarity, between different religious traditions?

Then comes the "Romance," a gentle, consoling melody that seems to say: Don't worry about it, relax, life can be beautiful. But there's a restlessness here, too, and soon the music grows more and more dissonant, until it reaches an anguished climax. The cello, soaring high into the treble clef, seems to be screaming in agony. But the tension subsides, and we're back to the opening oratoriolike chords. Now, though, the violin recitative has taken on an air of tragic defiance. Time seems to stand still. We feel as though this solitary violin could spin out its sad tale forever. Then, a masterstroke: The violin plays its last phrase entirely on the G string—giving it a darker color—and *muted*. I have to be quiet now, it seems to say; I have to hide my sorrow, and step back into the shadows. And the rest of the quartet ends the movement softly with a formal Bachian "amen" cadence, almost as though nothing had really happened.

Of course, this is all pretty subjective, and someone else's interpretation may be different from mine. But I think I'm on the right track, and I don't think there's any doubt that a subjective, emotional response is what Shostakovich wants. And if you're still not convinced that this music has meaning, consider when and where it was written: the Soviet Union in 1944. Anti-Semitism was virtually an official government policy, and despite being on the opposite side, Stalin was only too happy to help Hitler out when it came to the "Jewish Problem." Uncle Joe had his beady eye on Shostakovich, too. The composer lived in constant fear. Many of his friends had been shot or dragged off to Siberia. For a long time, Shostakovich kept a suitcase packed and ready by the door. Often in his music there are long, lonely, rather empty passages, with an underlying tension that never seems to resolve. I sometimes think it's the sound of insomnia.

In the Second Quartet, Shostakovich created a powerful musical drama, which would have been intensely moving to his audience. But in drawing explicitly on Jewish folk style, he was also making a statement of compassion and principle that took enormous courage.

I find all this incredibly inspiring. I know that plenty of people wouldn't. Too gloomy, they'd say, or too complicated. They probably wouldn't go to see *Hamlet* because they've heard it doesn't have a happy ending. Maybe you either get it or you don't.

Either way, this just isn't the kind of thing you *discuss* in English working-class circles. Portsmouth now has less sailors and more students, and where there was once just fish and chips and greasy curries, there are now Thai restaurants and tapas bars. But there are still doors—doors in people's minds—that are supposed to stay closed. Even now, my background makes me suspicious of "arty" people. It came as a shock to meet those Russians, who were more rooted in a gritty and impoverished reality than I was in Paulsgrove, and to find that they wanted to stay up all night quoting Pushkin and discussing, with burning intensity, the meaning of life. In some ways, I felt like I'd finally met my true peers.

At twenty, I was becoming so blindly submerged in the pop world that it would be years before I'd listen to anything like a Shostakovich quartet again, let alone ponder deeper philosophical questions, about music or anything else. And quite apart from the dictates of class and fashion, it's a sad irony that I'd been further alienated from "classical" music by the very thing that should have made it more alive than ever: my time at the Royal Academy of Music.

The burning questions in my musical life would now be things like: What shall I wear on stage? Which song should be the single? Shall we split the money from this gig, or put it towards a new PA amplifier?

This doesn't mean I'd become shallow. I was a certain age in a certain place at a certain time, doing the best I could. My passion for music was very much alive. It was just the outer form that changed, like a snake shedding its skin, and there were quite a few changes yet to come. And if Edward Bear wasn't plumbing musical depths, life was getting richer and stranger all the time.

The summer of 1975 would contain a number of notable events. Some of them were so rich and strange that I can hardly believe they happened even now.

Ladies' Problems

RIGHT AFTER the Welsh Tour debacle, Clive Bates sat in on a soundcheck and blew us all away. We couldn't really afford a fifth member, but we had to have Clive.

Clive had several nicknames: "the Whistling Plumber," because of his day job, and his talent for melodious whistling; "Plunger Bates," for obvious reasons; and "Buggsy," for a protruding front tooth. It was "Buggsy" that stuck, maybe because there was also something dark and gangsterish about him. He was a quiet, mysterious character, quite a few years older than the rest of us, who rarely uttered a word unless it was absolutely necessary. To this day I'm not sure whether Clive was a man of rare spiritual depth, or whether the lights were on but no one was home. One thing was for sure, though: He was a great rock 'n' roll guitarist.

Clive played with an urgency that immediately turned up the intensity of the whole band by several notches. He was a technically accomplished player who practiced classical and flamenco pieces on acoustic guitar in his spare time. But he also drew tough, gritty sounds from a Gibson SG, and he could actually be trusted to take a solo. He was in a different league from Mark, although Mark would have been the first to admit it. It wasn't playing that interested Mark, but writing songs and being a performer. Now he could concentrate on being the star of the show.

Clive made his debut on a gig at the Checquers Inn. Freed for a good part of the evening from the restricting role of guitarist, Mark climbed on top of the PA speakers, threw tambourines, leapt into the audience, and generally posed outrageously. It was great fun. Mark was a good poser, and the band felt like an enormous, throbbing machine behind him, flexing muscles it never knew it had.

I sold my Pianet and bought a synthesizer. A nasty, cheesy little thing it was, too: an early Korg, with a three-octave keyboard and red and blue knobs. It made sounds that all the subsequent digital technology in the world could not reproduce, and probably wouldn't want to either. I wish now that I'd kept it, if only to have it stuffed and mounted as a trophy. But it sounded good at the time, and some of the sounds it made in combination with Clive's guitar would, I'm sure, still sound impressively nasty today.

Edward Bear—the name, impossibly, was still clinging to us like a bad smell—was starting to find an identity. Our influences, at least, were pretty clear. There was the Alex Harvey Band, whom we'd all seen two or three times and loved for their combination of toughness and campy humor. Then there were bands on the emerging "pub rock" scene in London: Brinsley Schwartz, Eddie and the Hot Rods, and especially Dr. Feelgood. We played a couple of the Feelgood's songs, and looked for similar ones to cover: aggressive, but with a touch of humor. Gradually the style of the cover versions we played started to mesh with the style of our own songs—or vice versa.

A couple of other elements were thrown into the mix, too. There was Dave Cairns's funk-influenced drumming, which, now that I think about it, was quite original in the context of a hard-edged rock band. It's only been picked up on more recently, by people like Living Color and the Red Hot Chili Peppers. Then there were my jazz-influenced chords and a way of weaving boogie woogie piano runs in and out of the arrangements, in which I'd been heavily influenced by Bill Payne of Little Feat.

Whatever uniqueness the band possessed, though, was nothing compared to what took place on the occasion of Buggsy Bates's third gig.

We were scheduled to play Nero's, on Southsea front: Portsmouth's premier night spot. The plushest disco in town, it was considered a prestigious gig, despite a predictable indifference toward live music on the part of its clientele. Our gig was more or less an audition. We were booked to play one short set, with the possibility of a "real" booking later if they liked us.

It was a Saturday, so everyone was picked up from their homes. Graham's wife Julie always came out to the van to see him off, often with a packed lunch for the journey. Not today.

"Where's Julie?" asked Dave.

Graham sighed wearily and said, "Ladies' problems."

Whatever had been happening at home, Graham seemed to be happy, for once, to be on his way to a disco.

Nero's had two stages, at opposite ends of the club, one for bands and the other for the DJ, who was known as Merrick. Merrick was a big name in Portsmouth, and he presided over Nero's, appropriately, like a decadent Roman emperor. He wielded absolute power, and he'd been known to pull the plug on bands he didn't like.

At soundcheck, Merrick looked at us with barely concealed hostility. Basically, he didn't believe in bands. We didn't much like the look of him either. He wore a velvet tuxedo with a shirt open almost to the waist, and a big gold medallion nestled in his luxuriant chest hair. If he'd been dressed like this as a joke, we would have respected him. But Merrick was dead serious.

Clive, in a rare outburst, summed up the situation by dubbing him "a greasy twat." Our stages faced each other like two warships waiting for the order to commence battle.

After soundcheck we went downstairs to the Gaiety Bar, which faced South Parade Pier from beneath the disco. We drank nervously, anticipating a tough night, and argued, not for the first time, about whether we should even be playing this kind of place at all. Then the barman announced there was a phone call for a Mr. Graham Maby.

Graham picked up the phone and an unfamiliar voice said: "Is that Graham Maby?"

"Yes, who's this?"

"I'm a neighbor of yours. Your wife's just had a baby."

Graham's mind went blank for a moment. Then he said:

"I think there must be some mistake."

"There's no mistake," said the neighbor. "Your wife Julie has just had a baby."

"But she wasn't even pregnant!"

The neighbor laughed. "I'm telling you, mate, she's just had a baby, and you'd better get over here!"

Graham came back to the bar looking seriously ill. Every milliliter of blood had drained from his face.

"What happened?" we gasped in unison.

"I'm a dad!" said Graham. He had to repeat this a couple of times. Then he went over to a corner of the bar and lay on the floor.

In the panic that followed, Graham's friend Pete Watkins, who was our current roadie, had the presence of mind to drag Graham to his feet and into the van. After promising to return or at least phone before show-time, they roared off to Gosport.

The rest of us ordered more drinks and discussed the situation. The more we discussed it, the less believable it seemed. We didn't know it was even theoretically possible for a woman to be pregnant for eight or nine months without knowing it; for her to continue to have periods, for the baby not to show, for her to be in complete denial about whatever other symptoms she might have had. But all the one-in-a-million circumstances had come together in this case, and Graham did indeed have a completely unplanned and unexpected son.

There didn't seem to be much hope of playing a gig that night, but in the meantime there was nothing we could do except wait and drink. Time seemed to stand still, except that somehow we still got drunk.

Graham arrived in Gosport to find no trace of his wife and child. They'd been taken to St. Mary's Hospital in Portsmouth. Graham had probably passed them in the van on the way over. He called the hospital: They were doing just fine. So he came back to Nero's, and since it was almost time to go on stage, he decided to do the gig before going to the hospital.

So a slightly shaky and none-too-sober Edward Bear took the stage. We played three songs to polite, scattered applause. Then, a gamble: We'd decided to do our a cappella number early in the set, to force some kind of a reaction. Clive, who couldn't sing, had been talked by Mark into doing a whistling solo. But whistling over a microphone is tricky. Something about this particular kind of air pressure tends to distort the sound. So instead of Clive's usual sweet piping tone, with its sensuous vibrato, which had provoked side-splitting stoned laughter and wild applause in the van, the audience heard a sound like a giant farting steam train.

As soon as the song ended—before the audience even had time to react—the club filled with deafening disco music. Merrick's voice boomed over the PA, sarcastically thanking us, and all the power lights on our amps blinked off. The bastard had done it again! After four songs!

Edward Bear immediately split into three factions. Dave and Clive struggled to restrain Mark as he ploughed through the crowd towards Merrick with murderous intent. Graham and Pete Watkins rushed to St. Mary's Hospital. I went back to the bar.

We didn't hear from Graham for a few days, but we saw him in the *Evening News.* The day after Nero's, he was walking down Station Road in Gosport carrying two bunches of flowers, which he'd bought for the two ladies from across the street who'd assisted at the birth. A car pulled up next to him and a woman wound down the window and said, "You must be Graham Maby!"

She was a reporter, and she wanted to interview him. Graham, obliging as always, invited her into his flat and made her a cup of tea. The headline the next day read: 8 LB. 3 OZ. SURPRISE FOR JULIE.

> 'We had absolutely no idea that my wife, Julie, was expecting,' a flabbergasted Mr. Graham Maby said yesterday. 'My wife is very small and she thought she had a bit of a weight problem, but no one else had noticed it.'

An ambulanceman is quoted as saying "that young lady will certainly have to do some instant knitting," and there's also a garbled quote in which Graham seems to be claiming that the relative ease of the birth was somehow connected to the fact that both parents were vegetarians.

The kid was named Christopher, and we carried on gigging. Shortly after Graham and Julie's brush with fame, though, it was the band's turn.

Andy Arthurs and Steve Stevenson got us a deal with MAM Records.

It wasn't quite as exciting as it might sound. Firstly, MAM wasn't the ideal label. They were too "poppy," and they had no acts we admired—their biggest seller was Gilbert O'Sullivan. Secondly, we wouldn't actually be signed to MAM, but to Glamswell, Steve and Andy's production company, who in turn had their own deal with MAM. And thirdly, no one was talking about making an album. The deal was for two singles.

Still, a two-single deal was what the Beatles started with. This could be our big break. At worst, we'd be getting a foot in the door. Steve Stevenson came down from London and we met him in one of the hotels on Southsea front to sign the contract. The mood was celebratory, although

Dave Cairns muttered something here and there about how we should be signing a *proper* recording contract. He was quite right, but the rest of us felt that we should grab any opportunity that came our way, and in retrospect I think we were right, too. I've seen too many people hold out for years for the *right* break, and just fade away waiting, sinking into bitter resentment. If you're going to be a cynic, better to be cynical about what was, or is, than what might have been.

I've also seen people struggle for years to get a recording contract and become more single-mindedly obsessive than it's healthy for anyone to be, about anything. As with money, it's too easy to convince yourself that the one thing you don't have is the thing that would make everything right with the world.

The reality is that, like having a baby, getting a recording contract can be just the beginning of a whole new set of problems.

Arms and Legs

In August, Jill and I scraped together as much money as we could, and with some help from friends and families, threw a party on board the *Gay Enterprise*, a harbor ferry (more recently renamed the *Solent Enterprise*) that was available for hire. The tenth of August was Jill's seventeenth birthday, and the eleventh was my twenty-first.

I also scraped some money together to buy Jill several presents, including a mystery parcel of lingerie, which, despite my protestations, she insisted on opening in front of her parents. As I hid my face in my hands, she tore open the package and held up a pair of black crotchless panties. Percy Maby, sitting in his usual eating-peanuts-and-farting chair, roared with laughter.

"Corr, look at that, Jill!" he said. "Just what you always wanted, eh? *A Batman mask!*"

The party was a great success, with live music all night. Edward Bear played, of course, and Drew Barfield came down from London with his band John Doe, which now featured Steve Tatler as second guitarist and vocalist. It was a hell of a party, and I don't know when I've ever been so deliriously happy. There are only a few times in our lives when the line on the graph is going steadily upward, and everything seems to be falling into place.

Then the line started to flatten out. The first hurdle came when Steve Stevenson discovered a Canadian band by the name of Edward Bear. The poor buggers, he said, had made at least one album. If we were going to sign a contract, we'd have to find a new name, and fast. No one had ever liked "Edward Bear"; we'd just stopped thinking about it. There was a fresh eruption of suggestions, but once again we couldn't agree on anything. At the last minute we came up with a compromise: the pathetically awful "Edwin Bear."

Why we couldn't find anything better than this, I can't imagine. But Edwin Bear we were, for a couple of months, during which we recorded a handful of songs for MAM. The first session was at AIR Studios, where Jeff Beck was recording in the next room. We never saw or heard him. But he was *there.*

Soon we had another problem: No one could decide what our first single should be. We recorded "Any More Wine," the song that had started all this, but it didn't turn out so well, and we were concerned that it wasn't representative of the band.

What's a newly signed band to do? Release the catchiest song, the easiest song to promote, the one that comes closest to what's currently popular? Or stick to your guns and make a statement, and put out whatever you feel is your best and most distinctive effort? In either case, who has the last word?

Then there was controversy over some of Mark's lyrics. "Any More Wine" included the lines "I'll tell you a story that's going round my head / it starts with a glass / and ends with us in bed." Steve thought this was risqué enough to keep us off of Radio One. After much debate, the last line was changed to the feeble "ends with us bein' wed."

After "Any More Wine" we recorded "Janie," a catchy new song of Mark's, and a song that Andy brought in, called "Heat of the Night," by Paul Nicholas, who'd just had a hit and was therefore thought to have the magic touch. The song wasn't bad, and suited the band well enough. Maybe some of the magic would rub off on us. But did we really want our first release to be someone else's song?

We also recorded two of my songs: "Boogie Woogie Joe" and "She'll Surprise You," which was inspired by my girlfriend and bore a passing resemblance to Steely Dan's "Rikki Don't Lose That Number." This probably wasn't very representative of the direction we were taking, either, but I was getting a definite feeling that my songs were going to end up as B sides, if anything. Alan Matthews and Steve Stevenson both argued that the focus should be on Mark. I agreed, up to a point. He was the star. But surely my *songs* were just as good as his? I found out later that there was an ongoing debate about who was the real talent in the band, with Andy voting for me, but Steve and Alan on Mark's side.

No one, except maybe Jill, saw that I was seething with frustration. I was in an impossible bind: I had to confront Mark, before my position in the band was steamrollered away. But how could I risk splitting the band, just when we were getting somewhere?

Mark trumped me by calling a "band meeting" at a Gosport coffee shop.

"I want more control of the band," he announced.

I wanted to pour his coffee over his head.

"What exactly does that mean?" I asked.

"I don't think we're going to get anywhere with two leaders," said Mark. "We have to be focused." He did seem focused, but just a bit nervous; this wasn't easy for him either.

"Look," I said, "you're the front man, that's fine. I just want an equal share of the songwriting. That was the idea all along, wasn't it?"

"Mark's songs are more commercial, though," said the practical Dave Cairns.

"That might be true, but Joe's can be album tracks," said the diplomatic Graham Maby.

"Yeh," said Clive.

"Of course," said Mark. "But for now, the focus should be on me. Alan and Steve both think so."

"What about Andy?" I protested.

"I'm more interested in what Steve thinks."

"Why? What's so great about him?"

"Steve Stevenson," said Mark with conviction, "has got *style*."

"Style?" For some reason this infuriated me. "Andy Arthurs is a recording engineer, and a producer, and a musician, and he knows how to write a song. Don't you think that's a bit more *real?*"

"Yeah, well, I'll go for the superficiality every time," said Mark.

So what you're saying, I thought, is that I haven't got style, and what I *do* have isn't important. I fumed, but I didn't back down, and the meeting ended in an inconclusive truce. It would have to be renewed on a day-to-day basis, while the rest of the band, not wanting to take sides, tiptoed nervously around us.

It helped that our prospects seemed to be constantly improving. There was a definite buzz around the band, and an article appeared in the *Evening News,* with the headline: Edwin Bear Out to Put Portsmouth on the Map. The writing was of the expected standard:

> Memo to radio producers: watch out—for Edwin Bear are out to prove they are not a fluffy local band of no substance . . . their music is not just bare bones, they manage to stuff it with living marrow.

The attention to detail was not much better:

> The lead singer Clive Bates has an aggressive vocal style, as he struts around the stage claiming his territory.

Clive was also named later in the same article as the lead guitarist.

By now we were regularly packing out quite a few venues, and obviously building a following. We played regularly at the Checquers, and the Badger Bar in Bournemouth, a cellar club where a studenty crowd would sit on the floor. Normally, to save money at gigs, I brought a couple of bottles of cheap supermarket cider along with me, but the Badger Bar's excellent beer was refining my tastes in the direction of real ale.

Then there was the John Peel in Gosport. They booked all kinds of people now. I saw a heavy metal band there called Snot, who had their own lights, all of which were green. The singer wore nothing but a pair of skintight leather pants and threw himself maniacally around the stage, shaking his shoulder-length black hair, until it suddenly fell off. He was an off-duty sailor wearing a wig.

We stole some lights of our own from a disco somewhere along the way, four light-boxes with a little control panel that turned them on and off. No faders. I operated them from behind my keyboards while playing, which reminded me of playing all the percussion parts—all those years ago!—in the Schools Orchestra.

I also had a brief reunion with the violin. I took some lessons from a woman in Fareham and attached a cheap pickup to the bridge. The pickup didn't work very well, and my playing was shaky, but it seemed to add a bit more color here and there.

Mark was more and more confident in his starring role. He seemed to have a rare sort of charisma, the sort that men find amusing and women find sexy. On more than one occasion I had to pretend to be asleep in the front of the van while he wrestled with some groupie in the back. Mark also redefined his image. He cut his hair very short and wore an impressive silver dagger earring which skewered, rather than dangled from, the earlobe. Apart from a touch of eyeliner, the glitter was gone, and he dressed in dungarees, with bare feet. He looked like a pirate, or some kind of louche sailor gone AWOL in Jacques Brel's Amsterdam. The look, simultaneously tough and slightly kitsch, was perfect for the band.

Not everyone got it, though. Some time in early 1976 we walked on stage at a pub called the Old Ash Tree in Chatham, Kent, and saw a sea of skinheads in front of us. Right from the start, they objected to Mark. What was this bloke doing with short hair, mascara, and no Dr. Martens? They jeered and threatened, but Mark played his part to the hilt, daring them to do something about it. Halfway through the set, the atmosphere was unbearably tense, and Mark pushed too hard. He pointed at a skinhead in the audience, and the skinhead responded by climbing onto the stage and punching him in the face.

Once again, an Edward, or Edwin, Bear gig suddenly exploded into a fight scene from a bad Western. Mark disappeared into the crowd and a glittering shower of beer glasses rained onto us. I looked down and saw broken glass and blood on my keyboards. I'd been cut, but I was too shocked to feel it. As Mark managed to climb back onto the stage, we ran for our lives—except for Clive, who for some reason stood rooted to the spot. And as the glasses, bottles, and garbage kept coming, nothing hit him. It was as though he was surrounded by a Star Trek force-field. Finally he turned around, noticed that the stage was empty, and ran.

As we hid in the beer cellar, the manager appeared and astonished us by asking us to go back on. It's not hard to guess how we responded. From then on this place would be known as "The Old Ash Tray." It could have been worse. As on other gigs where "trouble" had broken out, we escaped with only minor cuts and bruises.

It was taking forever to get a record out, but finally a consensus was reached: The first single would be Mark's "Janie," with my "She'll Surprise You" as the B side, and a release date was set for April '76. Steve and Andy were lobbying to change the band's name again before then. Andy suggested "Arms and Legs." No one particularly liked it, but no one had a better idea.

Dave Cairns got us our last gig as Edwin Bear, or any kind of Bear, at Fareham Technical College. We were paid the princely sum of twenty pounds, and one of our PA speakers fell off the stage onto the head of a girl who was happily dancing in the front, knocking her senseless. The following week "Janie" was released, and we played a promotional show at the Tricorn in Portsmouth—headlining, at last, as Arms and Legs.

There was another article in the local paper, an indifferent review in *Melody Maker,* and a few plays on local radio. And that was it.

We stiffened our upper lips and kept on gigging. There were still good gigs, like a support spot with an old progressive-rock hero, Kevin Ayers, at the Leascliffe Hall in Folkestone. And our shows at the John Peel were so jammed that crowds of people stood in the car park and watched through the window.

There were also terrible gigs, like Tracey's in Ipswich. This was a late-night disco at the top of a multilevel concrete pile similar to Portsmouth's Tricorn, where we had to lug our gear up an endless series of ramps, and then hang around for hours on end for the dubious pleasure of clearing the dance floor and being booed. There were horrible journeys, too: driving back from Ipswich or somewhere in Cornwall, surfacing into still-half-drunk consciousness as the sun came up, then realizing that we still had a good three hours to go. Late one night a steel girder fell off a lorry in front of us, and we ran over it, blowing out two tires. We had to take all the gear out, on the side of the motorway, to change them. Another time the van ground to a halt in the middle of a flyover in pouring rain and gale-force winds. We slept in the van too many times, and I suffered asthma attacks in the night and drove everyone crazy with my wheezing.

One night we arrived at the Elbow Room in Eastleigh to find another band already setting up. We'd been double-booked, and the gig went to the first band to turn up. We decided to go back to Dave's house, get some cans of beer and dope, and listen to music.

People used to do that in those days. Dave had a "music room" that he'd lined with mattresses, with a pair of enormous speakers hanging on chains from the ceiling. We listened to Little Feat and *Sergeant Pepper* at deafening volume, and as strange as it may seem, I think this was the first time I fully appreciated the genius of the Beatles.

Every gig from this era seems to have a story attached to it, and it's hard to resist telling them. Some great characters, too: for instance, the beetroot-faced and bewhiskered landlord of a pub we played in Taunton, Somerset, who refused to serve me a pint of the local cider. "You'll 'ave an 'aaarf," he said, shaking his head gravely. The cider was so strong that you only got a pint if he knew you.

We had a series of roadies, with unlikely names and nicknames: Phil "Geno" Washington, "Nobby" Wilkinson, Pete "Snowy" Crump. One of them, a great bearded hulk by the name of Titch Carter, was a "real" roadie, who'd toured with some big-time acts, and he bored me to tears by bragging endlessly about his sexual conquests. I was about to dismiss it all as fantasy until I spotted him sneaking out to the van one night with a girl he'd just picked up. The bastard, I thought, how does he do it?! Titch opened the back door of the van and vaulted dramatically over the seat, but he landed with a shocking crunch and a scream. He'd forgotten that he'd left a couple of empty pint glasses on the backseat earlier in the day, and the full force of his considerable weight shattered them into tiny pieces. Titch spent the next hour picking the pieces out of his backside.

On the way back from points west, we always stopped at Pat's Burgers, a late-night snack stand next to the Southampton Guildhall. Pat, an old bald fellow with a big nose, made special "nonburgers" for me and Graham—burger buns stuffed with everything he had except the meat. They were still a complete meal, bulging with cheese, tomato, onions, mushrooms, fried eggs, pineapple, mustard, and ketchup. Titch Carter always ate at least three burgers and farted all the way home. Pat himself never said much, but on one occasion when we must have been even more ravenous than usual he shook his head and said, "Y'know, if you buggers can play as good as you eat, you must be bloody good."

We *were* bloody good, but by mid '76 we'd reached our peak. I think we sensed it, too. Frustration was setting in, and disillusion lurked just over the horizon. The upward trend had slipped from our grasp, and we were struggling even to find some kind of consistency. We were always in the gutter one night, and the stars the next: jerked up and down like puppets on a string, until our heads spun and our stomachs churned and we didn't know which end was up.

It was time for the last act of this particular tragicomedy. If this sounds melodramatic, think again. I'd invested nearly three years of hopes, dreams, and sheer hard work in this band. It was the biggest project of my life up to that point. The last act wasn't going to be easy.

Winners and Losers

IF ANYONE ever made an Arms and Legs movie, Mark and I would eventually come to blows on stage in the middle of a show, and then one of us would take a drug overdose while the other drove the van off the edge of a cliff. The more prosaic reality is that we respected each other enough, and we were good enough friends, that our truce held up, more or less, to the end.

There were several other reasons that the band's days were numbered, and one was the total indifference of MAM Records. Even allowing for the fact that we were signed to them through middlemen—Andy Arthurs and Steve Stevenson—we thought it strange that we never even *met* anyone from "our" record company. Weren't they at least curious enough to come and see us perform?

At one of our rare London gigs, a representative of MAM did finally show up, but he was a nondescript character who knew nothing about what was going on at the label, and obviously had no power or influence. We descended on him and asked a hundred questions, which only seemed to embarrass him. He just smiled politely and hummed and ha-ed until we finally gave up. I think he was the guy who answered the mail or made the tea.

It might seem odd that a label would sign artists, or put out records, and then do nothing more about it. But bands get signed, for instance, as a tax loss. Or at the whim of one executive who promptly leaves the company, leaving them high and dry. Record companies have also been known to spend a fortune making an album, only to decide it isn't what they wanted after all and, rather than having to spend more money promoting it, refuse to release it. Thousands of records just get thrown against the wall to see if one will stick. Meanwhile, a select few are nurtured like pampered puppies, with lots of money and aggressive promotion, to make sure they're going to stick before they're even thrown. The trick is to be one of the puppies. Talent and dedication can help, or, then again, not make an iota of difference.

I should say that, although I'm no great admirer of the music business, I'm no conspiracy theorist either. Like governments, record companies are more likely to screw things up by disorganization, incompetence, and lack of vision than by evil intent. There are plenty of good people in record companies, but the industry as a whole suffers from something I call "the winning team syndrome."

For instance: In the States there are hundreds of rock radio stations for every one jazz station. This is supposed to reflect public taste, and it does —up to a point. If it were a *true* reflection, the ratio would be less extreme: a bit less rock, a bit more jazz. The distortion comes from the fact that, in a commercial culture, virtually everyone wants to take the most profitable route. If that seems to be rock, they all play rock, and what's more, they all try to play the most popular rock records, too. So jazz fans in smaller towns get nothing at all, and potential jazz fans have nowhere to start. Now you have a Catch-22 situation: If minority tastes are not catered to, the minority will keep shrinking, and the commercial music industry can then pat itself on the back and say "We told you so."

Speaking of radio, it's notoriously bad in New York City. You need $40 million just to *start* a radio station there, so advertising dollars rule, and everyone plays it safe.

They all want to be on the winning team.

The industry likes to say that it's really we, the public, who choose what is successful and what isn't. MTV claims to play videos purely on the basis of record sales. But how do people know which records to buy in the first place? It's a nice theory—the genius of the free market—but it's obvious, if you think about it, that large and wealthy corporations don't just reflect public taste but actually play a very big role in creating it.

In a capitalist society, this may all be inevitable. Maybe we can't change the system. But we can at least try to (a) keep a skeptical distance, (b) vote with our wallets, and (c) remember that art is not competitive. A league table makes objective sense in sports, where the team that wins the most games rises to the top, and can fairly claim to be the best. The Top 20, on the other hand, shouldn't be taken too seriously. There are all kinds of reasons that one record has sold more, this week, than another. But in the realm of music, there are no winners, and the only losers are those who aren't enjoying themselves.

As Arms and Legs prepared to release a second single, we were so desperate to be winners that we were starting to lose the plot. In June '76 we recorded a few more songs, including "Heat of the Night." Our manager and our producers were convinced that the Paul Nicholas song was a smash hit just waiting to explode. But we were still uneasy about releasing a cover version. We had just one more shot at getting our own material out there. Then again, we had one more shot at having a hit, too. Reluctantly, we joined what looked like the winning team, and agreed that "Heat of the Night" would be our second single.

Andy and Steve then threw us all for a loop by taking Mark aside and suggesting that our version of "Heat of the Night" could be even better, even more commercial, if we rerecorded it and made some changes. What changes? Dave's drumming, said Steve, although, of course, very good—no one was disputing that—was, well, letting us down a bit. And Andy knew a great session drummer, who had played on a couple of hits . . .

My heart sinks as I remember all this, but of course similar minidramas of desperation and betrayal are playing themselves out all around us, every day, both in the small time and the biggest of the big. Everyone knows, for instance, that Hollywood studios regularly spend $100 million on one blockbuster movie. They pay the stars obscene amounts of money, and then try to safeguard their investment with marketing budgets that could drag several Third World countries into the twenty-first century without too much trouble. Even so, a lot of these films are flops. I've had more than one conversation about this with people in the movie industry, and I always ask the same question: Why don't you scrap just one of your $100 million movies each year, and give twenty talented young directors $5 million each? My God, what they could do with $5 million! Surely at least a couple of them would turn out something really good, and at least one of the films would be a hit. But at this point, the movie people are looking at me as though I were pleading a passionate case for the true existence of Santa Claus.

It's too easy to lose sight of the rewards to be gained from getting involved with the second-place, or tenth-place, or hundredth-place team, and helping it to be all it can be. This isn't just childish idealism, and I can't think of a better example than a fellow student of mine who, around the time of Arms and Legs's second release, would have been graduating from the Royal Academy of Music.

He'd arrived in my second term, and immediately caught the attention of everyone in the place—even a skulking malcontent like me. He was a conductor with both talent and charisma, as well as a genius for organizing and motivating people. He was one of the few people I've come across who seemed to walk around with 'STAR' emblazoned over his head in flashing neon lights; it was that obvious. His name was Simon Rattle, and he could have had his pick of any of the world's great orchestras, or become a highly paid itinerant—one more *plat du jour* for the jaded palates of London, Paris, and New York. Instead he chose to take over a provincial orchestra, the City of Birmingham Symphony, and to devote many years of his life to building it into a world-class ensemble. Britain now has one more great regional orchestra than it would otherwise have had, as a result of which a new concert hall was built that is one of the finest in the country, attracting more great performers, and enhancing the pride and prestige of the city as a result. Oh, and Simon is now Sir Simon.

Well, okay, say the Winning Teamsters, but that's an exception. At which point I give up and wash my hands of the whole debate.

But I know there are good and bad guys on both sides of the art/commerce divide, and I don't protest out of mere sour grapes. I had the sour grapes early on, with Arms and Legs.

We hired the session drummer, but needless to say, it didn't go down too well with Dave Cairns. Rightly or wrongly, he saw himself as a prime mover in the band. We were all embarrassed, but Dave promised not to bear a grudge. It was Making It that counted, not doing our own thing, not keeping the band's identity, not staying friends with each other.

The session drummer did give us a different feel: harder, more solid, but stiffer, and somehow less human. Was that going to make the difference between a hit and a flop?

Meanwhile Mark's song, "Good Times," was chosen as the B side, and

I was unhappy about not getting another of my songs recorded. The single was released on 20 August and passed immediately into oblivion. Now we were all unhappy.

We were thrown against the wall and we didn't stick. I suppose we bounced off. Later in my career I would experience both sticking to the wall quite unexpectedly, and then sliding down it. Now I'm not sure *where* I am. In the last days of Arms and Legs, though, I was beginning to get the message: I had to get my priorities straightened out. Because the only way to win, at least for us musicians, is by keeping the faith. Keeping our faith with the one thing that has really mattered all along: the music.

We have to follow what excites us, interests us, challenges us, and makes us feel alive, and put aside whatever does not; and if we can't make a living out of it, we should hang on to our day jobs. We must be wary of facts and figures and pundits and PR, of critics both internal and external, and of all those cocksure movers and shakers who tell you they have their fingers on the pulse; they don't have a finger on *yours*. If you're doing what makes you feel alive, no matter how obscure or uncool it might be, you can be Gulliver while they're all just Lilliputians, trying in vain to tie down your toes.

And *this* is how you win.

This is the End

NINETEEN SEVENTY-SIX was an interesting year for pop music. Things that wouldn't have stood a chance a couple of years before, like Dr. Feelgood's scabrous R&B, and Graham Parker's gritty white soul, were huge. Every new band looked like a gang of louts in thrift-shop suits, but they were packing people into London pubs like the Nashville, the Red Cow, and the Hope and Anchor. There was a general feeling that it was time to cut your hair short and get "back to basics." Bob Marley was becoming a star, too, and Mark and I were big reggae fans, but the London pub-rock scene was where we wanted to be. We pestered Alan Matthews endlessly to get us London gigs, and we did play a few, but at totally inappropriate venues: nite clubs like Gulliver's in Mayfair, where we always seemed to go on ridiculously late, after most of the people had left, and play to a few stragglers at the bar.

Someone asked me recently if Arms and Legs were pub rock.

"Not really," I said. "We were just 'pub.'"

Nineteen seventy-six was also the year that punk, which looked to me like the bastard offspring of pub rock and glam, was struggling to be born. One of the midwives, according to some histories of punk that I've seen, was the grandiose Rolling Stones stint at the Earl's Court Exhibition Centre in that year. I was there, as the guest of Pete "Snowy" Crump, sometime Arms and Legs roadie, now working for the Stones' mobile recording studio backstage. The Stones outdid themselves, if not musically, then with the star-shaped stage and the samba bands marching up and down the aisles and Mick levitating over the audience on a wire, and the sound was so bad that they got two or three minutes into "Satisfaction" before I even recognized it. It was a great spectacle, sort of, but it sort of made you sick, too. Spectacles like it made you feel like going to see the rawest garage bands in the sweatiest pub cellars you could find, or better still, forming one yourself. I wasn't a punk rocker, but I could relate to them. There was something in the air. Who was a "real" punk rocker, anyway? People get so hung up on bogus notions of "authenticity" in pop music, as though no spiky-haired punk had long hair a year or two before, as though no working-class hero had a public-school accent offstage. As though we're all supposed to self-destruct, *Mission Impossible*-style, once we've had our five minutes of fame, or else stay frozen like bugs in amber, immune to the changing zeitgeist.

Arms and Legs wasn't a punk band, but we resembled one more and more with every gig. We were scruffier, harder, louder, and we were acquiring the appropriate antisocial snarl in all honesty; we really *were* broke, frustrated, and generally pissed off. We started kicking amps over or throwing beer around on stage, and Mark was less Mick Jagger and more Iggy Pop. He was a star, but the great wide world didn't know it.

Our manager didn't approve of the direction we were taking. When I wore a threadbare dressing gown on stage, or Mark told someone in the audience to fuck off, Alan was genuinely dismayed. He had old-fashioned ideas about professionalism, and kept booking us into disco clubs where we were hated. Official band policy was still to play every gig we could get. But there *were* gigs, I started to think, that were worse than no gigs at all.

Alan's limitations were becoming more and more apparent. ("Your manager," Titch Carter said one day, "couldn't manage a good shit.") But there was nowhere else to turn. Managers and agents weren't exactly beating a path to our door. With the right contacts, and in the right venues, we might have been like the Stranglers—a band not exactly *of* the punk scene, but able to coexist with it. I still felt sure that we had what it takes, but a sinking feeling in my stomach kept telling me that wasn't enough.

Some of the last gigs I played with Arms and Legs were truly depressing. Bad gigs are one thing when you're committed to a band. But when the band's singles have flopped, and you're thinking about leaving, and you keep having an uncontrollable urge to bend a mike stand over the singer's head, they're quite another. There was, for instance, a two-night stand at the Fiesta Ballroom in Plymouth. The manager, who looked like a professional wrestler stuffed into a rented tuxedo two sizes too small for him, was very insistent about the dress code in his club: no jeans. So, of course, Mark wore jeans on stage, and the manager said that if he did so on the second night, we wouldn't be paid a penny.

That night, the rest of the band slept in the van, but I found a big roll of carpet backstage at the Fiesta and slept inside that. I woke up early the next morning with an asthma attack, wheezing from the dust, my whole body aching. The windowless club was pitch dark and I was locked in for several hours.

Once I escaped, the rest of the day was spent sitting around, bored, in parks and bus shelters. Then, for our second night, Mark obeyed the no-jeans rule by wearing satin hot pants on stage, with bare feet. A terrifying fight broke out on the dance floor. Glasses and chairs flew, and the manager waded eagerly into the middle of it, throwing tables aside as though they were matchboxes and banging heads together. Our dressing room turned into a casualty ward, with a queue of people waiting to clean themselves up at our sink. There was blood everywhere. And then, a five-hour drive home, in what must surely have been the slowest van in all creation: There was always something wrong with it.

Was it at the Fiesta (which we renamed the Fiasco) that Mark had a dispute with the manager after the show, and got paid in 10p pieces? Mark very deliberately started to count them, and then the manager punched him and had him thrown out by bouncers. But that could have been somewhere else.

Everything started to unravel around this time. Jill and I lost our flat. Mrs. Diffey decided to sell the house, and we had to get out.

I'd been wondering, for a while, about me and Jill. We still got on well, in a basic, animal kind of way, like two rabbits in a burrow. In bed, we were fine. Eating curry or drinking in the pub or just walking together, we were fine. But conversation was limited, and when I talked about my ambitions—if I ever raised the possibility of living in London, for instance—she grew anxious and remote. I tried hard to imagine a future with Jill. What would it look like? Every time I tried to see it, my mind would go worryingly blank.

When we lost the flat, Jill was beside herself, and wailed "This is the end! This is the end!" over and over again. I tried to reassure her that it wasn't the end, that moving back in with our parents for a while until we could get some money together would be just fine. I must have sounded half-hearted. I *was* half-hearted; I just didn't know what else to say. Jill stopped sobbing and thought for a moment, then started wailing "This is the end!" all over again.

I didn't know what I really wanted, but I knew a bubble had burst, and I was less devastated than I would have expected. Maybe, like the failure of the band's singles and the terrible gigs we were doing, the loss of the flat was a sign, a sign that it was time to change my life. How could I go back to my parents? I didn't want to lose Jill, but maybe it was time to move to London, with or without her.

But moving back into my parents' house, for the time being, was the only option. I was broke. My best bet, I thought, would be to look for another band, or pub, or restaurant, or anything as long as it paid a bit more than Arms and Legs. Luckily, I found something pretty quickly.

I gave the band as much notice as I could. Everyone tried hard to be grown-up about it, but there was no mistaking the feelings of hurt and rejection and disillusionment that swirled around beneath the surface. The reaction surprised me: All the life seemed to go out of the band. Mark tried to rally the troops, but the troops didn't seem to feel like being rallied.

My last gig with Arms and Legs, in October '76, was at an air force base, RAF Benson in Wallingford. The room was long and narrow, and the audience--about twenty squaddies—spent the whole show huddled round the bar all the way down at the other end. A vast, depressing no-man's-land yawned between us and them throughout the evening. Anyone would have thought the dance floor was mined. During our second set, half-drunk, with a black thundercloud hovering over my head, I urinated into an empty beer glass on stage, just to see if anyone would notice. They didn't.

After I left, the band struggled on for a while with two new guitarists. Then Graham left, and finally Mark called it a day and started from scratch, putting together his own band.

In a bizarre postscript to the Arms and Legs story, MAM, having paid for the recording, released "Any More Wine," with a horn section over-dubbed by Andy Arthurs. It got quite a few plays, ironically, on middle-of-the-road Radio Two. Changing the lyrics must have worked.

As miserable as the situation was, I was determined not to waste too much time grieving for Arms and Legs. I just kept telling myself I'd done the right thing by leaving. It helped, of course, that I actually had. Besides, I already had a new job lined up.

It couldn't possibly have been a bigger contrast.

Playboy of Pompey

I'M OFTEN ASKED if it's true that I once played piano in a Playboy Club. I suppose the fact is strange enough to stick in people's minds. But it's stranger than they think. The Playboy Club was in *Portsmouth*.

A couple of years before I walked out of Arms and Legs in Wallingford, a Playboy Casino, as yet without live entertainment, had opened in Osborne Road, Southsea. Following the success of the London Playboy Club, a nationwide chain of casinos—complete with bunny girls—was planned. Portsmouth got the first (closely followed by Manchester) by sheer chance. A Pompey businessman by the aromatic name of Red Fennel was a regular at the London club and just happened to hold a gaming license in his hometown.

The Portsmouth Playboy Club was quite popular as a sort of smart members-only social club for local business types and social climbers, as well as hard-core gamblers. The gamblers were a mixed bunch, including officers of the Brazilian navy and Iranian students, who regularly blew five hundred pounds without batting an eyelid. (Quite a few of these students were later stranded in Portsmouth after the Shah's deposal, and nowadays they can be seen here and there running back-street newsagents and junk shops).

In the autumn of '76, the club expanded as the Playroom opened, featuring dancing, cabaret, and, of course, more bunny girls. It was also to feature its very own trio, and Mike Hutton, a veteran jazz drummer from

Southampton, was charged with hiring a pianist and bassist to play for diners and dancers, and, most importantly, to back the cabaret acts. How did Mike find me? For all I remember, some equivalent of the Bat-phone might have been used, and a silhouette of a piano projected by searchlight onto the clouds. However it happened, it was the excuse I needed to quit Arms and Legs, and make a bit of money for a change.

The Playboy was managed by a Florentine ex–cocktail barman by the name of Rudi Del Piccolo, and God knows what he thought of me when I walked in. But it didn't take long to establish that I was more than capable of doing the job, and I was hired, for five nights a week, at ten pounds a night. Fifty quid a week! This was about ten times what I'd been making with Arms and Legs. Money to make more demo tapes! Money to launch my own band!

But, first things first: I had to get a tuxedo and a bow tie. Just the thought of it made my skin crawl. After establishing that I'd probably be able to get away with wearing any dark suit, I went shopping. I bought a black suit with a light chalk-stripe, which I thought made it somehow more bearable.

I wore the suit to the first rehearsal, and Mike was dubious. The manager was sent for. Signor Del Piccolo was a quiet man, with a pale, petulant face fringed by a feeble light-brown beard. He sat down and studied me for several minutes, squinting slightly with what could have been puzzlement, shortsightedness, or disgust. Finally I asked whether the suit was acceptable, or wasn't it? Rudi stood up, shrugged his shoulders, sighed heavily, and walked out. Apparently the suit would do.

I dragged my Apollo Restaurant sheet music out of mothballs and prepared to rehearse the trio. I'd use my Fender Rhodes and my Korg synthesizer, and I rigged up a stand for the music. I was not only the pianist, but, as the pianist usually is in these situations, the "musical director"—the "MD." This meant that although Mike was technically the bandleader, and dealt with money, contracts, and the Musicians' Union, I was responsible for holding the trio together musically: choosing material and giving count-offs and cues here and there.

The Playroom had a low ceiling and garish purple and silver wallpaper, and the trio was squeezed into one corner, while the DJ, who also controlled the sound and lights, had a small booth in the opposite corner. The space in between was reserved both for the cabaret acts and for dancing—

there was no stage. I looked around and felt suddenly depressed. What had I gotten myself into? I was doing this purely and simply for the money, and that's never been enough to get me really enthused about anything. I took a deep breath and put the trio through its swing, ballad, and bossa nova paces.

And what about these two fellows I was going to be squeezed into the corner with, five nights a week? Mike was, I guessed, in his midforties, a wiry little guy who struck me somehow as an absolutely typical jazz drummer. He reminded me of Buddy Rich without the arrogance, or Gene Krupa without the flash. Instead he had a twinkle in his eye that suggested he'd done a gig or two in his time and probably had a few stories to tell. He wasn't a bad drummer, either.

Ray, the bassist, was less inspiring. A morose fortyish man with glasses, he was a merely competent player, and his sight-reading was not even that. When I expressed concern, he said, "Don't worry, I'll just follow your left hand." This made me rather nervous.

Every Tuesday there was a "band call" in the afternoon to rehearse the week's cabaret. For my first week, the act was Carlo Dini, who had long sideburns, sleepy eyes, and a paunch, and billed himself prosaically as "the Italian Tenor." Basically, he was a bargain-basement Mario Lanza, an operatically trained singer performing pop ballads and a few Italian songs. The charts were straightforward, and although Ray fumbled a bit, the rehearsal didn't last much more than an hour. We were all set.

The club started to come to life as other employees started to arrive. Mike, the South African doorman/bouncer, must have been seven feet tall. Frank, the DJ and MC, was nothing like the flashy poseurs who'd plagued my former band's career. He was soft-spoken, almost insipid, with a ratty little mustache. Jim, the casino manager, seemed tough and sharp, and Paul, the maitre d', was a lanky bespectacled American who was the spitting image of Hank Hogan from the old Dan Dare comics. Everyone wore tuxedos and an air of suave professionalism.

Several attractive girls also arrived, disappeared into the basement dressing room, and reemerged wearing rabbit ears, high heels, and fluffy white tails. Mike greeted them all by name. Not their real names, of course. The girls all had "bunny names"—Lauren, Carmen, Sandi, Hayley, and so on. I didn't know whether to laugh or cry.

The first night was quietly successful, and the trio was given dinner on the house, upstairs in the casino. We were served by bunnies. The casino had a small restaurant and bar at one end and blackjack and roulette tables at the other. Inspector bunnies presided over the action in high chairs, waitress bunnies glided around with cocktails, and croupiers with skinny bow ties crouped, or whatever croupiers did. I felt like I was on a slightly tacky movie set, the set for a low-budget rip off of James Bond.

Mike laughed and said, "Funny gig, eh?"

I agreed.

"It's a good one, though," Mike assured me. "The people are all really nice, and we get a free meal every night. And the cabaret changes every week, so you don't get too bored."

Mike's assessment was spot-on, if a shade more enthusiastic than mine would ever be. The people *were* nice. The bunnies, for instance, were uniformly charming. It's a terrible and patronizing cliché to say that they were "not sluts at all, just nice girls working their way through college," but it was one I had to repeat over and over. People were titillated by the club's sexy image, but "hanky panky" was frowned upon, except, apparently, in the case of the manager, who seemed to spend suspicious amounts of time alone in his office with Janice, the glamorous black bunny.

The second week's act was the first in a long line of comedians, and all he needed was a "play-on"—about sixteen bars of anything we liked as long as it was fast and noisy. Then, as the comedian launched into his act, Mike grabbed me and dragged me to the bar of the Queens Hotel next door, which is now a brash disco bar, but in those days served a pretty good pint. This was going to be an easy week.

Mike and I started to haunt the Queens Bar on our breaks, too. I don't know what Ray did. Either he didn't join us, or his personality was such that I don't remember him being there. But I liked Mike. He had a good sense of humor, and, as I'd suspected, some good stories, of romantic debauchery in nightclubs and brothels long ago, or of the foibles of various well-known people he'd worked with.

The cabaret standard at the Playboy varied widely, although most of the acts were well respected on the circuit, and some of them were pretty good. One was the Irish comedian Pat O'Hare, who told outrageous, stereotypical Irish jokes (Paddy to Murphy: "How d'ye like the toilet brush oi gave ye fer Christmas?" Murphy to Paddy: "Aaargh, it was turrible; oi'm back on the paper"). Another was Elaine Del Mar, an elegant, coolly professional black jazz singer with some genuinely challenging charts. (At one point at band call she turned a withering glance on Ray and said icily, "Just play what's *written*, please.")

Most of these acts have long since faded into obscurity. But thanks to Mike Hutton, I have a stack of 8 x 10 photos which, if nothing else, offer conclusive proof that the mid '70s was a fashion disaster area to chill the blood. Here are Clive Lea, impressionist, in a pinstripe suit with ten-inch-wide lapels and an eight-inch-wide tie; Kirk St. James, Calypsonian, in a skintight catsuit, showing off a vast expanse of bare brown chest; Kim Davis, chanteuse, in a thousand swirling sequins; Tom Browne, singer, with a horrific shaggy haircut, gazing soulfully at a spot just over the photographer's head, his enormous pointed shirt collar spreading all the way out to his shoulders—in a high wind, he'd have taken off. My favorite, though, is Johnny Hillyard, also a singer, who looks like a slightly buck-toothed and longer-haired Donny Osmond. He wears a velvet braided jacket and an elaborately ruffled shirt, and he's holding toward the camera something that looks like a sort of astrological talisman, a golden wheel about the size of his hand. I puzzled over this for a while, until I noticed the glint of light on a chain leading from this mysterious object to somewhere under his collar: Yes, Johnny wants the world to get a really good look at his medallion.

Mike's diaries teem with half-remembered and often unlikely names: Jabie Abercrombie, Chester Shadrack, Junior "the Maori King" Jonsen, Jean de Both, Trevillion and Nine, Friday Brown, Vince Everett, Love and Stuff, Pinky Steede. Where are they now? Sad to say, most of them were neither good enough nor bad enough to make a lasting impression.

The same can be said about the Playboy gig in general. Once I got used to it, and it started to feel less like some cruel kind of penance and more like a job, it was just okay. The best thing about it was the money. I was back at my parents' house for a while, Mike gave me lifts to and from the gig (in an old Humber Hawk, a great tank of a car that made me feel like Elliot Ness cruising around Chicago) and, with the free meals, my fifty pounds a week was almost pure profit.

Still, things weren't quite going according to plan. When I started at the Playboy I really thought I'd be in a studio within weeks, making the demos that would launch my career as a solo artist. But I was in a slump. I didn't particularly want to push the songs I'd written for Arms and Legs.

Those days were gone, and I convinced myself that I never liked those songs much, anyway. I was looking for a new direction. It would have to reflect the spirit of the time: high-energy, stripped-down, back-to-basics, and all the other stock phrases that were being bandied about already to describe something called the New Wave. But with my background—I had letters after my name, for God's sake—I could hardly be a punk rocker. The way ahead wasn't clear, and I found myself with a new problem: an agonizing case of writers' block.

Then there was Jill. Since we lost our flat, things just hadn't been the same. Had I been in love with her? I wasn't sure. When we'd first gotten together I'd been so cruelly frustrated for so long, so desperate for some kind of intimacy, that any reasonably agreeable partner would have seemed like a cross between Brigitte Bardot and Mother Teresa. Now we seemed to have less and less in common. I wanted to move to the big city, travel the world, hit the big time. Jill was destined to stay in Gosport and have babies. I didn't blame her. Her path would be a safe and time-honored one. I, on the other hand, was hurtling into the unknown.

We started to do that slow dance around each other that couples do when they sense that a relationship is winding down, but neither party wants to be the bad guy. Finally, I broke the stalemate by moving over to Southsea. I couldn't bear Gosport, or living with my parents, any longer. I told Jill that I wanted to be alone for a while. A couple of months later I had second thoughts and went to see her, only to find that she was now seeing someone else.

According to popular myth, splitting up with my girlfriend should have helped with the writer's block. It didn't. Sometimes suffering produces art, and sometimes it just produces . . . suffering.

More often than not, music refuses to follow the rules of cause and effect, and art doesn't imitate life. My favorite example of this is Mahler's most tragic work, the great Sixth Symphony, which he wrote at what was probably just about the only really happy time in his life. I instinctively understand this. I've written sad songs when I've been perfectly happy: happy enough, perhaps, to tackle tragedy with at least some degree of objectivity. I've also helped myself out of depression by working on happy songs. But in late '76 and early '77, I couldn't write a damn thing.

Hurtling into the unknown. I had to get back on track. But which track, and how the hell was I supposed to find it?

My Secret Identity

I'M GROVELING on the floor of a dark underground cave full of money. It's a vault somewhere in the bowels of Barclays Bank, Osborne Road, Southsea, and all around me are huge piles of pound notes that are growing and growing, piling up before my eyes. The Queen's faces on the notes speak in unison with voices like the Wicked Witch of the West. "Joe! Spend me!" they hiss. "Do something with your life!" "I'm sorry, Your Majesty," I sob pathetically, "I'm just not up to it." The Queen laughs a fiendish laugh and I wake up sweating. It was all a dream! Except that I still wasn't up to it.

I had no piano, no girlfriend, no songs, and no ideas, but I did have a new home in Southsea. It was cheap and convenient, in the same street as the Playboy, in a building called Serpentine Chambers. But despite the name, which sounded as though it could have been the residence of Conan Doyle's Professor Moriarty, it was a dump. I'd rented a squalid little bed-sitting-room on the top floor, sharing a bathroom with several other squalid little bed-sitting-rooms. The other tenants must all have been night watchmen or bedridden invalids, as the place was eerily quiet. Directly across the street, though, was a notoriously rough after-hours joint called the Bistro, which stayed open an hour or two after the Playboy. I was often woken up just as I was falling asleep by fights spilling out onto the street at closing time. They always sounded the same: a woman's voice screeching "Don't 'it 'im! Don't 'it 'im!" and a drunken sailor's voice shouting "I'll kill the cunt! I'll kill the cunt!"

Serpentine Chambers became stranger as I gradually made some contact with my neighbors. The first was a titanic Irishman who pounded on my door one night while I was playing Bob Marley's *Exodus,* and told me to "Turn that focken row off or else."

The only time I ever heard anyone else playing music was one morning, as I lay in bed, and the strains of Johnny Cash singing "I Walk the Line" drifted up from the floor below. Then I heard it again—and again. Someone was playing the single and couldn't get enough of it. I started to count. They played it *seventeen times.*

One day I locked myself out. This was a bad move, since there was no one available with a spare key, and I had to get in to change into the monkey-suit for the evening. But I'd left my window open, and after thinking it over I knew that, vertigo or not, the only way to get into my bedsit was from the adjoining one. It was time to meet my next-door neighbor, if I had one.

I knocked on the door, and it opened a crack. A very old, bald man peered out. I explained the situation, and he let me in without a word. The room smelled of mildew and cough medicine, and my host was wearing nothing but a pajama jacket—with no trousers. And as hard as I tried not to look, I couldn't help but notice that he had a pair of exceptionally large balls, swinging low around his thighs. He smiled vacantly at me. I smiled back, took a deep breath, and climbed out onto the ledge. Grasping the parapet—thank God there was a parapet!—I eased myself over to my window. I never saw or heard anything of my next-door neighbor again.

In spite of a certain *Twilight Zone* quality, my lonely existence at Serpentine Chambers gradually became rather pleasant. I learned something I'd never suspected: that both solitude and routine can have a soothing effect. Five nights a week I did my evening shift at the piano. During the day, I read a lot, and walked the streets of Portsmouth and Southsea just as I'd done as a kid, browsing in junk shops, occasionally buying a secondhand LP to play on the cheap stereo that was my only significant possession. I listened to Bob Marley, got my hair cut—a bit shorter each time—and had my right ear pierced. On Sundays and Mondays, my free days, I drank my way around every pub in Southsea, and occasionally I took a train to London to spend a night with Drew Barfield, or take in a concert—Graham Parker at the Rainbow, for instance.

One day I suffered an asthma attack so severe that I couldn't climb the five flights of stairs to my bedsit. I sat on the bottom step for an hour, alone, not knowing what to do, and finally went to the phone box around the corner and called my mother. I didn't have much to do with my family these days, but she came and picked me up and I spent a week in bed, with her as my nurse, just like when I was a kid. I felt pathetic and vaguely ashamed, but too ill to care much. My attacks were less frequent now, but when they came, they really knocked me for six.

Back in Southsea, I sat on the beach, watching the waves and the play of light and clouds over the Isle of Wight. I remembered that melancholy, too, could be pleasant. But sooner or later I was going to have to do something more with my life than backing dodgy cabaret singers and impressionists. I went over to the Playboy during the afternoons, and forced myself to sit at my Fender Rhodes and write. When inspiration failed me, I bashed away on Mike's drums for a while. Eventually, some songs got written.

I wasn't sure I would ever have an entirely original songwriting style, of the sort that's instantly recognizable and consistent from one song to the next. Ideally, one's style arises spontaneously, out of the depths of one's being. But my depths weren't exactly handing me a style on a plate, so I was just going to have to invent one.

It would, of course, be eclectic—even if the all-embracing eclecticism of my teenage years had given way to a pop eclecticism. My vision had steadily shrunk from wide-screen 70-millimeter to something more like TV. I would still be pretty free, but I decided to write for guitar, bass, and drums only, with a little bit of piano here and there. No synthesizers, no horns, no vocal harmonies, no violin. I hoped this would make everything sound cleaner, leaner, and more consistent.

While I was groping for a style, I at least found an Attitude. Lyrically, I was finding my voice, or at least a voice that would work for a while. It was a wry, ironic voice, not too serious about anything, but hard-nosed, and stripped of all sentimentality. I no longer tried to write the kind of thing I thought rock lyricists were supposed to write. Instead I wrote bluntly about things I observed, things that amused me, things that pissed me off. It felt right. I was growing another layer of my shell, and starting to see myself, like many twenty-two-year-olds, as a clever cynic.

My songwriting persona was a million miles from the world of the Playboy Club, but this may have been just as well. At least I had no trouble separating the two in my mind. The Playboy was a means to an end, but on the other hand, I allowed myself to enjoy it as much as I could.

The biggest problem was Ray, the bassist. He was an embarrassment at band calls, and much of the time he didn't even look at the charts, but made good on his threat to "just follow my left hand." This meant that I had to either play most of the bass lines myself, or play chords in simple, root positions that he could follow. I couldn't leave out a chord, ever, and I had to make sure to play a big fat obvious one on the downbeat of each bar, or wherever the chord changed. And every time I thought Ray knew where he was, and allowed my left hand a bit more freedom, he would go off the musical rails and I'd have to bail him out. I soon began to curse him under my breath as he peered over my shoulder. If I was going to stick this gig for more than a few weeks, Ray was going to have to go.

Mike agreed: Why suffer? So we placed an advertisement for a new bassist in the *Evening News*. Then the *News* printed the ad several days before it was supposed to, and before we'd actually spoken to Ray about it. There was a horribly embarrassing scene, not so much with Ray, who accepted his fate gloomily, but with his wife. This fire-breathing harridan stormed into the club and cursed me and Mike to every circle of hell, and from then on I seemed to constantly bump into her around town and she would start ranting at me again. One Christmas, while I was enjoying a quiet pint at the India Arms in Southsea, she seemed to materialize out of nowhere, like some Dickensian ghost, to wish me the very worst Christmas it was possible for a human being to have. She was a nasty piece of work, but I have to say that as far as I know she's the only person in my career whom I've managed to turn into a mortal enemy.

After a series of stand-ins, we found a good bassist, an earnest twenty-year-old called Pete, who moved down from Guildford for the gig. It was the first time, I realized, that I'd worked with someone younger than myself.

Pete was pleasant enough, but I got on better with Mike, who was twice my age. He called me "Ace," made me try several different kinds of snuff (we would sit in the Queens Bar and sneeze for half an hour at a time), and he cracked me up with his stories, and songs he would make up, with ridiculous titles like "The Shades Of Night Were Falling Fast (But I Still Got A Bloody Good Look)," "Leave a Fiver Under the Pillow and Piss Off Blues," "Don't Kiss Me While I'm Smoking (Kiss Me Between the Draws)," or "You Can't Fuck About with Love." (Some years later, in

Mike's honor, I composed a romantic ballad using this last title, and I have hopes that Tony Bennett will record it one day).

To keep the Playboy routine interesting, I expanded my repertoire of standards, many of which I wrote out and harmonized by ear, always in the "wrong" keys. Mike knew all the original keys from long experience, and when I would announce, for instance, "Misty" in F, he would protest: "'Misty' in *F*? 'Misty's' in bloody A-flat!"—and I'd ask what difference it made to his drums, anyway, or I'd tell him to carry on in A-flat while I played in F, and we'd see if anyone noticed.

I particularly enjoyed the bossa novas of Antonio Carlos Jobim, with their sinuous melodies and chord changes that seemed to wind their way through every chord known to man, while always seeming effortlessly logical. I also set myself musical challenges, like modulating a song through all twelve keys, or working out unusual arrangements, such as a suite of songs from *West Side Story* in which "Something's Coming" was played as a fast mambo and "I Feel Pretty" in the style of a Mozart minuet. Now that I had a decent bassist and could stretch out a bit, my improvisational skills improved, too. I've never been a better than average soloist in the jazz sense, but I pride myself on at least letting my ear lead my fingers into something melodic, instead of just waffling, as too many players do, up and down blues scales or in and out of generic riffs.

In March '77, I went to my first punk gig. It was probably the first punk gig in Portsmouth: the Damned as support act for Marc Bolan at the Mecca Ballroom. I didn't know what to wear, and ended up in my chalk-stripe suit with a skinny tie knotted around my neck, with no shirt. As it turned out, there weren't too many punks there. But the Damned, I thought, were hilarious. The drummer was called Rat Scabies and destroyed his kit, the bassist was called Captain Sensible and wore a nurse's uniform, and every notion of musical professionalism that I'd learned over the last decade was gleefully trampled into the dirt. I didn't take it seriously for a minute, and I loved it.

In the spring, my block seemed to lift and I finished several songs. I booked a couple of days in the eight-track studio above Telecoms, the biggest music shop in Portsmouth (now studioless and renamed, for some reason, Nevada). The band was basically Arms and Legs redux: Graham Maby (who'd been taking some time off from gigging to come to terms with parenthood), Dave Cairns, and Mark Andrews on guitar. Mark, I think, was surprised to be asked. But with no power struggles to get in the way, we were moving quickly into a new relationship, in which we could egg each other on as friends.

According to Dave's diary, we recorded four songs, including a fast and frantic number called "Got the Time," which gave Dave a lot of trouble. The style I wanted—fast, sharp, and intense—was a long way from Dave's loose, funky approach. This was one guy, I thought, who might not survive the transition to New Wave.

Telecoms studio was a stuffy little shoe-box of a place, which was rendered even more claustrophobic by having no window between the control room and the recording room. It was acoustically dead, something I didn't know how to cope with at the time, so everything tended to sound rather flat and dull. Otherwise the recording went quite well. My singing was still insecure, but it was getting better. At this point it was very much influenced by Graham Parker, with echoes of Donald Fagen. Oh well. You have to start off by imitating *someone.*

All in all, I was making progress, and I started to feel something like confidence trickling back into my veins. I'd found a secret identity: New Wave singer-songwriter. Or was the lounge lizard at the Playboy Club the secret identity? I didn't know which way round it was, but I had to admit it was pretty funny.

Chalk and Cheese

THE SUMMER OF '77 has become legendary. It was long and hot, the Royal Silver Jubilee was celebrated, and the Sex Pistols went to Number One, after being banned by the BBC, with "God Save the Queen." I saw the Jam at the Mecca, and the Damned again at the Marquee in London. Rat Scabies threw his snare drum about twenty feet into the air and it ricocheted off the wall and into the audience. I never went to the Roxy, the birthplace of British punk, but I did go to its younger sibling the Vortex. I saw a band there called the Unwanted, who did a memorable version of Nancy Sinatra's "These Boots are Made for Walking":

These boots are made for kickin'
And that's just wot they'll do
One of these days these boots are gonna
Kick shit out of you.

The Vortex was always packed and sweaty and there was a lot of pushing and shoving and spitting, but very little real violence. An exception was the night Sham 69 played and drew a mixed audience of punks and skinheads, who hadn't quite figured out whether to be friends or enemies. There were some nasty scuffles, the stage was invaded, and I remember Jimmy Pursey, Sham's singer, trying to unite the two factions. He held up the hands of a punk on his left and a skinhead on his right, like a boxing referee, and got the crowd to chant "Punks and skins together! Punks and skins together!" over and over. Very little music got played, but it was pretty entertaining anyway.

Meanwhile, at Hugh Hefner's smallest outpost, one cabaret singer after another sang "The Way We Were," "I Write the Songs," "What I Did for Love," and "Help Me Make It Through the Night." There was a lot of Neil Sedaka and—one of the few musical artists I've ever truly hated—Neil Diamond. As for the performers themselves, an excerpt from the cabaret program—in the inimitable prose of Frank, the DJ/MC—gives some of the flavor:

FORTHCOMING ARTISTS!!

★ NIGEL HELLERY! (Hypnotist).

The return of Mr. Nigel "Eyes" Hellery, for the non-believers to see, and for the believers to have it confirmed.

★ LINDA DUNN! (Vocalist-Entertainer).

Take talent, experience, personality and beauty, blend it together and you will have Linda—live on stage.

★ FRANK HOLDER! (Vocalist-Musician)

Your wish is our command! For nearly 9 months we have chased and finally got Mr. Holder to return to you with his voice and magic.

★ JANICE HOYTE! (Vocalist)

Another artist re-engaged specially for your pleasure. What applies to Frank, certainly applies to Janice.

The trio began to dread these vocalists, especially on their second or third visits. Comedians were better. We would stay and watch them the first night, and then disappear to the Queens Bar for the rest of the week. Some of them were funny: There was a Yorkshireman who told grim tales of Northern boardinghouse life ("The landlady came to t' door with a face like a slate-hanger's nail-bag . . . On a clear day, you could see the curtains . . .") and an outrageous gay impressionist called Dustin Gee, who was always accompanied by a pretty young boyfriend, whom he would fondle shamelessly just out of sight of the audience. Dustin did brilliantly incongruous impressions of macho men. With the aid of a cigarette and a

Stetson, he *became* Robert Mitchum. The audience gasped, and when the applause died down he said with a campy lisp, "I can't do the voice!"

It was interesting to observe how the better acts "worked the audience," and by now I had a large repertoire of jokes. But otherwise I was beginning to feel too much like a fixture at the Playroom, like some sort of chalk-striped garden gnome in my little corner. Sheer boredom was becoming an occupational hazard. Mike, Pete, and I tried to find strategies to cope. For instance, we would each take it in turns to play, at eight-bar intervals, a horrendous wrong note or chord or blatantly missed beat. The challenge was to keep a straight face for the whole song, which was almost impossible. But even when one of us cracked, no one seemed to notice.

Inevitably, the two sides of my double life became more and more polarized. I decided to form my own band. Then I decided, record company or not, to make an album.

I was bitter towards record companies in general. But people were now forming their own labels, running them from their garages, and putting out singles or EPs if they couldn't afford to make albums. Why shouldn't I record an album's worth of songs at Telecoms, and license it to one of these independents? And if that failed, what was to stop me from starting my own label?

Suddenly inspired by this plan, I decided not only to get back into Telecoms as soon as possible, but to look for a gig or two as well. The first person I called was Graham Maby, who was now playing in a resolutely small-time "cover band" called Jumbo Route (where do these names come from?!) with ex–Smiling Hard drummer Dave Houghton. Why did drummers all seem to be called Dave? Anyway, Graham loved working with this one and suggested that I give him a try. I finished a few more songs, and we rehearsed in a corrugated-iron Scout hut in Gosport.

Dave Houghton was a revelation. He and Graham had quickly become the best rhythm section I'd ever heard, and they're still hard to beat now. Dave's style, much cleaner and snappier than Dave Cairns's, was perfect for the new material, and once I'd got past feeling intimidated by an ex-member of Smiling Hard, we got on well. There was nothing intimidating about Dave. He was one of the friendliest and funniest people I'd ever met.

Dave and Graham were going to be my rhythm section. I had to make sure of that. For the time being the guitarist was still Mark, who, although he was busy putting together a new band, was delighted to be involved.

For once he could be a side man, he said, and just "dress up like an idiot and thrash away." On the other hand, he still struggled with some of my guitar parts. I couldn't really blame him. The guitar, which most people consider a simple instrument, has always baffled me—even the violin was more logical. I've tried to learn the guitar, but after twenty years I can just about manage three chords. Every guitarist I've ever worked with has cursed me as he's struggled to interpret my ideas, ideas conceived at the keyboard or in my head and frequently impossible for a guitarist to play.

The guitar wasn't going to be the star of this show, though. I was more and more influenced by the reggae concept of emphasizing the bass and drums, and, since I also had a great bassist, I made him the lead instrument much of the time. I had a new challenge: how to arrange for just guitar, bass, and drums, and keep it interesting. There was a song, for instance, called "Sunday Papers" in which I had the guitar play reggae "chops" on two and four, while the bass and drums played a funk rhythm underneath, technically at half the tempo. I wanted to keep things simple, but that didn't mean we had to sound the same as every other four-piece on the planet.

Strictly speaking, the band was to be a three-piece more often than not. I didn't want to sit behind the piano the whole time. If we got any gigs, I was going to stand out front and actually be the lead singer. Everyone thought this was hilarious. I would have laughed at the idea myself even a year earlier, but times had changed. It didn't seem necessary any more for a "front man" to be good-looking, stylish, charismatic, or even a capable singer. Lee Brilleaux stood in front of Dr. Feelgood with all the glamour of a degenerate used-car salesman, and even he was starting to look like a rock idol, compared to some of the punk singers I was seeing. If there was ever going to be a time in rock history when I could get away with fronting a band, this was it.

As it turned out, we'd be playing live before we got a chance to get back in the studio, as we managed to line up two gigs in August. Mike arranged for a pianist to stand in for me at the Playroom. Both gigs were at the Cumberland Tavern, a big Portsmouth pub that had recently established itself as a live rock venue. There was a good buzz about the place, which, combined with the local following that Arms and Legs had had, gave us a big crowd for our first gig.

We had just enough songs to play one set. There were half a dozen of my new songs, including "Sunday Papers," "Got The Time," and a new one called "Throw It Away," which was basically a high-energy thrash. A couple of the others would not survive very far beyond these first gigs. The set was filled out with two or three of my Arms and Legs songs, and finally a cover version or two, though no one can remember what they were.

We were billed as the Joe Jackson Band, and I was terrified. It had all happened so suddenly, and there were so many things I hadn't figured out about how to front my own band. I didn't even know what to wear. In a panic, I changed half a dozen times before the show, and ended up in my Playboy jacket with a black shirt, skinny silver tie, and drainpipe jeans. Mark, entering into the spirit of things in a characteristically irreverent way, wore a dog collar, no shirt, and wraparound shades.

The atmosphere was almost unbearably electric as we took the stage, to applause mixed with whistles and laughter. This was an audience that didn't quite know what to expect and wasn't quite sure how it felt about New Wave, but was certainly curious.

"In case you're wondering," I said, "we're Portsmouth's first Medium Wave Band." It was a pretty lame off-the-cuff joke, but it actually got a laugh.

Within a couple of seconds I realized, firstly, that I'd been in hibernation for the best part of a year; and secondly that, with an almost amphetamine rush, I was alive again. This was my show, and my audience. All I had to do was take control. I counted off the first song, not just with the authority of having written it, but with an intoxicating feeling of power. The band—my band—exploded into action and played like maniacs. The audience loved it. By the end of the evening, my voice hoarse, drenched in sweat, I felt like I'd just gone ten rounds with Muhammed Ali, but I was still high—I didn't want it to stop, ever.

I don't know how I managed to sleep that night. I had to quit the Playboy Club, move to London, make an album. How come I'd wasted so much time?

Finally, I could taste and smell and feel what I'd only glimpsed before: me, the band, and the audience all vibrating on the same frequency, linking arms in free fall, time standing still somewhere high above the clouds. Genius that I was, alchemist, wizard, mad professor, I'd found the cure for gravity.

The next day, I was Clark Kent again, back in my purple-and-silver-wallpapered corner, playing bossa novas and backing a "vocal stylist" by the name of June Ricci.

The following week, several interesting things happened. I celebrated my twenty-third birthday, Elvis Presley died, and Charles Hawtrey, of *Carry On* film fame, came into the Playboy and bought me a drink. He was very much the worse for wear, and told me in a cloud of brandy-breath that I was "the besht young pianisht he'd sheen in bloody yearsh." I didn't know whether to be flattered or not. Then came a visit from the local cabaret celebrities, Koffee'n'Kreme.

Koffee'n'Kreme were Lance Ellington and Bet Hannah, a vocal duo who fronted the resident band at the Mecca. It seems amazing now, but at that time ballrooms like those of the Mecca and Locarno chains still actually had large and versatile house bands that played for dancing, probably as a result of the same Musicians' Union strictures that had kept getting Arms and Legs booked and booed in discos. Portsmouth's Mecca band was led by that crowd-pleasing rarity, a female drummer, by the name of Christy Lee. She was also Lance and Bet's manager, now that they'd been winners on *New Faces,* the TV talent show, twice in a row. Seizing the day, Koffee'n'Kreme were about to launch themselves onto the national cabaret circuit, and they needed an MD.

I didn't know what to say. I could handle the gig in my sleep, and it would pay a bit more than the Playboy. But it was the right thing at the wrong time. Or was it the wrong thing at the right time? I could still do with a bit more money to finance my album. But how much longer could I stand the cabaret world?

I said I'd think about it, and I did, hard. Meanwhile the world of New Wave seemed to converge, just a bit, with the world of the Playboy. Nigel, a young gay croupier who was dressing in punk style (even monkey-suited for work, his spiky haircut and earring were conspicuous) came in one day with a black eye. He'd been beaten up, not, as I first assumed, for being gay, but for being a punk. A gang of punks from Paulsgrove started to hang out at our local watering hole, the Queens. And then there was Maynard Williams.

Maynard Williams was an actor, singer, and musician who was the son of the comic actor Bill Maynard. By inclination, he was more a rock 'n' roller than anything else, but he was "doing the circuit" for a while to raise some money. When he showed up at the Playboy, it was obvious within five minutes that we were both out of place there and had a lot in common.

Maynard was a skinny guy, a few years older than me, who seemed to bristle with energy. He had the disturbing intensity of someone on speed, but without the drugs—that was just how he was. He talked fast, in an effort to keep up with a whirlpool of a brain, and for some reason we were yammering on about punk bands we'd seen before we even started rehearsing his act. Admittedly, I was probably the only cabaret MD he'd come across who'd just turned twenty-three and wore a Maltese cross earring.

That night Maynard sang "I Got the Music in Me," "Candle in the Wind," "Solitaire," and a few other old chestnuts with what looked to me, if not the audience, like obvious disdain. Then he asked the audience if there were any Sex Pistols fans in the house, which drew a nervous titter from two or three people, and blank stares from everyone else. "Mandy" was applauded politely, but then Maynard confounded them again by launching into a sort of satirical punk-rock medley. He'd recently appeared in a deplorable comedy film called *Confessions of a Pop Performer,* about a rough-and-ready rock band, and he put together a couple of the songs from the film "for a bit of a laugh." The band in the film were called Kipper, and the first song was their anthem: "The name is Kipper, Kipper, mean as Jack the Ripper." This was followed by "Do the Clapham":

Here's a new dance that's going round
It's gonna be the rage of London town
. . . Grab a partner half your size
Then thump her right between the eyes
Then if you're bored and you want a laugh
Kick a few members of the catering staff
. . . There's one more thing that ought to be said
You can do this dance on someone's head.

Nervous titters from two or three people, and blank stares from everyone else. The week before, this medley had gotten Maynard kicked out of a smart club in Surrey—they weren't going to stand for any "punk filth." But Maynard finally won the Playroom over by ending with a Neil Sedaka medley.

That week, Maynard came to the Cumberland before his spot at the Playroom, and saw half of the second-ever gig by the Joe Jackson Band. The pub was even more packed than the last time, I felt a bit more confident, and Mark wore a turquoise off-the-shoulder crimplene catsuit, which he'd inherited from an eccentric friend who used to play bass in the '50s for Johnny Kidd and the Pirates. I dedicated the show to the memory of "a great star and a real hero of mine ever since I can remember"—the audience assumed I was referring to Elvis, but when I said the name of Groucho Marx, who'd died the day before, a cheer went up. (Shortly afterwards I saw a punk fanzine that gleefully celebrated Elvis's death. "His gut," it said, "was casting a shadow over rock 'n' roll.")

Our second show was every bit as exhilarating as the first. I'd never imagined it would be so easy to get a reaction out of an audience, and to get them on my side. After the show, it suddenly occurred to me that I might have learned something from all those cabaret acts after all. Nothing musical, but something, perhaps, about how to confront an audience? I'd never thought of myself as a "performer" before. All of a sudden, I didn't want to be anything else.

The next day, Maynard Williams, who'd been blown away by the gig, grabbed me and demanded, with even more than his usual intensity, "What the bloody hell are we doing at the Playboy Club?!"

A week later, he got a large gas bill and remembered. Many years later, he would make a fortune in the West End, performing in Andrew Lloyd Webber musicals for years before moving to the south of France. As for me, I quit the Playboy, after ten long months, but I still needed a bit more time, and money, to finish my album and launch myself onto the New Wave music scene. I gritted my teeth, prayed for strength, and became the pianist and musical director of Koffee'n'Kreme.

The Second Piece of Advice

KOFFEE'N'KREME were obviously going to be pretty corny. The name alone guaranteed it. It was both too cute and somehow crass, almost racist. Lance, who was the handsome and rather flamboyant offspring of the black bandleader Ray Ellington and a blonde actress, was "coffee," and Bet, who was a down-to-earth Glaswegian, was "cream." They both had shortish Afro hairdos and looked good together, in a cabaret sort of way.

What exactly *is* "cabaret," anyway? In the States the word suggests a rather classy performance by a singer in an intimate setting, drawing material from the worlds of jazz and the Broadway musical. In France it's more likely to involve satirical humor. And we all have some vague, romantically decadent idea of cabaret in the Berlin of the 1930s.

Cabaret in Britain, as typified by Koffee'n'Kreme, prided itself (sometimes misguidedly) on professionalism; and the musicians had to read music, which meant that a lot of them had a jazz or musical theater background. But otherwise, it was widely understood to be populist entertainment, with no pretensions to art: fun for all the family, often slightly tacky, but careful never to offend. It didn't have much to do with rock 'n' roll, but it wasn't entirely at odds with pop. In fact, most cabaret singers sang recent disco or ballad hits. No one, at any time, performed original material. Crowd-pleasing was the whole point, so songs were selected from a repertoire of proven crowd-pleasers.

Koffee'n'Kreme were going to travel with their own four-piece band,

and the act was to be based out of London. As I sat on the train en route to their first rehearsal, I reflected on the differences between me and them, and took stock of my career so far. The Big Questions I'd had when I started at the Academy seemed to have worked themselves out—but in ironic ways.

I'd started in music with high ideals. I wanted to excel at something, something meaningful, and I rejected—or was unaware of—petty restrictions based on class, age, or fashion. So I was drawn to "serious" music, "classical" music, "art" music. But as much as I loved the music itself, I became uncomfortable in that world and saw no future for myself there. I rebelled against it by becoming a populist. Now, confronted on a daily basis by the relentless, almost obsequious populism of the cabaret world, I wanted to rebel yet again. As I did at fifteen, I wanted to be a true, passionate artist in the face of mediocrity. Now, though, I wanted to do it with a rock band. In other words in a populist medium. Was it the right medium?

At the time, I thought so. So much about being a rock performer seemed to be a balancing act: between pleasing yourself and pleasing a mass audience, between being true to yourself and true to the medium, between the desire to revel in trash and kitsch and cheap thrills and the desire to excel, between celebrating youth and having to get a year older every year. I thought—fingers crossed, touch wood—that I could pull it off. I thought I could have my cake and eat it too. Stupid expression! Wasn't eating the cake the whole point? I mean, what else is a cake for?

I was still buzzing from my first shows with my own band. I'd come so close to what I *really* wanted. Koffee'n'Kreme would be a bizarre diversion, as though this London-bound train were to stop just before reaching Waterloo and then lurch off onto some obscure branch line. I made a solemn promise to myself: keep writing; keep recording songs, one at a time if necessary; don't let go.

My confidence level was better than it had been a year or two before, but it could still be shaky. Just before leaving for London, I had a long talk with Mark Andrews, and told him all my plans: making an album, taking it to independent labels but with a contingency plan to release it myself, moving to London, and having my own band standing by, ready for action. Mark was impressed. He said that, if nothing else, I didn't lack confidence. This surprised me, until I realized that once again, what looked like confidence to others felt like desperate, white-knuckled determination to me. I *had* to succeed in music. I was no good at anything else.

Things were simpler for Koffee'n'Kreme. They may have been a bit nervous about launching their act—they were only human. But there was no question in anyone's mind about who they were and where they were going. They didn't have the sense, as I'd always had, of being on some sort of mission. They were just trying to cash in on a bit of TV exposure. In a way, I envied them.

At a rehearsal room somewhere off Tottenham Court Road, I met the rest of the entourage. It was bigger than I'd expected. K'n'K's act wasn't just *their* act. It was being professionally produced, at considerable expense. There was a producer, a musical arranger, and a choreographer, all of whom seemed like stock characters—you knew at a glance who did what. Then there was a Russian-Jewish booking agent, from the Mecca organization, called Ivor Rabin, who was even more archetypal. Big, cigar-smoking, wearing an astrakhan overcoat, a fur hat, and the air of an old-fashioned impresario, he could have played the part of an agent in any movie musical of the '30s.

Rehearsals, for Lance and Bet, were as much about dance steps and gestures and looking at each other in the right way as they were about music. Koffee'n'Kreme's act was planned with military precision: exactly forty-five minutes, and nothing left to chance.

The band, luckily, were all nice guys, cabaret veterans who knew each other from years of holiday camps, variety shows, and Christmas pantomimes. Tony, the guitarist, was the oldest, in his midthirties, with a sad Buster Keaton face, a cockney accent, and a very dry sense of humor. Dennis, the bassist, was a bit younger and also a Londoner. He was smartly dressed, good-looking, smoothly professional, and a good player. Jimmy, the drummer, was a year or two older than me. He was a friend of Bet's from Glasgow, from a theatrical family—his father was a well-known Scottish comedian—and very friendly, with an infectious goofy grin.

The Koffee'n'Kreme show started, ambitiously, with Stevie Wonder's "Sir Duke," but then settled into more predictable fare: obvious duet choices like "Don't Go Breaking My Heart," an Abba medley, a '50s medley, and something or other by Neil bloody Diamond. Lance would leave the stage while Bet sang Boz Skaggs's "We're All Alone," and Lance's solo was Elton John's "Sorry Seems to Be the Hardest Word." It could have been worse. At least they both had decent voices and sang in tune, and at least we'd be traveling all over the country, and going to quite a few places

I'd never been. We'd be playing week-long residencies, for instance, in some of the big northern working-men's clubs, which were quite classy compared to the ones I was used to.

My chalk-striped suit was deemed not good enough, and I was told to get a "proper tux." I said, more-or-less truthfully, that I couldn't afford it, so Christy Lee reluctantly decided that "the act" would pay for one. It was, inevitably, the cheapest one they could find, made of stiff black cardboardy material, with too-short sleeves and braiding around the lapels. I hated it.

Koffee'n'Kreme hit the road in a green Sherpa van, which Tony the guitarist drove for a few pounds extra. The first warm-up shows were two nights at the Starlight Rooms in Enfield. Lance was scared stiff, although Bet, more experienced and more professional, seemed calm. During the show, Lud Romano, their choreographer, sat a couple of tables back, prompting them with what looked like semaphore signals, regardless of the punters around him. I felt a bit sorry for Lance and Bet. This wasn't really their show at all. It wasn't really anyone's. The audience response was what it would be on every gig from now on: warm but never quite ecstatic.

Lance offered to put me up for the first couple of weeks, as we did a string of one-nighters within an hour or two of London. Mostly we had his mother's Bloomsbury flat to ourselves, with occasional visits from the startlingly young and sexy mother. Lance's parents were divorced, and as far as I could gather, he'd grown up alternately spoiled and neglected. He turned out to be much younger than I'd thought—only twenty—wore silk shirts, gold chains and bracelets, and always seemed to be admiring himself in a mirror. I couldn't relate to him at all, but he laughed easily, at least, and we got on well enough.

I soon began to notice that Koffee'n'Kreme's public image didn't reflect their true relationship. Privately, they couldn't have been more different. Bet was twelve years older than Lance. She was tough, practical, and straightforward, and a seasoned veteran, whereas Lance seemed to treat the whole thing as a bit of a lark. Onstage, they looked like a cute young couple in love. Offstage, they steered clear of each other. To add irony to irony, Bet was a lesbian, and if she *had* been interested in men, Lance would probably have been the last man on earth she'd have picked.

The backing band cultivated a faintly amused neutrality toward the stars of the show, while I was teased good-naturedly about being the only punk MD in the business. There was none of the pumping adrenaline and passionate determination of a rock band like Arms and Legs. This band was friendly but slightly detached.

No one thought the show itself was any big deal. As Dennis said, it was just a forty-five-minute interruption of the main business: chasing girls and drinking. The show, after all, was the same every night, exactly to the note, even down to the patter between songs. This deliberate avoidance of all spontaneity was pure cabaret, although over the years I've realized that a lot of rock 'n' roll shows are equally choreographed.

In other words, you can't distinguish the Artists from the Entertainers by genre. Every musical category contains some of each. Cab Calloway and Duke Ellington can both be categorized as big band jazz, but Cab was unambiguously an Entertainer, while the Duke was an Artist of the highest caliber.

So what *is* the difference?

Maybe they were born under different signs. I've been skeptical of astrology ever since I found out that I share a birthday with both Enid Blyton, quaint old-fashioned author of the quaintest of quaint children's books, and a notorious German serial killer known as the Butcher of Cologne. Nevertheless I can imagine two extra signs of the Zodiac:

* *The Entertainer* (Jan 1–Dec 31)—you want to make people happy. You want to be accepted. You think your best-selling work must be your best—the one where you got it *right*—and you feel obligated to give people more of the same. You enjoy applause as an end in itself, and the more applause there is, the better job you feel you've done. The face you present to the world isn't necessarily you. It may well be an act, a routine, a *shtick*. You are likely to be a conservative or traditionalist, more likely to take the easy or proven route, and you don't want to change the world. You just want to enjoy yourself and make a few quid along the way. And if you can bring enjoyment to others, too, why then, what could be better?

  Your weak point: Paranoia. You may become a superstar, but still lack self-esteem. This is because your guiding lights—applause, box office receipts, good press—are all outside yourself, and ultimately out of your control.

* *The Artist* (Jan 1–Dec 31)—you are interested in the pursuit of truth, beauty, and new insights and connections. You want to be an individual,

> rather than run with the pack. You ask questions and don't necessarily accept the answers you get. You may like applause, but it's not an end in itself. You don't necessarily consider your best-selling work to be your best, especially since you're always striving for something better. What you do is not an act. It's *you*. And you don't want people just to have fun, but to join you in thinking, feeling, and exploring. Your ultimate goal may even be almost religious: not simple pleasure, but transcendence.
>
> Your weak point: Self-indulgence. That is, a tendency to think that every lame or trivial idea that comes into your head is important, just because the muse brought it along with all the good ones. Remember that an artist needs an audience, too, and a ruthless internal editor to make sure your work is as good, as focused, and as accessible as it can be —on its own terms.

Of course these stereotypes don't always hold up. Many of us are both, just as we're both masculine and feminine, or introvert and extrovert. For some, the balance comes naturally. But every creative person should know which side they ultimately come down on. What's your "bottom line?" It was pretty obvious what Koffee'n'Kreme's was. But working with them, ironically, was going to help me to define my own.

Knowing your bottom line gets more important as you get older, and more important still if you have some success. Money and success don't change you, but tend to reveal you for who you really are. And few things are more revealing, in the wake of success, than the way you answer the inevitable question: And now what?

This brings me to the second, and last, piece of advice that I'm prepared to give to aspiring musicians—or anyone else. Be yourself, and as far as possible, try to do something wherein you can give the *best* of yourself. It's harder than it sounds: "Be yourself" has been reduced to a slogan, but knowledge of any kind takes some work, and self-knowledge is no exception.

In the meantime, don't use Madonna as a role model if who you *really* relate to is Joni Mitchell. Or vice versa. Don't mutilate your foot, trying to squeeze it into Cinderella's slipper. I've tried to do some of that myself, but nowadays there's no doubt in my mind: I'm one of the ugly sisters.

And *proud* of it.

Life in a Suitcase

I DECIDED to let go of my bedsit in Southsea. I wasn't going to be spending much time in any one place for a while, and the next time I had a flat of my own, I wanted it to be in London.

I stored my few belongings in my parents' attic, and, for the first but by no means the last time, packed the suitcase out of which I was going to live. The suitcase contained several copies of my Telecoms tape, and not a whole lot else. The last thing I did before leaving for a week at the Talk of the North in Manchester was to buy a black leather jacket. Most of the time I wore it with black drainpipe jeans.

In Manchester we stayed in a boarding house presided over in motherly fashion by a lady called Winnie, who cooked us massive roast dinners in a cozy room with a roaring fire. Unfortunately it was the only room in the house that was heated. The bedrooms were chilly but tolerable under a pile of blankets and eiderdowns, this being October—we didn't know yet that we'd be back in January, which would be a different story. After Winnie's, it was mostly downhill. I hadn't realized that we were expected to pay for our accommodation out of our wages. Since no one wanted to spend any more than they really had to, we would always be sleeping two or three to a room in dreary places with cold bedrooms and nylon sheets, living on toast with margarine and queuing for bathrooms.

Standing luxuriously in between our Manchester digs and the club were a fish-and-chip shop and a magnificent old pub called the Packet

House, where several pints of Boddingtons bitter before the show were de rigueur. After the show there'd be several more of whatever the club was serving, along with a couple of brandies or whiskies. And this was a mere aperitif compared to the Rabelaisian excesses to come. These guys were just getting started.

Every situation I'd found myself in as a musician had involved the consumption, sometimes the excessive consumption, of alcohol. But Koffee'n'Kreme were the champions. Lance got through a bottle of scotch a day, and Bet always seemed to have a glass of something in her hand. Jimmy drank anything, but Dennis and Tony were beer connoisseurs and members of the still-young Campaign for Real Ale. A well-thumbed copy of CAMRA's *Good Beer Guide* lived in the van, and it was religiously consulted every time we got to a new town. I liked a good pint of bitter myself, and now that I had the opportunity to educate my palate further, I became a lifelong devotee. I still love traditional English beer more than most things in life.

At the Talk of the North we set up in the basement on a platform that would then rise dramatically up to the stage. Away from London, with nothing else to do but relax and get to know each other, the band members started to reveal idiosyncrasies. The dashing Dennis, for instance, made good on his threat to chase girls—preferably nubile teenage ones. His lady-killer image was offset, though, by a schoolboyish enthusiasm for steam trains, and he would occasionally show up with an LP of train noises under his arm.

His good friend Tony had opposite tastes in women. Although he was married and didn't chase them, he had an obsession with "matrons"—mature women of some physical stature—preferably dressed in some kind of uniform, or, better still, rubber. He called Bet "Auntie Betty" and seemed to be the only one of us who lusted after her. If she wasn't quite a matron, she apparently had the makings of one.

Tony's sense of humor was as dry as the Sahara, and he often talked in a world-weary, philosophical way. We would be heading up the M1, and he'd look around at the autumn scenery and say solemnly, "Y'know, there's something about this special time of year that stirs a special feeling in the depths of my miserable fuckin' soul." No one was ever quite sure if he was joking or serious. In fact, Tony was warm-hearted but prone to melancholy. He was also, though no one acknowledged it, an alcoholic.

Jimmy was the most accessible member of the team, always "up," never a problem. Bet had frequent bad moods, and I didn't realize at first that they usually had something to do with her partner. Lance and Bet weren't just two very different personalities; it was increasingly obvious that they couldn't stand each other. It could only get worse.

On the way out of Manchester I was talked into playing my tape in the van. Bet said nothing, Lance giggled, and the boys in the band all laughed and cheered and said it was great, but didn't seem to take it very seriously. Good for you, Joe, now, where's that *Good Beer Guide?* This was fine with me. I knew going into this gig that we were from different musical planets, and it was enough for me that there was no hostility.

Our next residency was in Dublin. It was the first time I'd been out of Britain, and the first time I'd flown, which terrified me. But Dublin was fascinating. It struck me as a smaller, darker, quirkier, more Victorian version of London. We were booked for a week at a club called the Chariot Inn, which had just reopened after burning down, under mysterious circumstances, for the fourth or fifth time.

We were to stay in a guest-house in Rathmines run by a Mrs. Flaherty. In a matter-of-fact way she explained that there was a man dying in a nearby hospital, and that she was renting a room to his wife until he did. Since the "ould feller" was taking a bit longer to pop off than everyone expected, she was one room short. So I ended up staying in a house around the corner but joining the others for breakfast, along with a wild-looking hairy man with no shoes and smelly feet.

I saw the hairy man again at the upstairs bar of the Chariot Inn after our first show. He introduced himself as Ray Azala, finished his drink, then took a bite out of the glass and chewed it with horrific crunching noises. "Mmmm, delicious!" he said, took another bite, and wandered off.

Ray Azala, it turned out, was our opening act, whom I'd missed. He was a Strong Man, who broke chains on his chest, ate fire, and smashed his face into a pile of broken glass. His act was very strange indeed. It ended with Ray on his knees with an iron sword against his throat, and half a dozen burly volunteers from the audience pushing against it. After a few minutes of grunting and straining, the sword would bend.

The next morning Ray Azala stumbled down to breakfast, once again in his malodorous bed-socks, and once again Mrs. Flaherty served, for some reason, fizzy orangeade with our bacon and eggs.

"I'm turribly sorry, Joe," she said to me, straight-faced, "But dat feller's not dead yet. I'll be sure to let ye know as soon as he is." She left the room and there was a moment of stunned silence.

"Still not dead, eh?" said Jimmy.

"Not very thoughtful, is he?" said Dennis.

"The bloody cheek of the man!" said Tony.

"Inconsiderate bastard," said Bet.

After breakfast we wandered around the town. Dennis would shake his head at some odd piece of local color and say, "Blimey, it's another country, isn't it?"

"Dennis," I said, "it *is* another bloody country."

Afternoons and early evenings were spent in a doomed attempt to have at least one pint of Guinness in every pub in Dublin. I got to know and love Ireland better in years to come, but this first visit went by in a bit of a daze.

By now I was practically counting the minutes until I could get back to playing my own music. But first: Blackpool, a town that seemed to take an inordinate pride in its own sheer ugliness. It was "out of season," of course, and every day brought gale-force winds and rain. We sheltered in a Yates's Wine Lodge, one of those bizarre northern institutions dedicated to the pursuit of cheap, quick, and total alcoholic oblivion. A rough, basic place with the atmosphere of a railway station, it served luridly colored "cocktails" with names like "Mermaid" and "Green Goddess," which made everyone giggle within minutes—God only knows what they put in them. We swapped and found they all tasted exactly the same.

The next day, there was a major storm that swept away half of one of the piers. I stood in a seaside pub with Dennis, pints of Thwaites bitter in hand, watching awestruck as forty-foot waves came crashing over the road. Little old ladies were lifted off their feet by the wind and blown into the paths of oncoming cars. Next morning, the streets were littered with broken roof-slates, and beautiful white swirling patterns had been salt-blasted into the windows of nearly every house.

I had to admit, working with Koffee'n'Kreme wasn't all bad. It could even be fun. And I was getting a taste of something I'd be doing a lot of in the not-too-distant future: touring. Not a bad way to make a living, albeit hard work, and not without its scary moments. Like waking up in a hotel room you don't remember checking into, and not being able to remember what town or even what *country* you're in. Then looking out the window and *still* being none the wiser. It usually turns out to be Belgium.

After Blackpool, a whole week off, and my first priority was to find a guitarist.

It had always been understood that Mark was a temporary stand-in. Besides, he now had his own band, the Gents. I managed to catch one of their first gigs, and I liked their image. Mark had apparently picked four of the meanest, ugliest, most degenerate-looking characters he could find—the drummer looked like an ax-murderer—and dressed them in cheap tuxedos and frilly shirts. I was probably more amused by this than most, since they looked exactly like a bunch of escaped convicts who were dodging the cops by masquerading as Koffee'n'Kreme's backing band.

I called the best guitarist I knew, Gary Sanford, who'd played on my Surrey University demo a couple of years before. I spent a night at his flat, which was close to Drew Barfield's in Camberwell. Gary impressed me by having an LP of the *Rite of Spring* and also by having become a big fan of both punk and reggae. He agreed to be the standby guitarist for the standby Joe Jackson Band and went down to Portsmouth with me on the train to rehearse for a couple of days in the scout hut.

Graham Maby and Dave Houghton welcomed Gary enthusiastically. Here, at last, was a band with no weak link, a band that showed all the signs of being the best band I'd played with so far. If I could only hold on to these guys! We recorded a couple of new songs. Even in the curiously deadening environment of Telecoms, they sounded great.

One of these songs was called "Is She Really Going Out With Him." Everyone liked it. It was catchy, they said, and had the makings of a hit. I wouldn't know a hit, I protested, from a hole in my head. I liked all my songs, and if I'd written a hit it was by accident. But I appreciated the enthusiasm, and something else, too: a growing feeling that I was Onto Something.

I got the song's title from a line on the Damned's first album, and they, of course, had got it from an old hit by the Shangri'Las. I thought it would be a good title for a funny little song about watching couples and wondering what the girls could possibly see in the guys.

People still occasionally tell me that this song is the best thing I've ever done. I'm certainly not ashamed of it, and I thank them, but I have to admit I sincerely hope they're not right.

Survival

NIGHT AFTER NIGHT, Koffee'n'Kreme gazed lovingly into each other's eyes, while all around us, punk was having its Summer of Hate. Maybe every summer has to be the Summer of Something. But the music scene of the late '70s was more diverse than a lot of people remember. You could do pretty much what you liked as long as you didn't wear flared trousers.

Punk was the point at which pop/rock music finally split into what would become an infinite number of subgenres. It was certainly cracked, but now, like Humpty Dumpty, it broke into little pieces, and nothing could put it back together again.

Not that it was planned that way. Even in its earliest, purest form, punk wasn't a political movement, or even a unified front. The Sex Pistols were anarchists and provocateurs, the Damned were a kitsch cartoon, the Ramones played bubblegum pop really fast, and the Clash were a high-energy rock band, not so different, if you think about it, from the Who.

I first saw the Clash some time in 1977, in Guildford. I took Jill, my ex-girlfriend, with me. We were experimenting, briefly, with "being friends." Jill was frightened from the minute we got off the train by the purple-haired, leather-and-chain-clad mutants hanging around on every corner. But I'd seen more violence around sailors' pubs in my hometown than I was ever going to see at a punk gig. And I was mesmerized by the sheer intensity of the Clash. These guys, I thought, *meant* every note.

How different were the Clash from the Pistols, really? It's a question of perspective: how you focus that zoom lens. Anyway, everything is eventually subject to revisionism. A few years ago, *Rolling Stone* published a critics' poll of the 100 Greatest Rock Records of All Time. And what was Number One? *Never Mind The Bollocks,* by the Sex Pistols.

I got a good laugh out of this. The conventional wisdom here is that punk reinvigorated rock—reconnected it with its pure essence. Maybe, seeing the Clash in 1977, you could have believed it. But the Pistols came not to save rock but to destroy it. Or at least, to take the piss. Their music is a vicious, sneering travesty of rock, and saying that they made the greatest rock album ever is like saying the San Francisco Earthquake was a great day for architecture.

Most punk bands were dreadful. They were lucky to get fifteen seconds, let alone fifteen minutes, of fame. I didn't care. In between Koffee'n'Kreme gigs I locked up my tux, put on my leather jacket, and went to as many gigs as I could. I saw the Vibrators, the Slits, Chelsea, Siouxsie and the Banshees, and quite a few bands whose names we've all forgotten. Some of my friends and colleagues were surprised at me. Arguments erupted: How could I, a music college graduate, support musicians who, in some cases, barely knew how to strap on a guitar, let alone play it?

Irony, in my musical life, seemed to keep piling on top of irony. A lot of my musical training had been in storage, in the attic of my brain, while I played with rock 'n' rollers. But now I liked music that many of them considered beyond the pale. Now *they* were the snobs! They'd spent years trying, as they saw it, to be real musicians. Who did these spiky-haired upstarts think they were?

Actually, from the point of view of pure musicianship, it's possible to see the whole history of popular music in the twentieth century as one of steady decline. Ragtime was played by classically trained musicians at a time when classical training, for anyone with a serious interest in music, would have been taken for granted. The big band jazzmen of the '30s and '40s may or may not have had such training, but they certainly mastered their instruments, read music, and could improvise well or even brilliantly. Many early rock 'n' rollers had jazz chops but made a conscious choice to keep things simple. You can see where this is heading. Punk was the end of the line.

Mark Andrews had come over to my Southsea bedsit one day to listen to the first album by the Damned. I grinned through the whole thing, while he half-smiled and half-frowned.

"What do you think?" I asked.

Mark thought for a moment.

"It's the last word," he said, half-seriously pretending to be an old fart, "the last word in nasty, loud, horrible pop groups."

You couldn't get more raw, more primitive, more unschooled than this —or so we thought.

We couldn't have foreseen the advent of music video, or the phenomenal advances in music technology. It's now possible to be a star on the basis of just looking the part and pressing a few buttons—or having someone press them for you. I'm exaggerating a bit, of course. But technology now allows almost anyone to make a record that doesn't sound much different from the records on the radio. In New York recently I saw a band —though not a "band" in the traditional sense—called The Prodigy, three members of which played nothing and could hardly be called singers either, and one of whom only danced, and not exactly brilliantly at that, on just three or four songs. Hardly anything was actually played "live."

I didn't care. I thought they were great. But the bass-playing friend I'd gone with wasn't quite so sure. He wore the same half-and-half expression afterwards that Mark had done after listening to the Damned, and he reminisced about the heady days of punk.

"At least then," he argued, "you had to play an instrument, just a little bit, to get into a band. Now it seems like all you have to do is be a buddy of the guy who makes the drum loops."

"I know what you mean," I said, "but so what, really?"

The bassist frowned.

"I suppose I just worry," he said, "that most people don't know the difference."

My head told me that he had a point, that it *is* harder and harder for the general public to sort the wheat from the chaff. It would be nice to see people paying their musical dues again, really learning their craft, not as an end, but as a beginning.

But my heart said: What the hell, I *liked* the Prodigy. They were exciting and fun and the guy making the drum loops was much more than that, and actually quite brilliant. And I seemed to be having the same arguments with "real" musicians in 1997 as I did in 1977, as I defended, for instance, the best electronic dance music for being inspired on its own terms.

I'll still take "amateurish but entertaining" over "worthy but dull" any day. I also think that, humans being human, every genre will ultimately (once the feeding-frenzy of hipness fades away) be found to contain about the same proportion of the good, the bad, and the yawningly mediocre. Besides, if you don't like the music of the moment, all you have to do is stick around. Every trend, when carried far enough, grows within itself the seeds of a backlash.

Back in 1977, the bad bands could still be fun, and the good ones—who were too musical to be classed as punk and came under the heading of New Wave—were getting really interesting. Especially Television, the Talking Heads, and Elvis Costello. Inspiring, too. Here were people, I thought, doing things not so far removed from what I was trying to do, and if they could make it, why not me?

I should have realized even then that comparisons between me and Elvis were inevitable. At first I was irritated. Over the next few years, as the comparisons kept dogging me, I would start to develop a nervous tic that would flare up murderously at the mere mention of his name. Elvis? I'd say; wasn't he that fat bastard who died on the toilet? Nowadays I'm more philosophical. After all, we *do* have a lot in common, and the comparison is actually flattering.

Apart from shattering whatever unity or cohesion rock might have had, punk was also the point at which rock realized that desperate measures were needed to prolong its rebellious youth. Afraid that it was getting too respectable, it stuck safety pins through its cheeks, said "fuck" on the telly, beat up people it didn't like, and spat at those it did.

As much as I enjoyed the whole circus, though, I didn't, even at twenty-three, think that being provocative just for the sake of it was particularly clever. Provocation without some greater sense of purpose is ultimately empty. Many great works of art have been provocative. The *Rite of Spring* caused a full-scale riot at its first performance in 1913. But Stravinsky didn't write it just because he wanted to start a riot. He'd come up with something provocative in a deeper sense: by having brilliant ideas that a lot of people weren't quite ready for. To use a more recent example, Bob Dylan caused an uproar in 1965 by "going electric." In both cases, the riots were broken up, but the music survives.

Punk wasn't really a revolution. It was phase three of a revolution which started back in the '50s, when white kids in the American South started playing black music. That was pretty damn revolutionary. Those middle-aged rednecks we see in old newsreels, railing against "nigra music" and burning records, weren't just comic fuddy-duddies. They thought their whole civilization was crashing down in flames around them, and in many ways, they were right.

Since the '70s, pop music's efforts to stay "bad" have seemed more and more desperate. Recently we've seen hard rock bands who may (or may not) be practicing satanists, and the Gangsta Rapper, a music star who not only looks and sounds like a murderous sociopath, but may (or may not) actually *be* one. Where do we go from here?

Maybe, in a few more years, rock concerts featuring live on-stage disembowelings will be all the rage, and I'll look like a naive old buffer. But somehow I think it's more likely that we've hit the wall. Forty-year-old writers for established newspapers commend young bands for being suitably anti-Establishment, and teenagers listen to Jimi Hendrix. Someone, somewhere, will probably always come up with a way to be provocative just for the sake of it. But to take it as seriously as those *Rolling Stone* critics apparently did, as the whole point of rock 'n' roll, will surely seem more and more desperate, too. If they were right (or even serious) about *Never Mind the Bollocks* being the pinnacle of rock, they should all have quit their jobs and folded the magazine the next day, because neither they, nor any of us, had anywhere to go from there, or anything to build on.

The Summer of Hate was the point at which the fatal poison got into the blood of rock 'n' roll: the bacteria of irony, self-parody, and cynicism. The Death of Rock has been announced many times, and I don't want to add yet another obituary. I think it's the heroic myth of rock that's dead. No form of *music* ever dies. It becomes an ingredient of something new, of forms we can't yet imagine; or it survives as a classic style. Bebop, bel canto, calypso, rock 'n' roll. Future generations will thrill to their first exposure to loud electric guitars, just as I thrilled to my first exposure to an orchestra, playing Beethoven's Seventh at Portsmouth Guildhall.

In the light of this, the Brit-Pop of the mid '90s, with its self-conscious evocations of the Beatles, Kinks, or early Bowie, makes perfect sense for its time. It's as though we'd come far enough to see some value, not just in revolution, but in some sort of continuity.

And, getting back to punk: The Clash's first album holds up better than the Pistols'. Why? Because the tunes are better. The music survives. The music *always* survives.

Out of the Woodpile

AS CHRISTMAS approached, I kept hearing Ian Dury singing "Sex and Drugs and Rock 'n' Roll," but I kept putting on my cheap tuxedo and playing schmaltz. There wasn't too much rock 'n' roll in Koffee'n'Kreme, but there were certainly drugs (if you counted alcohol) and sex (if you counted me out). Several times I had to pretend to be asleep while people did it in the next bed. I realized that one of the greatest gifts that money might be able to buy was privacy. First it was Dennis, in Eastbourne, and then Nick in Hereford. Nick was our new roadie, although he had no qualifications for the job, apart from his dedication to the pursuit of girls and booze. On the night in question, I not only had to put up with what seemed like hours of gasping and slurping, but also with Nick talking about me when they finished, telling his conquest what a weirdo I was. Thanks a lot, Nick. You were a lousy roadie, by the way.

Meanwhile I rebelled against the schmaltz by writing a song called "Fools in Love." Over a loping reggae bass line, which I hoped was vaguely sinister, I cataloged all the sick and deluded things that lovers did to each other, but ended each chorus with a twist: "I should know because this fool's in love again." I wasn't in love, but the juxtaposition of the romantic and the cynical suited my new style to a tee.

How much longer could I stand this split existence? The bow tied Dr. Jekyll and leather-jacketed Mr. Hyde? I resolved to take at least one step in the right direction by finding a flat in London. I couldn't go on abusing people's hospitality. I had to have my own place, or at least my own room somewhere. I put an advertisement in *Time Out*, and shortly afterwards I met Maura Keady.

Maura was just starting her career as a teacher and had managed to get a two-bedroom council flat in East Dulwich. We met at Waterloo station to discuss the possibility of sharing it, me in my leather jacket, her in an afghan coat that had seen better days. I liked Maura immediately. A few years older than me, she was from a big Irish family—both her parents were from Connemara—but had grown up in Battersea. She was a down-to-earth working-class Londoner through and through and obviously no fool. She had a forceful personality, without being intimidating; the kind of person who made me forget my shyness. We immediately established a bullshit-free zone. It was as though we'd known each other for years.

Koffee'n'Kreme soon had a week off, owing to the mysterious cancellation of a residency in Guernsey, so I went with Maura to look at the flat. It was on a rough housing estate on Dog Kennel Hill. I seemed to have a talent for finding nasty domiciles with picturesque names. We climbed a piss-stained and graffitied stairway to the third floor, only to find that Maura had been given the wrong key, and couldn't open the door. I peered through the letterbox and decided that the flat would do just fine, anyway. It was cheap, and convenient, since I was comfortable in southeast London —my friends in Camberwell were just down the road. There were no other promising candidates—I'd gotten some pretty strange replies to my ad—and besides, it felt right. Fate seemed to keep dragging me to this part of town, and fate seemed to want to entwine my life in some way with Maura's.

Maura was moving in the following week. We agreed that, because of my schedule, I'd wait until the new year. Koffee'n'Kreme had another string of one-nighters coming up, followed by a Christmas residency in Sheffield.

We headed up the M1 on a cold, gray day—we *always* seemed to be heading up the M1 on a cold, gray day, and I was depressed. Not by the weather, but at the thought of all the London gigs, and London adventures, and London opportunities I was missing out on.

But what the hell, it was Christmas, and at the Fiesta Club in Sheffield a festive mood prevailed. There was always some kind of party going on in the spacious backstage area. Halfway into the week Jimmy and I, prowling around, found Dennis holed up in a dressing room with the pianist of the house band. Dennis had discovered, quite by chance, that the pianist shared his passion for steam trains, and they bonded like brothers. Tonight was a special occasion. The pianist had brought his film projector in, and the two of them sat, pints in hand, watching priceless footage from the Age of Steam, and I swear I saw a tear in Dennis's eye.

Touching though this was, Jimmy and I decided to move on. From the next dressing room we heard the razzing sound of a party noisemaker, and knocked on the door. "Oh hello lads, come in," said the house bassist, casually, so we did. In front of us stood the house drummer with his trousers round his ankles, and a very fat, completely naked girl on her knees in front of him.

"Oh, this is Janice, lads," said the bassist, still completely casual, as if absentmindedly introducing an old friend at a polite wine-and-cheese party. Janice actually tried to reply, and said something with her mouth full, which sounded like "Gmmmph." Meanwhile the house trombonist knelt behind her, blowing the noisemaker, in and out, at her enormous quivering arse.

After a while—how much of this sort of thing can you watch?—Jimmy and I paid our respects and left. Hardly daring to knock at the next dressing room, we headed for the bar. On the way we passed Tony, who was holding court at a table of old ladies. The youngest of them couldn't have been under eighty.

"Christ," said Jimmy, "I knew he liked older women, but . . ."

More and more, Tony sought out the oldest women he could find. There was nothing sexual about it, he protested. He just liked the company of old women more than anyone else. You could look into their eyes, he said, and see nothing but kindness.

We spent Christmas Day in the pub where we'd found our digs courtesy of the *Good Beer Guide*, drunk, singing around an old piano, then attempting Christmas carols in four-part harmony. After a particularly poignant rendition of "In the Bleak Midwinter," Bet looked at me, slightly cross-eyed, and said: "Ye know, when ye were singin' that, a completely different expression came over yir face."

"What d'you mean?" I asked.

"Well . . . sort'ae peaceful. Sort'ae innocent. Beautiful."

"Bloody hell," I said. I had no idea what my face was doing, since I'd lost control of it, along with most other parts of my body, at least an hour ago. But I could see why my relationship with Bet had always been polite but cool. She couldn't understand how she'd ended up with an MD who wore a leather jacket and a Maltese cross or a paperclip in his ear.

Bet just didn't *get* New Wave. One day in the van she snatched a copy of the *NME* from me, with the Damned scowling and mugging on the front page.

"What's the *matter* with these people?" she demanded. "Why d' they have to look as *ugly* as possible? Why are they always making *stupid faces?*" (In her accent, it sounded like "stew-pit feces"). Bet, a cabaret trouper to the end, would never let a camera within miles of her unless she'd had her hair done and was wearing her best dress. I really didn't know how to explain my perversity to her, and I regretted it, because as distant as her sensibility was from mine, I liked her.

As we left Sheffield for a residency in Lancashire, I was finally overwhelmed both by a heavy cold and a monstrous asthma attack that had been building for a couple of days. I could barely stagger onto the stage, and Lance and Bet were so worried they decided to bring in a "dep" and give me a week or two of sick leave. Since I was going to have to go to my parents' house to pick up my things anyway, I spent a miserable day taking various trains all the way down to Gosport.

Back in my old sick-bed again, feeling ten years old, miserable and defeated. It was the second-to-last big attack of my life. A year or two later I had one that put me in hospital for two weeks. Since then, apart from a bit of wheezing here and there, triggered by cold weather, flu, or allergies, I've been pretty healthy.

In January '78 I officially moved to London. The flat turned out to be comfortable enough, and just big enough for Maura and me to stay out of each other's way. I didn't mind sharing at all. In fact, I liked knowing that I wasn't completely alone, and I knew already that we were going to be good friends.

I bought a cheap secondhand upright piano and worked on a song called "One More Time," with a driving guitar riff and anguished lyrics about the end of a relationship. The guy can't believe the girl wants to leave: Tell me one more time, he says, one more time, one *more* time. I'd taken a little piece of my breakup with Jill, one moment, one feeling, and embellished it into something else. I guess that's how fiction works: not creating something false, but creating new truths out of bits of old ones. Just as we create new music by endlessly reshuffling the same old chords and scales.

With the last verse still unfinished, I was off to Nottingham and then once again to Manchester, where the drinking was now reaching epic, Viking Saga proportions. I was woken daily at around half past ten, and after a breakfast of porridge and toast to soak up some of the damage, I was dragged out for a lunchtime pub crawl and put away four or five pints. Then back to Winnie's for a nap. I'd wake up again around six, have a bath, and, feeling almost human, meet Tony and Dennis in the Packet House for a couple of pints of Boddingtons. After the show, we hung around the club drinking until they threw us out; then back to Winnie's, where the bedrooms were so cold you *had* to be drunk. The blankets and eiderdowns were now piled practically to the ceiling, but the starched sheets were like slabs of ice which never, ever, seemed to thaw out. Peering out from under them, I could actually see my breath forming a cloud of vapor over the bed. This time I was sharing with Jimmy, who swayed from side to side and said, "Right! The next time that bed comes roond here, I'm on it!"

I can drink a lot without getting obviously drunk, and when I do get drunk, my personality doesn't change dramatically. I just feel relaxed and laugh more easily. It just so happens that I have a high tolerance for alcohol. I don't say this as a boast, since I've never been quite sure whether it's a good or a bad thing. But in the case of Koffee'n'Kreme, it was a matter of sheer life-and-death necessity.

Over the next couple of months the rot set in. Tony started to grumble about the disorganization and bad digs; we would often arrive in a town center before we realized that no one had booked any accommodation, and one of us would have to get out at a phone box and consult the yellow pages.

Dennis badgered Ivor Rabin and Christy Lee for more money, to no avail. The act had cost so much to produce that it never made a penny, and pretty soon Lance and Bet would be stuck in the bind of needing a new act in order to keep going, but not being able to pay for it.

Bet was permanently furious at Lance. He showed up late or not at all for personal appearances they were supposed to make together for charities. Money went missing, all kinds of small things went wrong, and Bet blamed all of them on Lance—often, I suspect, with good reason. Even their agent, Ivor Rabin, said that Lance was "the nigger in the woodpile." This astonishing statement wasn't meant to be racist. It was just an expression, like "a spanner in the works."

At one gig, we met the housewife's favorite drag artiste, Danny La Rue, who had another way of putting it. Shockingly attired in a man's suit but still quite a long way from butch, he took Bet aside after the show. He was quite drunk.

"Dahling," he said, "you *have* to get rid of your *paht-nah.*"

"Oh yeah, why's that then?" asked Bet, more-or-less rhetorically.

"Because your paht-nah," said Danny, "is a *fucking wank-ah.*"

Neither of them knew that Lance was standing right behind them.

Lance didn't seem to care. More and more, he just did as he pleased. He started driving the van, and he was a frighteningly bad driver, one time trying to get out of a traffic jam by driving on the wrong side of the road. When there was only one mirror backstage—which was quite often—Lance would take it over, and Bet had to get to the club earlier and earlier to prepare for the show. But no matter how early she arrived, Lance would be there, preening. And the last straw: People constantly told Bet how wonderful it was to see a young couple on stage together who were so obviously in love. We can tell, they said, by the way you look at each other.

In February, a three-week residency at the Savoy Hotel in London, where the band played behind a mesh curtain. Several times, when I arrived for work in my leather jacket, I was turned away by a supercilious doorman and had to find a back way in. Then a week in Glasgow, and Bet and Jimmy spent the train journey telling us what a great place their hometown was. All that stuff about drunkenness and murder, they said, was a myth. Eventually we got off the train and stood at a taxi rank, where a crazy-eyed man in a filthy old overcoat accosted Lance and pointed at his, Lance's, gold bracelet.

"What the fuck d'ye call that?" he snarled.

"Errr ... a bracelet!" said Lance, flustered.

"Ye'd better get it off pal," said the crazy man, "they'll cut yer fuckin' hand off furrit roond here." It was the one time I saw Lance's face turn from coffee to cream.

Despite this rude introduction, we had fun in Glasgow. But by March and April I was really struggling. Rock bottom probably came in Workington, surely the ugliest and most boring town in England, where

Jimmy and I walked around in such a state of ennui that we resorted to desperate measures to keep our spirits up: going into a ladies' clothes shop, for instance, and trying to keep a straight face while Jimmy tried on a dress.

Then, at a swanky London nightclub, I did the show seriously drunk, and afterwards realized that I didn't remember playing a note of it. I'd done the whole thing on autopilot. This scared me. I told Lance and Bet to start looking for a new MD.

My farewell to the cabaret world was a posh black-tie function in the ballroom of the Grosvenor House Hotel, Park Lane. Before the show, the stars had a blazing row in their dressing room. Ivor Rabin tried to calm things down but eventually gave up and left them to it. Lance was poised to hit Bet, until she told him to go ahead, since she was just dying for an excuse to sue him. Lance dropped his fist, whereupon Bet punched him.

Lance stormed out of the dressing room, smashing glasses and overturning tables. Then, for forty-five minutes, Koffee'n'Kreme were lovebirds again. After that, Lance picked up where he'd left off, and overturned a grand piano.

"I knew he was the nigger in the woodpile," said Ivor.

I walked out in disgust, never to return.

Cogs and Gears

AT DOG KENNEL HILL, reggae music boomed through my bedroom wall, courtesy of the Jamaican family next door. Our upstairs neighbors were Turkish. They worked in an all-Turkish factory and spoke no English, but they took a liking to Maura and would invite her up for dinner. They communicated in sign language and Maura was allowed to sit at the table with the men while the women stayed in the kitchen.

It was a rough estate. Drug dealers lurked in corners, and hard-bitten twelve-year-olds trundled pushchairs around loaded with knocked-off radios and stereo components. But it didn't actually feel dangerous, as long as you used some common sense. It was certainly no worse than where I'd grown up, and besides, I liked the reggae music. Maura helped me to fit in, too. If someone knocked on the door wanting to use the phone, I thought they had a bloody nerve, but she'd invite them in for a cup of tea, and we'd get to know them. A born-and-bred south Londoner, she seemed completely at home, and she also had the gift of being able to turn strangers into friends. It was a gift I'd never really had, but after a while I got the sense that our neighbors assumed, since I lived with Maura, that I must be alright.

Drew Barfield had the same gift, and it was thanks largely to him that I had a rich social life in London. Pretty soon I seemed to know everyone who was worth knowing in the Camberwell area. Our meeting place was a large pub called the Grove House, which was always full of art students, actors (including Ian McKellen and a young and struggling Tim Roth), and musicians (including Wreckless Eric and members of Squeeze). Drew seemed to be the catalyst, the one person everyone knew, who introduced everyone to everyone else.

Drew and my other old friend, Steve Tatler, were doing all kinds of strange gigs these days. At one point they took off for a month-long tour of Finland with a '50s rock 'n' roll revival band. The drummer, Jeff, was a notorious thief, so skillful and daring that you had to admire him, even though he'd done two stretches in prison. He set off for Finland with nothing but a pair of sticks and a change of clothes, and came back on a motorcycle followed by a vanful of drum kits, furniture, and gardening equipment.

When Drew and Steve played the London pubs, their roadie was usually an extraordinary character called Mr. Beverage or Bevo, who was named after his habit of asking, "Anyone care for a beverage?" This had an oddly quaint ring to it, since Bevo could neither read nor write and for the most part even had a hard time with speaking—he called monitors "mollitors," and once, when an amp fell out of the back of a truck and narrowly missed his head, claimed he'd almost been decaffeinated. He also had a snake tattooed on an unusual, though actually quite appropriate, part of his anatomy. Bevo was no fool, however, but the kind of guy who usually manages to end up laughing at the people who once laughed at him. Nowadays he runs a successful equipment hire company.

Extraordinary characters seemed to be everywhere. There was the Greek barber in Camberwell Church Street who would cut your hair for a quid. He was cheap because he was cross-eyed and would always leave one side of your hair about an inch longer than the other. My favorite character, though, was the bassist of an Irish country and western band with whom Steve Tatler played one gig. He was painfully out of tune, and he obviously didn't know it. He was a big guy, and Steve didn't want to offend him, so he asked if he could try out his bass, so that he could tune it surreptitiously. The bassist agreed. But when Steve tried to turn the machine heads, they wouldn't move. All four of them were jammed tight.

"What the hell . . . ?" said Steve.

"Ah, there's a reason for that," said the bassist with a wink. "Y'see, 'twas in tune when I bought it, so I had 'em *welded.*"

I was becoming a passionate urbanite. I no longer saw the point of being anywhere but London. It would be a good ten years, for instance, before I'd even attempt a walk in the country, let alone enjoy it. The only time I left London was for Telecoms Studio in Portsmouth.

Gary Sanford and I went down on the train for more rehearsals at the Scout Hut. The Joe Jackson Band, despite its uncertain prospects, was starting to sound very good indeed. And it was all so easy! Not just because they were great players, but because there were no debates over strategy or musical direction or even the band's name—and no power struggles. The whole point of the band was to play my music.

As for me, I'd assumed the role of leader without even thinking about it, and that was easier than I would have expected, too. I wasn't the leader type, I thought—loud, dominant, intimidating—but I could lead simply by knowing what I wanted and asking for it politely. People who were players, rather than songwriters in their own right, responded. Someone has to tell them what to do. Human nature: Most people, in fact, are glad when someone steps forward and says, right, this is the way it's going to be.

After one rehearsal, Gary and I went to the Mecca ballroom to see the Buzzcocks. The gig was so-so. What really interested me was a girl I spotted in the crowd: surely the only black girl in Portsmouth, slender, just a little bit awkward, with close-cropped hair, standing all by herself in a bright yellow sweater. Gary and I soon found out that her name was Ruth Rogers-Wright.

She was a curious character. Instead of the West Indian patois I expected, she spoke with a laconic middle-class accent. Her mother was from Sierra Leone; her father was a black American who'd disappeared before she was born. She'd grown up mostly in Germany, but somehow ended up in Portsmouth, and she stood out like a whole fistful of sore thumbs. She seemed rather hard and cynical, but I sensed a vulnerability, too. She intrigued me, and she was also, I thought, heartbreakingly beautiful.

After a while I realized that Ruth was one of the very few women on planet Earth who didn't particularly fancy Gary. She was definitely interested in me. We exchanged phone numbers. I couldn't stop thinking about her. I had a strange feeling, a feeling that I've only had a few times in my life: a sense that something big was happening, an awareness of fate, like massive cogs and gears turning and clicking into place. I was probably in love and definitely in trouble.

I started submitting tapes to record companies. There was no point in waiting any longer, I thought. I was as ready as I'd ever be. The record companies didn't scare me. I wasn't afraid of rejection, since I liked the idea of putting out the record myself, anyway. But first I went to my two favorite boutique labels, Stiff and Chiswick, and to the major label I thought was the "hippest" at the time—Virgin. All three turned me down.

I tracked down Andy Arthurs and Steve Stevenson, no longer working together but still plugging away in the business. They both liked my tape, and they'd see what they could do, but I didn't expect much. There is a Japanese Samurai motto: "Expect nothing, but be ready for anything." I like that. It's definitely how I started to feel at this point of my life, and for the most part, how I still feel now.

Around this time I went to see Maynard Williams at the Young Vic, playing the Fool in a highly entertaining production of *Twelfth Night.* Freed from the clutches of the cabaret circuit, we met occasionally for a drink or a gig, and had some wild evenings. Sometimes Maynard's crazy friend Terry came along. Terry was an out-of-work actor, and a nice guy, until he'd had about fifteen pints, when he was liable to do just about anything. We went to see Generation X at the Roundhouse, and Terry started a loud drunken tirade about punks, what a bunch of wankers they were, especially this twat of a singer with Generation X who called himself Billy Idol. Any fuckwit could be a punk, shouted Terry, even him, at which point he decided to pierce his own ear with a safety pin. With his head down on the bar, knocking drinks all over the place, he tried to force the safety pin through his ear, and blood squirted everywhere.

"Terry, you mad bastard, for Chrissake stop it!" begged Maynard, trying to restrain him.

"Fuck off! It's punk, innit!" screamed Terry, as he was dragged out by bouncers. Years later Terry was to become a regular on *Coronation Street.*

By the end of May, my album was recorded and ready for mixing, which meant it was as good as finished, since I didn't see any reason that mixing should take more than a couple of days. I even hired a photographer I'd met through someone at the Playboy Club, to take some pictures for an album cover. Tongue firmly in cheek, we tried some wildly different looks: in one I wore a Teddy Boy drape coat, in another a hippie caftan. I'd been thinking about my "image," trying to decide whether I even wanted one.

I had a vague notion that I wanted to send up the whole idea of having an image, but I hadn't quite figured out how. I just wanted to be *sharp*. I started wearing black jeans with white shoes. It was a time, I thought, for black and white instead of color, mono instead of stereo, hard instead of soft, fact instead of fiction. "Sharp"—that was what I wanted to be, how I wanted my music to sound, how I wanted to look—you could be sharp even in clothes from Oxfam; it was all about attitude. I tried to sum up the attitude in a song called "Look Sharp," and I thought it might be a good title for the album, too. Then I decided to call my own label, if I started one, Sharp Records.

My funds were dwindling, though, and I signed on the dole. I hadn't saved as much money as I'd hoped—I was always spending it on beer and concerts. Once I'd paid off Telecoms, I'd probably be all right for a couple more months. I was trying not to think about what would happen after that.

I needn't have worried. It's strange, as I retrace my past, how much it reads like a novel. Everything seems to have happened when it was supposed to happen, and each step seems to have been the logical next step. Maybe everyone's life would seem that way, if they took the trouble to write about it. At any time, though, it could have gone in a thousand different directions. Maybe they would all have seemed logical, too, in retrospect.

Sometimes I think I believe in fate and sometimes I don't. Sometimes I think that fate is not some supernatural force, but the outcome of all the people in the world just being who they are. Responding to each other in their own particular ways and constantly setting off chain reactions that take on a kind of inevitability. When those chain reactions get so complex or so far removed from us that we can't see them, we just look at the end results and say: It must be fate.

As I was hawking my tape, an American record producer by the name of David Kershenbaum was spending a few months in London, under the auspices of A&M Records, looking for new talent. He was fed up with the American rock scene, which at that point had gotten pretty stale, and he was convinced that the best new stuff was going to be coming out of England for a while yet.

While Kershenbaum was hitting the clubs, a young man called Howard Berman had just been promoted to Label Manager at United Artists Records. He'd worked on a demo a while back at Telecoms Studio, with a band from the Isle of Wight. So, when he got a call from Mike Deveraux, the owner of Telecoms, telling him to watch out for a bloke called Joe Jackson, he said he'd see what he could do.

I went to see Howard and, although the album was virtually finished, gave him a "sampler" tape of four tracks, which he loved. Fresh and exciting and very "now," he said. Give me a deal then, I said. But it wasn't that simple.

Howard was the first record company person who helped and encouraged me, and I'll always be grateful to him. But he had no power to sign anyone. That was the prerogative of the A&R (Artists and Repertoire) department, and the A&R man didn't like my tape. Hang on, said Howard, he's leaving soon. I hung on, the A&R man left, and a new A&R man arrived. He didn't like the tape either.

Frustrated, Howard decided to pass me on to Albion. Albion was a company run by Derek Savage and Dai Davies, which was known mainly as a booking agency, but had recently started its own record label. Albion Records was marketed and distributed by Howard's company, United Artists. Howard was hoping that if Albion signed me, he could still be involved somehow.

Derek and Dai were very interested. So was a guy called John Telfer, who they'd just hired to run Albion Publishing. I wasn't sure how I felt about Derek and Dai at the time, and now, I think it's perhaps best to follow an old adage: "If you can't say something good about someone, say nothing." But I hit it off with John Telfer right away.

John was an impressive figure, tall, with an enormous beard, but with a surprisingly soft voice and gentle manner. He was passionate about music (not always true of people in the music business) and especially, at that point, about bringing great but obscure reggae artists over to the UK from Jamaica. He also wore a lot of black and had a predilection for white shoes.

As wary and cynical as I was, I felt that I could trust John. We discussed the possibility of my signing, if nothing else, a publishing deal with him. I'd never even thought about my publishing rights and royalties. But sooner or later I was going to need an ally in this business, and I had a good feeling about John.

Meanwhile, David Kershenbaum was about to throw in the towel. He hadn't found anyone he wanted to work with, and Jerry Moss—the "M" of A&M—wanted him back in LA. But a couple of days before he was due to leave, John Telfer played him my tape. John wasn't even aware that if David wanted to produce me, it was a pretty safe bet that he could also get me signed to A&M Records.

All this time, I'd been going backwards and forwards between London and Portsmouth, doing final mixes at Telecoms, and pursuing the enigmatic Ruth Rogers-Wright. She lived in a flat in Purbrook, on the outskirts of Portsmouth, and her mother lived just around the corner. Cyrillia Rogers-Wright was quite a character, too. She'd been a nightclub singer (sometimes billed as "Schwarze Venus") in Germany for many years—Ruth had spent a large part of her youth in Aachen, near the Dutch border. Now Cyrillia was nursing at a Portsmouth hospital. The first time I met her, she'd just gotten out of the bath and was relaxing with a joint. She was a voluptuous woman with huge breasts, and she didn't look much older than Ruth. Very black, her hair twisted and braided in a bizarre African style, she sat wrapped in a towel, an enormous spliff in one hand, dealing tarot cards with the other.

She was no more psychically aware than I was, though, that I had connected, in just a few months, with my future producer, my future record company, my future manager, and my future wife.

Some Bloody Yank

IN THE SUMMER of '78, everything suddenly came together. I decided to sign a publishing contract with John Telfer, but before the contract was even ready, he'd set up a meeting with David Kershenbaum, who was apparently so keen to produce me and get me signed to A&M that I thought there had to be a catch somewhere.

Ruth became my girlfriend and started spending weekends with me at Dog Kennel Hill. It was an odd relationship, though, progressing in fits and starts. We obviously fascinated each other, but for some reason, neither of us could quite relax.

Where Jill had been warm, Ruth was cool. Sexually, we couldn't quite seem to get off the ground, and it often seemed to me that even her body felt cool, beautiful and cool like black marble. I started to see her as a challenge. I would thaw her out.

Maura didn't really warm to Ruth. Not many people did, at first. "Be careful of her," she said, to my surprise. It wasn't like Maura to act like my big sister, even if, secretly, I rather liked to think of her that way.

"Why?" I asked, and I realized I was more troubled by doubts about Ruth than annoyed with Maura.

"Just be careful, that's all." And that was all she'd say.

John Telfer and I went to meet David Kershenbaum, and I didn't know what to make of him. He was a neat little man with big glasses, who spoke a language that I didn't really understand, or trust: Californian.

Still, he was obviously excited by the current music scene in London, even if, like most Americans, he found Elvis Costello and Squeeze and the Police more appealing than, say, Sham 69. He was looking for something not just new and hip and colorful, but melodic and musically accessible.

This kind of attitude was sneered at in the UK at the time. The bloody Yanks, people said, want everything bland and homogenized and watered-down. In my ignorance, I probably went along with this. Like most people close to the British pop world, I wasn't objective enough to see that the music was dependent to a huge extent on its context: the social climate, the fashion, and so on. This has always been truer of Britain than the States. The appeal of American music—and for that matter American cinema, TV, and so on—tends to be straightforward and universal, while the Brits tend to be quirky or ironic or referential in a way that assumes an audience attuned to cultural nuance. Then, as now, British artists have lost their context as they crossed the Atlantic, and the music has had to fend for itself.

John Telfer was excited by David's enthusiasm. He thought we'd stumbled across the ideal producer, because every album David produced sounded different. It sounded not like *him*, but like the artist in question. I was excited too, but also wary. Why did I need a producer, anyway? I already had a finished album, and it sounded pretty good to me. I didn't want to sign to a major label if it meant starting all over again with some bloody Yank telling me what to do.

David was patient and diplomatic. He loved my tape, he said, and he would hardly change a thing. He just felt that it could be "presented" a bit better. When I said I didn't know what he meant, he suggested that we go into a studio for a day, and he'd show me.

So, the following week, I took my eight-track master tapes from Telecoms to meet the Yank at a London studio called Pathway. David made discreet suggestions and gradually got me to relax a bit. We tried redoing some vocals, and David did a couple of quick remixes on the spot, changing little things—an EQ here, a reverb there—nothing drastic, but I had to admit that everything sounded better. David wasn't trying to turn me into Fleetwood Mac after all, and I began to trust him. He asked if my band could be ready to record in the next couple of weeks. I said yes. Emphatically.

But first, I signed my publishing to Albion—a bad move, as it later turned out—and received an advance of one thousand pounds. In the scheme of things, this wasn't a very big advance, but it was more money than I ever thought I'd see in my life.

I went out to celebrate with some friends, including Ruth, who glowed with a happiness that was more drug-induced than I realized. But, oh my God, whenever she thawed out a bit, my temperature seemed to go up by a hundred degrees. We went to see a reggae band called Culture at a venue called the Venue. I checked my precious, nicely broken-in leather jacket at the door, and when I came back for it, drunk and happy, two or three hours later, it had disappeared.

Sometimes a crumb falls from God's table, and sometimes He takes the food from your mouth. I was furious, but then I took it as a sign: I mustn't get too bigheaded, and anyway, a leather jacket wasn't my image any more.

I had my image figured out, I thought, along with everything else. Sharp, sarcastic, dressing in black and white and clashing pinstripes and polka dots, I was smart, and yet sending up smartness at the same time. Almost a mod, but mods were cool, and I wanted to be more ironic, just a little bit deliberately uncool. Another image came to mind: the sort of small-time crook or shady character played by people like Harry Fowler in British movies of the '40s or '50s. The pencil-thin mustache, the loud tie, the suit not as stylish as he thinks it is, the contraband stockings or cigarettes hidden in the lining of the jacket: a *spiv.* When people wanted to know how to label me, I'd tell them "spiv rock." I never thought for a moment that anyone would take me seriously, but quite a few people did. A year or two later, I would see an advertisement saying *Bass player wanted for Spiv-Rock band* in a music paper in San Francisco.

My band was ready to spring into action at any moment. How did we feel, now that everything was falling into place so easily? The phrase that comes to mind is "slightly stunned euphoria." We were like four people who'd just had three or four quick drinks without having had a chance to eat first.

I knew we'd be playing live soon, probably playing a lot, and I had that figured out, too. The band would wear black and white and use the absolute minimum of equipment. I would be myself on stage. Exaggerating myself a bit, perhaps, but there'd be no contrived moves, no posing, no script. Every show would be spontaneous. If I didn't know what to do with myself, I'd just stand with my hands in my pockets. Otherwise, I'd do or say whatever I felt like at the time. Sometimes I'd be provocative, but with the aim of grabbing the audience and involving them as much as possible, raising the energy level, making something *happen.*

My biggest influence as a stage performer was probably Mark Andrews. When people ask who has influenced me, I always sense that they're expecting to hear certain names: John Lennon, David Bowie, Graham Parker. The truth is that I'm influenced by everything, but especially by the people I've worked with closely, people no one else has heard of, people like Martin Keel, Yannis Grapsas, Mike Hutton, and the Barfield brothers.

And Mark, who got up there night after night with no idea of what he was going to do, but with a fierce determination to make something *happen.* Only once, he explained to me his attitude towards the audience, which was: "Okay, so you think I'm a wanker. So what? *Come on in!*"

A year or two later, Mark Andrews and the Gents made an album for A&M. In the wake of its failure, unscrupulous management, and other problems, Mark eventually quit the music business in disgust and became a chef. He still plays a gig here and there, but mostly in the background, as a rhythm guitarist. The man everyone assumed would be a star decided that he didn't want to be one, after all.

But Mark's philosophy worked pretty well for me, even if it tended to be misunderstood in America, where being ironic or sarcastic or challenging is often construed simply as having "a bad attitude."

Americans seemed to assume, too, that what I did was an "act." On my first visit to Los Angeles, a session was booked for me with a famous photographer, who set up a microphone, played my album, and told me to go into "the act" while he snapped away. I had no idea what to do. After about five minutes I told him to stuff it and walked out.

But before that could happen, I had to sign with A&M Records. The circumstances of my signing were unusual. For one thing, the head of the company, Derek Green, was away on vacation at the time. David Kershenbaum pushed the deal through by himself, despite not officially having the authority to do so. He was not even an employee of A&M, but he claimed (more-or-less truthfully) that Derek had authorized him to sign whoever he wanted to produce. David just had the appropriate department draw up a contract, which I signed in a pub in the middle of rerecording my first album. There was no champagne signing ceremony. In fact, it was something of an anticlimax.

John Telfer went, in a matter of weeks, from being my publisher and acting as my manager to actually being my manager. His first decision in that role turned out to be a brilliant one. He didn't ask for an advance from A&M, but just a monthly wage for me, Graham, Gary, and Dave—the minimum we could give up our day jobs and live on—until further notice.

Why was this so brilliant? Firstly, the paltry sums we were taking from A&M (the album cost a mere £7,500 to make) meant that Derek Green, when he came back from wherever he was, had nothing to complain about. Secondly, I became one of a very select group of artists to be "fully recouped" on their first royalty statement. I didn't owe the record company a penny.

A&M actually owed me a favor or two, and every time we wanted anything extra from them, we got it—including, after a while, a much better royalty rate. But more important, over the years, has been my ability to maintain complete creative control. Most people ask for as much money up-front as they can get away with. What they don't always realize is that this puts the record company in the driver's seat. But when the company has spent very little and your records make a profit, however small, they have no leverage. I've *never* owed my record company money, and although that doesn't guarantee they'll do a good job, it does guarantee that I can do pretty much whatever I like.

My first album was recorded at Eden Studios in Chiswick, west London, in August 1978. Dave Houghton came up to London and stayed with me at Dog Kennel Hill, while Graham stayed with Gary in Camberwell, thus creating two pairs that would persist for the life of the band, as we shared motel rooms or formed pool or table-football teams.

Kershenbaum's choice of studio—he was very particular—was fine with us, but the recording schedule would not be ideal. David had to get back to the States and Eden was only available at odd times—mostly, to my chagrin, in the morning. Some of the afternoons were already booked by a certain Mr. Costello.

There was no way I could get out of bed and sing right away, so I got up very early and eased into consciousness in the company of burly *Sun*-reading workers in a caff near the studio. Then I had to try to sing on a gutful of eggs, beans, and fried bread. I still had so much to learn!

The album would be virtually the same as what I'd made in Portsmouth: the same songs in the same order, but recorded better, the bass fuller, the drums harder, the guitar sharper, the reverbs bigger. My singing, thanks to Kershenbaum's tactful prodding, was better, too, better than it had any right to be. Despite the restrictive schedule, we still managed to get the whole thing done in two weeks.

I turned twenty-four during the recording. I was still just a kid, really, but it felt like the culmination of a lifetime of struggle. I was certainly ready for it. I'd reinvented myself, and quite consciously become exactly what the pop world loves: A fresh young face with some catchy tunes, a definite look, and a definite sound, all of which were just right for the time.

I don't mean to suggest that I was a phony. This was very much what I wanted to do, it was great fun, and I don't regret one note of it. In some ways it was a compromise, but one I was happy to make at the time. I was doing my own music my own way, and I soon acquired—especially in America—a reputation for being independent and stubbornly uncompromising. On the other hand, I wanted very much to be part of "the scene," to be accepted and applauded, to belong. So I mastered the balancing act. I was doing my own thing *and* "giving the people what they wanted."

In the back of my mind, I still had doubts. I was limiting myself, and I don't mean to sound either boastful or dismissive of my early work when I say that I was using only a small percentage of my musical talent and skill. Only now can I be honest enough to admit that this was partly because of the voices of Pompey hardnuts still echoing in my head, jeering at the poncey kid with the violin.

I actually tried to conceal, for instance, the fact that I had a diploma from the Royal Academy of Music. My whole attitude, even the way I dressed, had hardened into something too contrived, too one-dimensional, to be sustained for very long. After all this time, there were still unanswered questions, after all.

I decided to seize my moment, and think about them later.

Look Sharp!

I'M LISTENING to an album called *Look Sharp,* by a guy called Joe Jackson. Despite the fact that he has the same name as me, and even looks a bit like me, I'm trying to pretend that I've never heard of him, and that I'm hearing this music for the first time.

So how does it strike me?

It positively reeks of the year 1978, although it wasn't released until the beginning of '79. It sounds like it was made in just a few days, and I laugh as I'm reminded that most of the time it's actually in mono.

As for the style of the music: There *is* no style. The late '70s vintage, and the general rawness of the sound, place it more or less in the New Wave. But a genre-spotter could find bits of jazz, reggae, latin, '60s pop, R&B, punk, funk, and even disco. There are echoes of the Beatles, Steely Dan, and Graham Parker. What I hear, I think, is a guy with eclectic tastes, who, by sticking mostly to just guitar, bass, and drums, and by keeping everything almost obsessively simple, has created the *illusion* of a style—and a style that would have been very much in sync with its time. He's also created the illusion of being just a bratty rocker with a few snappy tunes. In fact, as his choice of chords and his jazzy piano-playing suggest, he's a much more accomplished musician.

I hear a voice that is a bit strained, and has a limited range, but is quite distinctive. I hear some good tunes and some awkward, childish lyrics, although they at least demonstrate, here and there, the saving grace of humor. And I definitely hear the cynical worldview of a man in his early twenties. At twenty-three or twenty-four it seems very clever to say that the world is just a bag of woe. By the time you get to, say, forty, you've seen some woe, and it's not so funny anymore.

Along with the cynicism I hear a lot of irony, which is not the same thing. Irony is a legitimate device, a way of being funny and serious at the same time, a subtle way of making a point. But irony should be handled with care. All too often, it's used as a defense. We use it to hide the fact that we don't have the courage of our convictions, the nerve to say what we really think or how we really feel. If irony hardens into habit, we become stiff, restricted, emotionally constipated. I like to think that hasn't happened.

All in all, I like *Look Sharp.* It makes me smile more than it makes me cringe. But it surprises me, in retrospect, that more people didn't see through the illusions—illusions that I wasn't going to be able to keep up for more than another album or two. Once the fuss died down, and I was no longer the flavor of the month, I would have two choices, neither of them easy. I would either have to turn *Look Sharp* into a formula and crank it out indefinitely, becoming a cartoon character in the process; or do some growing up in public.

A lot of people like my first album more than I do, and that's fine with me. There's no question of right or wrong: They are entitled to a subjective opinion about it.

And so am I.

It was strange to finally hear my own record on the radio, and I've never really gotten used to it since. I don't even know how to describe the feeling. You know it's your record within a second, and it's definitely a thrill. But you're hypersensitive to how it sounds, and to how people are reacting. And sometimes, especially when it's old music, there's a feeling almost of embarrassment too, or at least of vulnerability: as though someone had discovered the teenage poetry you'd hidden in a drawer, and read it on the air.

That's another reason that artists aren't always as confident or as pleased with themselves as you might expect. There's nothing so impressive as someone doing something you can't do, or having an idea you didn't have. But when it's your own brainchild, you may love it with all your heart, but you still see every tiny flaw. Out it goes into the world, and you can't take it back. You can only pray that the world will be kind.

Look Sharp would be successful beyond anything I could imagine. And at this point my story, if I decided to continue it, would have a different resonance, because it becomes what you might call a matter of public record. I stepped out of the wings and into the spotlight, and that seems to me a perfect place to end.

I can't help feeling that what happened in the wings was more interesting anyway. In the spotlight, the Joe Jackson Band did all the things every other band in the spotlight has ever done. We quickly worked our way up from support spots to headlining on the club and pub circuit—the Nashville, the Hope and Anchor, the Marquee—and then up to theaters and concert halls. We toured all over Europe, and were tourists at the Berlin Wall, or the Vatican, or the red light district of Amsterdam. We went to America and found out that you could party all night in New York, that you could drive across Colorado and Arizona for days without actually getting anywhere, that Chicago was windy and Texas was hot. We drank Aquavit in Stockholm and Weissbier in Munich and Tequila in LA. The drummer took speed, the bassist took quaaludes, and I took cocaine but liked it too much to let it become a habit.

We had hangovers and road fever and jet lag, but for a while we could do nothing wrong. A blonde in New Jersey came up to me while I was watching our support band and stuck her tongue in my ear; a black girl in Kansas introduced herself as an "exotic dancer" and insisted on demonstrating her act in my hotel room shower. Gary fell in love with a girl in Pittsburgh, Graham fell in love with a girl in Chicago, and I fell in love with New York City. We met some big stars and they were all shorter and less interesting than they seemed on TV. We made a second album, *I'm the Man*, which was basically the same as the first, and then a "difficult" third, *Beat Crazy*, in which we tried to change the formula a bit, without being quite sure of how. We worked nonstop for three years and burned ourselves out.

Ruth Rogers-Wright and I got married, a leap of faith that seems in retrospect to have been more an act of desperation. I couldn't thaw her out, after all, and we would be divorced within a couple of years. Things got pretty ugly. But I'm not interested in settling scores, or in titillating anyone with gory details. Suffice it to say that if Ruth was, at that time, a troubled woman, I was a fool. I flattered myself that I could give her some sort of stability at a time when I was blatantly incapable of it.

In some ways my relationship with Ruth was like the dark counterpoint to my moment of shining success. She has been living for many years in Australia, and although we're not exactly friends, I hear intriguing things: she's become a writer, a singer, a Buddhist, a mother. Has she changed? I really couldn't say. Has anyone?

The Joe Jackson Band split when our drummer decided he was happier in the Small Time, after all. These days Dave Houghton runs a drum shop in Portsmouth, plays local gigs, teaches young drummers, and seems to me a pillar of the community. Gary would go on to work with Joan Armatrading and Aztec Camera, and the last I heard, was playing heavy metal. Graham continued to work with me, for many years, and is very much in demand today, touring with Marshall Crenshaw, They Might Be Giants, or Natalie Merchant.

Most of the musicians I've known are still at it in some way or another, although there have certainly been some casualties. Bet Hannah, sadly, died at fifty, of a stroke that followed on the heels of a hereditary liver condition. Meanwhile her exguitarist, Tony, was drinking himself to death in Blackpool.

But the rest of the Koffee'n'Kreme team are still working, as are members of Edward Bear and Smiling Hard and Arms and Legs. Drew Barfield has been a sideman and cowriter for various artists, including most recently Paul Young. Steve Stevenson lives in France, Andy Arthurs in Australia. Alan Matthews seems to have vanished without trace. Martin Keel has never been abroad, and barely been outside of Portsmouth, but travels widely in his mind, having become a student of Eastern philosophy and mysticism. Some of my nonmusical friends, too, seem to have gotten what they wanted: Jill Maby has three kids, and Maura Keady is now the head of a south London school.

As for me, I spent the '80s recording and touring, and pushing the outside of the pop envelope: trying to find ways of being more true to myself while holding on to that mass audience. It didn't always work, of course. Sometimes I lost the audience, and sometimes I lost myself, but I learned a lot along the way, and made at least a couple of records (*Night and Day* and *Blaze of Glory*) that I'm still proud of.

One of the things I learned is that although pop success can be manufactured to a certain extent, it's often a shallow kind of success. If you're the right age, in the right place, and doing the right thing at the right time, you can't fail. It's hard not to let it go to your head, thinking that it's all happening because you really are a genius. But it doesn't last. It *can't.*

A few years of glory.

And then what?

And Then What?

I'M CHECKING my e-mail, and here's a good one. A man in Detroit, who saw my last show there, wants half his money back. The show, two hours long, was equally divided between new and older music, but that wasn't nearly enough old stuff for him.

This raises some interesting possibilities. I must admit I like the idea of a sliding scale—paying according to how much you like something. For instance, I saw a pretty good movie last week that was rather let down by the last ten minutes. So, according to my calculations, they owe me sixty-five cents.

More exciting, though, is the fact that a lot of people came to see my last tour and liked it *more* than they expected. I have plenty of proof: letters, e-mail, and yes, even reviews.

These people owe *me* money.

I can laugh this sort of thing off much more easily than I used to. I'd love to please everyone, but trying to please everyone, like trying to hold on to pop success, soon becomes too desperate a game to be any fun at all.

I got this message once and for all around 1992. I was on tour, the latest of many world tours, and in great danger of just going through the motions. I was exhausted, sick of the music industry, my head too full of chart positions and marketing plans and radio formats and video rotation to be able to remember why I was doing this in the first place.

At the end of the tour I found myself in Sydney, editing film of our concert there for home video release. As the tape rolled, I saw six people on stage, all very nice people and good musicians, working hard to deliver a show that was solid, musical, and professional. It also tried, here and there, to offer something a bit different from your average rock show. But it wasn't different enough to be playing by a whole new set of rules. The more I watched, the more it seemed too safe, stale, and somehow *unnecessary.*

That show, and the whole tour, had been well received, but trying to sell the latest record—at least, on the kind of scale that qualifies as pop success and keeps the media interested—was a struggle. But why shouldn't it be? Even real fans might have four or five of my albums already. Why should they buy another one, when newer, younger, hipper, sexier, more widely hyped acts were coming up behind me every week?

After Sydney, I took some time off to rethink and then plunged into depression. I couldn't write anything. But this went way beyond writers' block. After a while I realized, to my horror, that I couldn't even *listen* to music. It had all started to sound like noise.

It's hard to adequately convey in words what a frightening experience this is for a musician.

It felt like a loss of faith. What could possibly bring it back? Booze or sobriety? Sex or celibacy? Friends or solitude? Yoga, drugs, psychotherapy? I tried just about everything. But the music was dead, and I had to seriously consider doing something else with my life. Like what? I didn't have a clue.

At one point, convinced that New York was part of the problem, I moved to Paris. Poor old Joe, said friends sarcastically, living in Paris with nothing to do except eat, drink, and be merry. What a life, eh? In reality I was completely lost. Some days I couldn't even get out of bed. I was sick of French cuisine within a month, and I had to stop drinking because alcohol took me even lower.

But this isn't another "recovered addict" story, and good beer and whiskey are still friends rather than masters. I just had to let some false friends go: the guiding lights of applause and record sales and airplay and critical acclaim. Those lights had all been gradually going out, anyway, though some of that may have been just my own paranoia. Either way, it had gotten pretty dark.

How I worked my way out of depression could be a whole other book, and not an easy one to write. Suffice it to say that I was able to climb out of that bottomless pit once I'd convinced myself that Joe Jackson, Pop Star, had to die; but that as a human being—and even as a musician—I didn't have to die with him. Then the music came back. After a loss of faith, I experienced something like Grace.

Two years after Sydney, I was testing myself, as I did from time to time, by listening to some music just to see if I might enjoy it, and I suddenly realized that I *did*. It was a new album by a brilliant young jazz pianist called Marcus Roberts. Then I listened to one of my favorite Brazilian records, Milton Nascimento's *Anima*, and once again it sent delicious shivers down my spine.

I tried to register those moments when music touched me on the deepest level. Which music did I *really* love? I found that maybe half of it was "classical." I listened to a lot of string quartets—Shostakovich, Beethoven, and an underrated composer who fascinates me, Leoš Janáček. And I found that I still liked latin music. I was energized for weeks by a rare performance by the Cuban group Los Munequitos de Matanzas. Although the music was superficially minimal—just percussion and vocal chanting—it was actually rich and complex. The interlocking rhythms that can sound mechanical and clattering in the hands of a run-of-the-mill salsa group became, in the hands of these old masters, pliant, sensuous, and playful. As I listened I seemed to feel lighter and lighter until I was floating way up in the sky.

At first I couldn't listen to pop/rock music. I'd simply heard too much of it. But gradually that changed, too. It's hard to pick examples, but one occasion that sticks in my mind is seeing the Australasian band Crowded House on the same day that a confused young man called Kurt Cobain put a bullet through his own head. Rock seemed to be living up to all its worst stereotypes. Then Crowded House seemed to redeem it, playing with real spirit and a sense of fun, their songs echoing the Beatles and everything that has become "classical" in rock, but still distinctly their own, glittering with melodic beauty and intelligence.

Since then, I've enjoyed a lot of new records by new bands. As I write this in 1998, I'm listening to Radiohead and Massive Attack, like everyone else. But I've lost whatever urge I might once have had to compete with them, and that's very liberating.

Liberating, too, to realize that if no one else liked the music I liked, I really didn't care. I let go of trying to be clever, trying to be objective, trying to stay on top of it all. There's so much hype around, so much snobbery, so much mindless worshiping of celebrity and success. We all have to make an effort now and again to shut it all out, be *sub*jective, and ask: What's really important, and meaningful, to *me?*

And that's the story of how I found my way back from the musical wilderness. Just as I started to feel something like solid ground beneath my feet, though, I was hit by another earthquake.

My father and I had both mellowed a bit over time, and we got on better. My parents were proud of my success. My dad never said so, of course, but I could tell. He never said much of anything, although I'd try to trick him into opening up a bit by, for instance, asking him to explain the rules of cricket, or debating the merits of different single malt scotches. This strategy seemed to be paying off, here and there, until he was diagnosed, aged sixty-five, with an incurable cancer.

He didn't have long to live. Surely there were explanations, secrets, something he wanted to get off his chest? But he became more silent and unreachable than ever. He just didn't *want* to talk, and trying seemed so painful to him that I eventually gave up.

Instead I learned something I'd never suspected: We could communicate through music. My father had a barely concealed sentimental side, and certain pieces of music clearly moved him. When words seemed futile, we listened to music together. Later, when he was too weak to move and confined to bed, I played the piano, the same piano I'd learned on back in the hallways at Paulsgrove and Gosport. It was now basking in the living room of a newish house back in Portsmouth, and it was holding up remarkably well. I played Beethoven, Mozart, Chopin, the old pub songs I'd played at the Wicor Mill, the ragtime I'd played at the Admiral Drake, the standards I'd played at the Playboy. I wished I could be in two places at once, because both my mother and my dad's nurse told me that when he heard the music, his face lit up, and he seemed to be at peace.

It's pretty hard to hold on to any lingering resentments after that.

When I started to compose again, it was with a new attitude. The music was coming from a deeper place now, and perhaps for the first time, I started to find a style of my own. Eclectic, for sure. But no two people are eclectic in the same way. Hard to categorize, too, and therefore hard to sell; but I was willing to accept that, if it was the price of feeling comfortable inside my own skin.

I was fully aware of being a musical misfit. I loved both "classical" and "pop," without completely belonging to the world, the culture, the tradition, of either. But I started to think: So what? I am what I am. And besides, all those worlds and cultures and traditions were blurring together more and more each day.

So I'm still making music, no longer a pop star—if I ever really was—but just a composer, which is what I wanted to be in the first place. In many ways I feel closer now, in my forties, to the person I was at fifteen than to who I was at twenty-five or thirty-five.

One difference is that my ego has, at least to some extent, gotten out of the way. Not that my musical career was ever an ego trip, exactly. Early on, as far as I can figure it out, it was an attempt to *connect*, to have some communication with my fellow human beings that felt more meaningful and more alive than what I experienced at home or at school. Later, it became more about wanting to be accepted and applauded. Nowadays it's more about connection again. And now that I have what I suppose I must call a more mature perspective, I'm less interested purely in my own career and more interested in the survival of the art of music in general.

Why should I be concerned?

Because our cultural agenda is no longer being shaped either by "elitist" experts or by "the will of the People," so much as by the bottom lines of big corporations who want to sell us stuff, and preferably stuff that's easy to sell. Those of us who care about music have to stand up and be counted. We're going to have to rebel, and we can't do that by dying our hair green and thrashing electric guitars, not anymore. That kind of rebellion is already packaged and labeled and available at your local supermarket at the special bargain price of $9.99 (plus tax). No: in the Corporate Age, the rebels must be people with not only passion but intelligence, discernment, and good taste.

We—those of us who care—must always seek out and proclaim excellence rather than simply accepting what's popular or well promoted. So we also need to keep a cool head when people start calling us "elitists."

Perhaps I *am* an elitist, but if so, it's in the sense that if I go to see Manchester United, I want to see the elite of football. I'm not going to apologize for that. What, after all, are artists *for*? I don't think they're there to be the "voice of the People," even if it sometimes seems to work that way. I think artists are there to amaze, to inspire, to challenge, and to open our minds and hearts. On a basic, tribal level, I think the artist should be the shaman. All too often, in our culture, he's the village idiot.

What I'd like to see is an aristocracy of music, but one that is meritocratically elected and democratically accessible. Why not? These no longer have to be contradictions. We have the technology to make all kinds of culture available to everyone, and snobs of every stripe are running out of excuses.

Admittedly, this breakdown of old boundaries is more likely to be reflected in, say, massive coverage of the Spice Girls in *The Guardian* or *The Times*, than it is in millions of Pompey hardnuts grooving to Shostakovich. The cynical artist sees this as evidence for an old complaint: The Masses Are Stupid. But more and more I see this kind of cynicism as a cop-out and a bore, and I can't go along with it. The fact is that people *en masse* can't be expected to be connoisseurs, or passionate about what I happen to be passionate about. They're not stupid: They just have different priorities.

Everyone, though, should have some music education. One reason that working-class kids like me are usually more likely to appreciate the subtleties of Manchester United than the subtleties of Mahler is that they've all played a bit of football, so they know what's going on. But few young people today even have the musical opportunities I had at the Tec.

If we want music to survive, we must teach kids to appreciate it, before it's too late, before songs become nothing more than units of currency, and instrumental music exists only to accompany car commercials. My concern isn't just for the music, but for the kids, too. What kind of kids do we want, after all?

And with that, I'll get down off my soapbox. I don't like to sound so pessimistic: For the most part, it's not how I feel. The art of music may be in a state of flux, but it won't be extinct any time soon. Schoenberg once said that there were still plenty of good tunes to be written in the key of C major; that is, on just the white notes on the keyboard. He conspicuously failed to write any, but I think he was right.

I've heard it said that a pessimist is never disappointed. It's a cute line, but I think it's wrong. A pessimist is someone who is *permanently* disappointed.

An optimist is only disappointed now and again.

Epilogue: Of Mice and Mozart

I'M SITTING in a Portsmouth pub—how very original of me!—deliciously anonymous, listening to tonight's band. They're called Dave and Jim, and I'm thinking: That's one way to solve the old band-name dilemma. Dave is my old friend Dave Houghton, drumming as well as ever and singing, too. Jim is a keyboard player and vocalist who manages to create a big fat bass sound with his left hand, so that this duo, if you weren't looking, could easily fool you into thinking they were a quartet. They play only cover versions, but I'll take a pub gig like this over some big-time stadium rock extravaganza any time.

Then Dave—who does all the talking and could probably have yet another career in stand-up comedy, if he wanted—announces a special guest. Ladies and gentlemen, Portsmouth's very own, Shakin' Jimmy!

I've heard of this guy, but never seen him in action until now. He sits in with local bands here and there, and the bands always welcome him warmly to the stage, not so much, I suspect, because of his musical ability as the fact that Jimmy is a very big bloke. Big, and determined. His acoustic guitar looks like a ukulele on him, and if he helps you pack up your gear, you will find that any hardware involving wing nuts or screws will have been snapped and bent into submission.

Jimmy's speciality is Elvis numbers, and tonight we get a passable version of "Gotta Lotta Livin' to Do." We're spared the legendary spectacle of Jimmy doing the splits, though. Just as well. I don't think the stage in this place could take it.

Shakin' Jimmy's most impressive performance, though, comes at the end of the evening, when he packs up and leaves. He does his own solo gigs, you see, playing electric—or, as he says, a Lectric guitar rather than a Coustic one—so he needs an amp, a PA system, a drum machine, and some presumably very heavy-duty stands. And he's built a little trailer, which he tows behind his bicycle. Jimmy piles everything on to it, and away he goes. The last we see of him is a fluorescent "Long Vehicle" sign disappearing into the misty night.

Pompey characters—and there are still plenty of them—are one of the pleasures of my transatlantic existence, but there's actually a New York equivalent, more or less, of Shakin' Jimmy. His, or rather her, name is Baby Dee, a buxom transsexual who rides around the Village on a tricycle with a platform attached to the back. On the platform stands a full-size concert harp, which she plays rather well. But she also sings, to her own accordion accompaniment. Always the same song: "Lydia, the Tattooed Lady," in a strange falsetto voice. The tourists gape and reach for their cameras. New Yorkers, of course, have seen it all before; and they're all too busy, anyway, bashing each other with briefcases and fighting over yellow taxis.

Bloody mad, these musicians. How many times have I heard that from musicians themselves? It's always said with an expression of pure glee: Bloody mad, aren't we, the lot of us, but who wants to be normal, eh? And what they really mean, of course, is that they're a lot saner than most people, and having a lot more fun.

Stories of art as divine madness are entertaining, full of wild-eyed absinthe-drinking bohemians and glamorous suicides, but I for one see music more as divine sanity. In other words, I'd be a lot crazier without it.

But it's time for me to admit, having already laid out all the cause-and-effect psychobabble I can muster, that I never did really figure out *why* I'm doing what I do. Yes, it's about connection: I've made many friends through music, and many more I've never even met. Not only that, but I've made friends—through their work—with musicians who *I'll* never meet either; some of them from radically different cultures, and some of them long since dead and buried. But still, beyond all that, lies the mystery of music itself. I don't know why musical ideas grow in our heads. And I don't know, either, why grass grows, or trees grow, or babies grow in the womb. All I know is that it all just keeps on happening, and there doesn't seem to be a damn thing we can do about it.

Just the other day I was amused to read in the paper how scientists have discovered that mice who were treated to regular doses of Mozart grew up smarter and happier than mice who were musically deprived. So it seems likely, say the scientists (I imagine lightbulbs appearing above their heads) that the same thing might apply to humans.

I could have told them this for nothing. But we seem to need things sanctioned by the priests of the god of science, and if that's what it takes for people to let their kids have clarinet lessons, I suppose it's all right.

In the end, music doesn't *have* to make sense: You just have to believe, and good stuff happens. Through music I've connected to people, to places, to the past, and to the future. And through music (to paraphrase Oscar one more time) I've been able to connect the gutter to the stars.

It's been as good a religion as any.